Foundation Chemistry

For Class X

Part-1 of 2

NOTION PRESS

NOTION PRESS

India. Singapore. Malaysia.

ISBN xxx-x-xxxxx-xx-x

Dedicated to our Beloved Prime Minister Shree Narendra Modi ji, whose life gives the Inspiration to every Individual

*If a Man **Decides** to achieve something in his life nothing is Impossible*

कर्मण्येवाधिकारस्ते मा फलेषु कदाचन।

मा कर्मफलहेतुर्भूर्मा ते सङ्गोऽस्त्वकर्मणि॥ २-४७

Karmanye vadhikaraste Ma Phaleshu Kadachana,

Ma Karmaphalaheturbhurma Te Sangostvakarmani

You have the right to work only but never to its fruits.

Let not the fruits of action be your motive, nor let your attachment be to inaction.

CONTENT

TOPIC NAME	PAGE NO.

1. CHEMICAL REACTIONS AND EQUATIONS

2. ACIDS, BASES AND SALTS

3. METALS & NON-METALS

1 CHEMICAL REACTIONS AND EQUATIONS

CONCEPT TREE

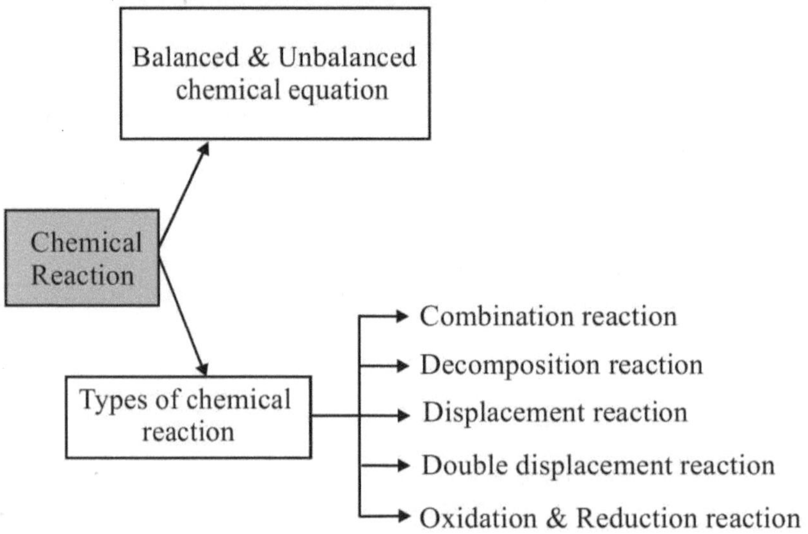

1.1 INTRODUCTION :

Any change with the formation of new substance is called chemical reaction. There are many type of chemical reaction e.g. displacement reaction, combination reaction etc. A chemical equation represents a chemical reaction. In a chemical reaction balancing is very important. It can be done by various methods. Oxidation and reduction reaction are also the types of chemical reaction. These reactions can be balanced by ion electron method and oxidation number method. Corrosion and rancidity are the effects of oxidation reactions.

Change is the law of nature.

There are so many situations of daily life, where we can observe various changes.

Like,

(i) Conversion of tea into vapours from a cup of hot tea.

(ii) Corrosion of iron articles (rusting) if exposed to humid atmosphere.

(iii) Cooking of food.

(iv) Digestion of food in our body.

(v) Breaking

(vi) Combustion of fuel in our vehicle.

Scientist classify these changes as :

⇨ Physical changes

⇨ Chemical changes.

(1) Physical changes : A change in which physical properties of the substance changes but the chemical composition does not change.

Examples

Freezing, melting, boiling, condensation etc.

Characteristic features of physical changes :

(i) The identity of the substances is maintained.

(ii) The change may or may not take place.

(iii) Heat change may or may not take place.

(iv) Only the physical state or some of the physical properties of the substances are changed.

(2) Chemical Changes : A change in which one of more substances changes into new substances with a different chemical composition.

Examples.

Burning of candle, rusting of iron, calcination of lime stone etc.

Characteristic features of chemical changes :

(i) The identity of original substance is completely lost.

(ii) The change is permanent.

(iii) The change is generally accompanied by energy change.

(iv) The change cannot be reversed.

1.2 CHEMICAL REACTION :

A chemical reaction is a process which transforms one or more substances into new substances. During chemical reactions, new substances with new properties are formed . The substances which take part in chemical reactions are called **reactants** and the substances which are formed as a result of chemical reactions are called **products**. For example, in the reaction between sodium hydroxide and hydrochloric acid to give sodium chloride and water.

$NaOH$	+	HCl	$\rightarrow$	$NaCl$	+	H_2O
Sodium Hydroxide		Hydrochloric acid		Sodium Chloride		Water
	(Reactants)				(Products)	

The chemical reactions involves the breaking of bonds between the atoms of the reacting substances and making of new bonds between atoms of products.

Reactant : Substances which take part in a chemical reaction.

Product : The new substances which is formed as a result of chemical reaction.

The following observation helps us to determine whether a chemical reaction has taken place.

⇨ change in state ⇨ change in colour

⇨ evolution of a gas ⇨ change in temperature

⇨ formation of precipitate

The important characteristics of a chemical reaction : -

(i) Change in state : The physical state of the substance normally changes.

e.g. (a) Formation of solid MgO from solid Mg and gaseous O_2.

(b) Formation of solid PbI_2(ppt) from liquid solutions of $Pb(NO_3)_2$ and KI.

(c) Formation of H_2 gas form the reaction of solid Zn with liquid H_2SO_4.

(d) Two volumes of hydrogen gas react with one volume of oxygen gas to form two volume of water.

$$2H_2 (g) + O_2 (g) \longrightarrow 2H_2O (\ell)$$

or when electric current is passed through water it splits into its elements .

$$2H_2O (\ell) \xrightarrow{\text{Electric current}} 2H_2(g) + O_2 (g)$$

(e)

$$\underset{\text{Ammonia}}{NH_3(g)} + \underset{\text{Hydrochloric acid}}{HCl(g)} \longrightarrow \underset{\text{Ammonium chloride}}{NH_4Cl (s)}$$

(ii) Change in colour : In some of the chemical reactions change in colour can be observed.

e.g. (a) Formation of brown rust on black iron nails.

(b) Formation of yellow ppt. of lead iodide from colourless solution of $Pb(NO_3)_2$ and KI.

(c) When red lead oxide is heated strongly it forms yellow coloured lead monoxide and gives of oxygen gas.

$$\underset{\substack{\text{Lead oxide}\\\text{(Red)}}}{2Pb_3O_4(s)} \xrightarrow{\text{heat}} \underset{\substack{\text{Lead monoxide}\\\text{(Yellow)}}}{6PbO(s)} + O_2(g)$$

(d) When copper carbonate (green) is heated strongly it leaves behind a black residue.

$$\underset{\substack{\text{Copper}\\\text{carbonate}\\\text{(Green)}}}{CuCO_3(s)} \xrightarrow{\text{heat}} \underset{\substack{\text{Copper oxide}\\\text{(Black)}}}{CuO (s)} + \underset{\text{Carbon dioxide}}{CO_2(g)}$$

Other such examples are -

$$\underset{\substack{\text{Lead (II) nitrate}\\\text{(White)}}}{2Pb(NO_3)_2(s)} \xrightarrow{\text{heat}} \underset{\substack{\text{Lead (II) oxide}\\\text{(Yellow)}}}{2PbO(s)} + \underset{\substack{\text{Nitrogen}\\\text{dioxide}\\\text{(Brown)}}}{4NO_2 (g)} + O_2 (g)$$

$$\underset{\substack{\text{White}\\\text{sugar}}}{C_{12}H_{22}O_{11}(s)} \xrightarrow{\text{heat}} \underset{\substack{\text{Carbon}\\\text{black}}}{12C(s)} + \underset{\text{Water}}{11H_2O(g)}$$

(iii) Evolution of a gas : In some cases, a gas may be evolved.

(a) Reaction between a metal such as zinc, magnesium, or iron and dilute sulphuric acid produces hydrogen gas.

$$\underset{\text{zinc}}{Zn(s)} + \underset{\text{sulphuric acid}}{H_2SO_4 (dil)} \longrightarrow \underset{\text{zinc sulphate}}{ZnSO_4 (aq)} + \underset{\text{hydrogen gas}}{H_2 (g)}$$

(b) Reaction between iron sulphide and dilute sulphuric acid produces hydrogen sulphide gas.

$$\underset{\text{iron sulphide}}{FeS (s)} + H_2SO_4(dil) \longrightarrow \underset{\text{ferrous sulphate}}{FeSO_4 (aq)} + H_2S (g)$$

(c) Heating a mixture of potassium chlorate ($KClO_3$) and manganese dioxide (MnO_2) gives oxygen gas.

$$\underset{\text{Potassium chlorate}}{2KClO_3 (s)} \xrightarrow[MnO_2]{\text{heat}} \underset{\text{potassium chloride}}{2KCl (s)} + \underset{\text{oxygen gas}}{3O_2(g)}$$

MnO_2 is used as a catalyst in this reaction.

This reaction is used for the preparation of oxygen in the laboratory.

(iv) Change in energy : Most of the reactions are accompanied by energy change i.e. gain (endothermic) or release(exothermic) energy during a chemical reaction.
On the basis of energy changes, there are two types of reactions :

(A) Endothermic reaction : A chemical reaction which is accompanied by the absorption of energy is called an endothermic reaction.

(a) $N_2(g) + O_2(g) + Heat \longrightarrow 2NO(g)$
(Nitrogen) (Oxygen) (Nitric oxide)

(b) Light energy is essential for biochemical reaction, photosynthesis, by which green plants prepare their food from carbon dioxide & water.
$6CO_2 + 6H_2O + energy \longrightarrow C_6H_{12}O_6 + 6O_2$

(B) Exothermic reaction : A chemical reaction which is accompanied by the release of energy is called exothermic reaction.

(a) When magnesium wire is heated from its tip in a bunsen flame, it catches fire and burns with a dazzling white flame with release of heat and light energy.

$$2Mg\,(s) + O_2\,(g) \xrightarrow{Heat} 2MgO\,(s) + Energy$$

(b) When quick lime (calcium oxide) is placed in water, the water becomes very hot and sometimes starts boiling. It is because of release of heat energy during the reaction.

$$CaO\,(s) + H_2O \longrightarrow Ca(OH)_2\,(aq) + \text{Heat energy}$$
Calcium oxide, Water, Calcium hydroxide

(v) Formation of precipitate : Some chemical reactions are characterised by the formation of precipitate (an insoluble substance), when the solutions of two soluble chemical compounds are mixed together.

(a) When silver nitrate solution is mixed with a solution of sodium chloride, a white precipitate of silver chloride is formed.

$$AgNO_3\,(aq) + NaCl\,(aq) \longrightarrow NaNO_3(aq) + AgCl\,(s)$$
Silver nitrate, Sodium chloride (Colourless), Sodium nitrate (Colourless), Silver chloride (White precipitate)

(b) A dirty green precipitate of ferrous hydroxide is formed, when a solution of ferrous sulphate is mixed with sodium hydroxide solution .

$$FeSO_4\,(aq) + 2NaOH\,(aq) \longrightarrow Na_2SO_4(aq) + Fe(OH)_2\,(s)$$
Ferrous sulphate, Sodium hydroxide, Sodium sulphate, Ferrous hydroxide (Green precipitate)

(c) $BaCl_2\,(aq) + \text{dil } H_2SO_4 \longrightarrow BaSO_4(s) + 2HCl(aq)$
Barium chloride, Barium sulphate (White precipitate)

1.3 CHEMICAL EQUATION :

Symbolic representation of chemical reaction in terms of symbols and formulas of reactants and the products which will give idea about true chemical change.

Chemical Equations or Equations for Chemical Reaction

We have seen that all chemical changes are accompanied by chemical reactions. These reactions can be described in sentence from but the description is quite long. Chemical equations have been framed to describe the chemical reactions.

A chemical equation links together the substances which react (reactants) with the new substances that are formed (product)

The chemical equation are of two types :

(i) Word Equation

(ii) Symbol Equation

Let us briefly describe these two types of equations.

➤ **Writing Word Equations :** A word equation links together the names of the reactants with those of the products. For example, the word equation when magnesium ribbon burns in oxygen to form a white powder of magnesium oxide, may be written as follows :

$$\underset{\text{(reactants)}}{\text{Magnesium} + \text{Oxygen}} \longrightarrow \underset{\text{(product)}}{\text{Magnesium oxide}}$$

Similarly, the word equation for the chemical reaction between granulated zinc and hydrochloric acid may be written as :

$$\underset{\text{(reactants)}}{\text{Zinc} + \text{Hydrochloric acid}} \longrightarrow \underset{\text{(products)}}{\text{Zinc chloride} + \text{Hydrogen}}$$

In a word equation :

- ⇨ The reactant are written on the left hand side with plus sign (+) between them.
- ⇨ The product are written on the right hand side with plus sign (+) between them.
- ⇨ An arrow ($\longrightarrow$) separates the reactants from the products.
- ⇨ The direction of the arrow head points towards the products.

➤ **Writing Symbol Equations :** A chemical equation can also be described in terms of symbols and formulae of the reactants and products taking part in a particular reaction. This is known as symbol equation.

In the symbol equation, the symbols and formulae of the elements and compounds are written instead of their word names.

For example, burning of magnesium in oxygen to form magnesium oxide may be written as follows :

$$Mg + O_2 \longrightarrow MgO$$

The symbol equation for the reaction between zinc and hydrochloric acid is :

$$Zn + HCl \longrightarrow ZnCl_2 + H_2$$

Both the symbol equations are not balanced which means that the number of different atoms on both sides of the equation are not equal.

Essentials of Chemical Equations :

Essentials of chemical equations are :

(i) It must represent a true chemical change.

(ii) All the reactants and the products of the chemical reaction must be in the form of their representative chemical formulae or symbols.

(iii) The total number of atoms of all elements must be same on both sides.

(iv) It must be molecular.

If equation is not satisfying any of the above conditions it cannot be termed as chemical equation.

For example

$Pt + 4HCl \rightarrow PtCl_4 + 2H_2$, though a balanced equation algebraically, is not a true chemical reaction and hence, not a chemical equation since platinum does not react with hydrochloric acid to give hydrogen.

$KClO_3 \rightarrow KCl + 3O_2$ is a true chemical reaction and balanced too, yet oxygen is not shown its molecular form, hence, it is yet an incomplete chemical equation.

1.4 UNBALANCED AND BALANCED CHEMICAL EQUATIONS :

In an unbalanced equation, the number of atoms of different element on both sides of the equation are not equal. For example, in the first equation, the number of Mg atoms on both sides of the equation is one (same). But the number of oxygen atoms are not equal. It is known as unbalanced equation.

$$Mg + O_2 \longrightarrow MgO \text{ (Unbalanced equation)}$$

An unbalanced equation is also called skeletal equation.

In a balanced equation, the number of atoms of different elements on both sides of the equation are always equal. The balanced equation for the burning of magnesium ribbon in oxygen may be written as:

$$2Mg + O_2 \longrightarrow 2MgO \text{ (Balanced equation)}$$

The atoms of one element do not change into the atoms of the other element. Similarly, the atoms neither disappear from the reaction mixture nor do they appear from somewhere. Actually a chemical reaction simply involves an exchange of partners during the reaction. As a result, no change in mass occurs and the law of conservation of mass hold good. This can be illustrated by the reaction between hydrogen and oxygen to form water.

$$\text{Hydrogen} + \text{Oxygen} \longrightarrow \text{Water}$$

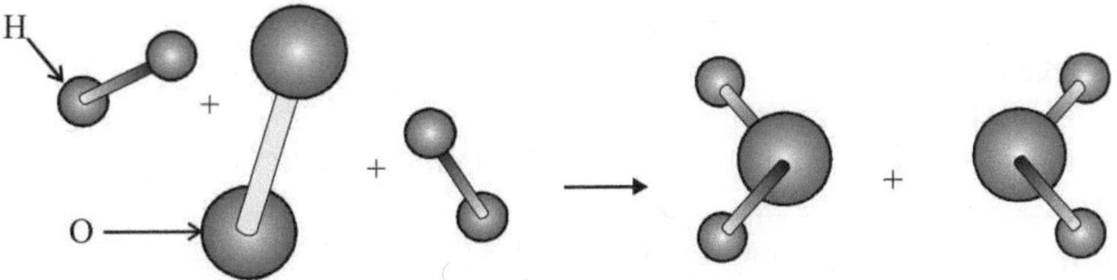

Each molecule of water (H_2O) contains one atom of oxygen (O) and two atoms of hydrogen (H). This means that one molecule of oxygen (O_2) which contains two atoms will combine with two molecules of hydrogen ($2H_2$) to form two molecules of water ($2H_2O$).

$$2H_2 + O_2 \longrightarrow 2H_2O$$

This represents a balanced chemical equation.

In a skeletal equation law of conversation of mass is not followed.

The balancing of a chemical equation is essential or necessary to fulfil the requirement of the law of Conservation of Mass. The law may be stated as : The total mass of all the products of reaction in a chemical reaction is equal to the total mass of all the reactants.

Keep in mind that the key feature of balanced chemical equation is the conservation law.

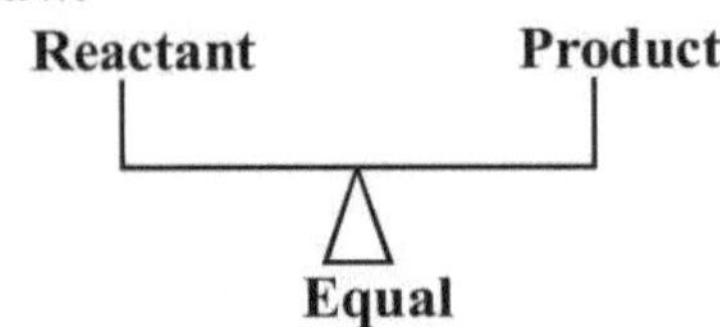

➤ Balancing of Chemical Equations :

The process of making the number of different element on both sides of the equation equal.

The balancing of a chemical equation can be done with the help of **Hit and Trial method**. In this method, the coefficients before the symbol or formulae of the reactants and products are adjusted in such a way that the total number of atoms of each element on both the sides of the arrow head become equal. This balancing is also known mass balancing because the atoms of elements on both sides are equal and their masses will also be equal.

The major steps involved in balancing a chemical equation are as follows :

1. Write the chemical equation in the form of a word equation. Keep the reactants on left side and the products on right side. Separate them by an arrow head ($\longrightarrow$) pointing from the reactants towards the products.
2. Convert the word equation into the symbol equation by writing the symbols and formulae of all the reactants and products.
3. Make the atoms of different elements on both sides of the equation equal by suitable method. This is known as balancing of equation.
4. Do not change the formulae of the substances while balancing the equation.

To understand this, let us consider the following word equation.

Zinc + Sulphuric acid $\rightarrow$ Zinc Sulphate + Hydrogen

Chemical equation for the above word equation will be,

$Zn + H_2SO_4 \rightarrow ZnSO_4 + H_2$

Let us examine the number of atoms of different elements on both sides of the arrow.

Element	Number of atoms in reaction (L.H.S.)	Number of atoms in products (R.H.S)
Zn	1	1
H	2	2
S	1	1
O	4	4

As the number of atoms of each element is same on both sides of the arrow the equation can be said, a balanced chemical equation.

Let us balance some of the chemical reactions by following the above steps.

(1) Magnesium metal reacts with hydrochloric acid to form magnesium chloride and hydrogen.

- **Step-1 :** Word equation.
  Magnesium + Hydrochloric acid → Magnesium chloride + Hydrogen

- **Step-II :** Chemical equation,

$$Mg + HCl \longrightarrow MgCl_2 + H_2$$

- **Step-III :** Enclose all formulae into boxes.

$$\boxed{Mg} + \boxed{HCl} \longrightarrow \boxed{MgCl_2} + \boxed{H_2}$$

- **Step-IV :** Count the number of atoms for all elements.

Element	Number of atoms in reaction (L.H.S.)	Number of atoms in products (R.H.S)
Mg	1	1
Cl	1	2
H	1	2

We can see that number of Mg is same on both side but Cl and H atoms differs on both sides.

- **Step - V :** As the number of atoms is deficient at reactant side, lets begin from here. At reactant side HCl is the bigger formula, so we will start with it.
- **Step-VI :** Put coefficient 2 before HCl to make chlorine equal to reactant side

$$Mg + 2HCl \longrightarrow MgCl_2 + H_2$$

  Here, we can seen that H automatically gets balanced.

- **Step-VII :** Now check the number of atoms of different elements on both sides of the equation. These are equal.
  This means that the equation is balanced.

(2) Steam is passed over heated iron to form Iron oxide and hydrogen,

- **Step-I :** Iron + Steam ⟶ Iron Oxide + Hydrogen
- **Step-II :** $Fe + H_2O \longrightarrow Fe_3O_4 + H_2$
- **Step-III :** $\boxed{Fe} + \boxed{H_2O} \longrightarrow \boxed{Fe_3O_4} + \boxed{H_2}$

Element	Number of atoms on (L.H.S.)	Number of atoms on (R.H.S)
Fe	1	3
H	2	2
O	1	4

- **Step-IV :** Formula selected Fe_3O_4 to start balancing oxygen,
  (i) To balance O-atoms, multiply H_2O on LHS by 4.

$$\boxed{Fe} + 4\boxed{H_2O} \longrightarrow \boxed{Fe_3O_4} + \boxed{H_2}$$

  (ii) Now balance Fe atoms.

$$3\boxed{Fe} + 4\boxed{H_2O} \longrightarrow \boxed{Fe_3O_4} + \boxed{H_2}$$

  (iii) Balance H atoms.

$$3\boxed{Fe} + 4\boxed{H_2O} \longrightarrow \boxed{Fe_3O_4} + 4\boxed{H_2}$$

- **Step-V :** On checking the number of all elements we found that equation is balanced now,

$$3Fe + 4H_2O \longrightarrow Fe_3O_4 + 4H_2$$

Note : Fe_3O_4 is also known as magnetic oxide of iron.

Illustrations

Illustration 1 : Balance the given equation

(i) $CH_4 + O_2 \longrightarrow CO_2 + H_2O$ *(not balanced)*

(ii) $Fe + O_2 \longrightarrow Fe_2O_3$ *(not balanced)*

Solution : (i) $CH_4 + 2O_2 \longrightarrow CO_2 + 2H_2O$ (balanced)

(ii) $4Fe + 3O_2 \longrightarrow 2Fe_2O_3$ (balanced)

Illustration 2 : Why it is necessary to balance a chemical equation ?

Solution : In order to make law of conservation of mass, applicable on the given chemical equation, it is necessary to make number of atoms of all elements equal on L.H.S. & R.H.S. Thus balancing is required.

➤ Making a chemical equation more informative :

We have studied that a chemical equation is the true representation of a chemical reaction. It is always better to make the equation is informative as possible to get a better picture of the chemical reaction. The various steps in this direction are :

1. Write the state symbols for the reactions and products participating in the reaction.
   Writing Symbols of Physical States : The chemical equations or symbol equations which we have enlisted donot mention the physical states of the reactant and product species involved in the reaction. In order to make the equation more informative, the physical states are also mentioned with the help of certain specific symbols known as 'state symbols'. These symbols are :
   - ⇨ (s) for solid state
   - ⇨ (ℓ) for liquid state
   - ⇨ (g) for gaseous state
   - ⇨ (aq) for aqueous solution i.e. solution prepared in water.
2. Indicate the gas evolved in the reaction by an arrow pointing upwards ($\uparrow$)
3. Represent the precipitate if formed in the reaction by an arrow pointing downwards ($\downarrow$) or by using the abbreviation 'ppt'.
4. Mention the actual heat evolved in the exothermic reaction by plus (+) sign and heat absorbed in the endothermic reaction by negative (–) sign on the product side.

$$C(s) + O_2(g) \longrightarrow CO_2(g) + 393.5 \text{ kJ} \quad \text{(Exothermic reaction)}$$
$$C(s) + 2H_2(g) \longrightarrow CH_4(g) + 74.8 \text{ kJ} \quad \text{(Exothermic reaction)}$$
$$N_2(g) + O_2(g) \longrightarrow 2NO(g) - 180.0 \text{ kJ} \quad \text{(Endothermic reaction)}$$

5. In some chemical reactions conditions of temperature, pressure, catalyst etc. are mentioned either above or below the arrow head that separates the reactants from products. For example,

$$N_2(g) + 3H_2(g) \xrightarrow[\text{Fe (catalyst)}]{500^\circ C, 200\ atm} 2NH_3(g)$$

$$6CO_2(g) + 6H_2O(\ell) \xrightarrow[\text{Chlorophyll}]{\text{Sun light}} C_6H_{12}O_6(aq) + 6O_2(g)$$

6. Certain chemical reactions can proceed in both the directions. The reactants change into products in forward reaction. The products are converted into reactants in the backward reaction. For example :

$$N_2(g) + 3H_2(g) \longrightarrow 2NH_3(g) \quad \text{(Forward reaction)}$$

$$2NH_3(g) \longrightarrow N_2(g) + 3H_2(g) \quad \text{(Backward reaction)}$$

Such reaction are also called reversible reactions and are indicated by the symbol ($\rightleftharpoons$).

$$N_2(g) + 3H_2(g) \underset{\text{Backward}}{\overset{\text{Forward}}{\rightleftharpoons}} 2NH_3(g)$$

➤ Significance or Important Information Conveyed by a Chemical Equation :

A balanced chemical equation conveys a lot of other informations, in addition to its telling about the feasibility of a reaction.

Some important information conveyed by a chemical equation is given below :

1. An equation, tells us the names of the reactants and the products. For example, chemical equation.
   $CaCO_3 + 2HCl \rightarrow CaCl_2 + CO_2 + H_2O$
2. It conveys to us the relative number of molecules of the reactants and the products.
   $Zn + H_2SO_4 \rightarrow ZnSO_4 + H_2$
3. It conveys to us the relative number of moles of reactants and the products.
4. Relative masses of reactants and the products become known to us.
5. It also tells about the relative volumes of reactants and the products, if they happen to be gaseous.

Now Consider the following chemical equation :

$N_2 + 3H_2 \longrightarrow 2NH_3$

⇨ It tells us that nitrogen and hydrogen react to form ammonia.

⇨ Formulas of nitrogen, hydrogen and ammonia are N_2, H_2 and NH_3 respectively.

⇨ One mole of nitrogen reacts with three moles of hydrogen to form two moles of ammonia.

⇨ 28 g of nitorgen react with 6 g of hydrogen to form 34 g of ammonia.

⇨ 1 volume of nitrogen reacts with three volumes of hydrogen to form two volumes of ammonia.

N_2	+	$3H_2$	$\longrightarrow$	$2NH_3$
Nitrogen		Hydrogen		Ammonia
1 mole		3 mole		2 mole
$14 \times 2 = 28$ g		$3 \times 2 = 6$ g		$2 \times (14 + 3) = 34$ g
1 volume		3 volume		2 volume

➤ Limitations of a Chemical Equation :

A chemical equation does not gives the following informations :

1. **Physical state of reactants and products :** It is not possible to know the physical state of reactants and products whether these substances are solid, liquid or a gas.
2. **Conditions necessary for a chemical reaction :** A chemical equation does not indicate about the condition necessary for the reaction i.e., about temperature, pressure or presence of a catalyst.
3. **Rate of reaction :** It does not give any idea about the rate of the reaction whether slow or fast.
4. **Change of heat :** An equation fails to give any indication whether the heat is absorbed or evolved.
5. **Concentration :** It does not give any indication about the concentration of the reactants.
6. **Mechanism :** It fails to give any idea about the mechanism of the reaction.
7. **Nature of reaction :** An equation fails to give any indication about the nature of reaction whether it is reversible or irreversible reaction.

➤ Removal of Drawbacks of a Chemical Equation :

Limitations of chemical reactions have been partially removed.

1. To express the concentration of the substances the word 'conc.' for concentrated and 'dil' for dilute are written just below the reactant.

$$\underset{\text{(conc.)}}{Cu + 2H_2SO_4} \longrightarrow CuSO_4 + SO_2 + 2H_2O$$

2. If a substance formed in the reaction is gas, it is indicated putting an arrow pointing upwards after the formula.

$$CaCO_3 \longrightarrow CaO + CO_2\uparrow$$

If a substance is precipitated in the reaction, it is indicated by putting arrow pointing downwards after the formula.

$$NaCl + AgNO_3 \longrightarrow AgCl\downarrow + NaNO_3$$

3. Physical states of the reactants and products are specified by the letter **s**, **g** and ***l*** denoting solid, gas or liquid respectively. The word aq (aqua-water) is usually placed within small brackets after the formula to indicate that the water solution of the compound is used.

$$2Na\ (s) + 2H_2O\ (l) \longrightarrow 2NaOH\ (aq) + H_2(g)\uparrow$$

4. Reversible reaction is indicated by the sign of reversibility ($\rightleftharpoons$)

$$N_2(g) + O_2\ (g) \rightleftharpoons 2NO(g)\uparrow$$

5. If a reaction take place at a particular temperature or pressure, it is expressed by writing on or below the arrow head.

$$N_2 + 3H_2 \xrightarrow[450°C]{200\ atm} 2NH_3$$

6. If the reaction is exothermic the energy released is expressed by plus (+) sign and if the reaction is endothermic, it is expressed by putting minus (–) sign.

$$C + O_2 \longrightarrow CO_2 + 94300 \text{ calories. (exothermic)}$$

$$N_2 + O_2 \longrightarrow 2NO - 83200 \text{ calories. (endothermic)}$$

1.5 DIFFERENT TYPES OF CHEMICAL REACTIONS :

During a chemical raection some bonds break and some new bonds are formed this result in redistribution of atoms in different ways.

Accordingly the reactions are classified in different types.

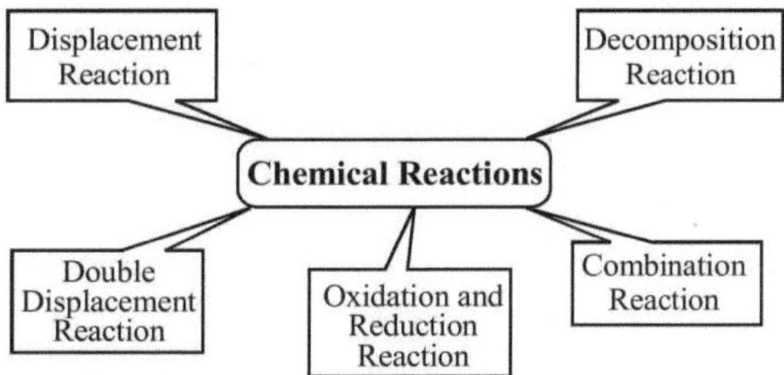

➢ Combination Reactions :

Those chemical reactions which involve the combination of two or more substances to form a single new substance are called **combination reactions**. Combination reactions may involve either :

(i) Combination of two elements.

(ii) Combination of an element and a compound to form a new compound or

(iii) Combination of two compounds.

Let us now discuss all these types of combination reactions one by one.

(i) Combination reactions involving two elements : Some examples of combination reactions involving two elements are :

(a) Carbon (charcoal) burns in air to form carbon dioxide

$$\underset{\text{Carbon (Charcoal)}}{C(s)} + \underset{\text{Oxygen}}{O_2(g)} \longrightarrow \underset{\text{Carbon dioxide}}{CO_2(g)}$$

(b) Hydrogen burns in oxygen to form water

$$\underset{\text{Hydrogen}}{2H_2(g)} + \underset{\text{Oxygen}}{O_2(g)} \xrightarrow{\text{Electric spark}} \underset{\text{Water}}{2H_2O(l)}$$

(c) Buring of magnesium in air

$$\underset{\text{Magnesium}}{2Mg\ (s)} + \underset{\text{Oxygen}}{O_2(g)} \longrightarrow \underset{\text{Magnesium oxide}}{2MgO(g)}$$

(ii) Combination reactions involving an element and a compound : Some examples of combination reactions involving an element and a compound are :

(a) Nitric oxide combines with oxygen at room temperature to form brown fumes of nitrogen dioxide (NO_2)

$$\underset{\text{Nitric oxide}}{2NO(g)} + \underset{\text{Oxygen}}{O_2(g)} \longrightarrow \underset{\text{Nitrogen dioxide}}{2NO_2(g)}$$

(b) Carbon monoxide combines with oxygen to produce corbondioxide (CO_2)

$$\underset{\text{Carbon monoxide}}{2CO(g)} + \underset{\text{Oxygen}}{O_2(g)} \longrightarrow \underset{\text{Carbondioxide}}{2CO_2(g)}$$

(c) Sulphur oxide raect with oxygen to yield sulphur trioxide (SO_3)

$$\underset{\text{Sulphur dioxide}}{2SO_2(g)} + \underset{\text{Oxygen}}{O_2(g)} \longrightarrow \underset{\text{Sulphur trioxide}}{2SO_3(g)}$$

(iii) Combination reactions involving two compounds : Some examples of such reactions are :

$$\underset{\text{Quick lime}}{CaO(s)} + H_2O(\ell) \longrightarrow \underset{\text{Slaked lime}}{Ca(OH)_2(s)}$$

⇨ Activity :

In order to illustrate a combination reaction, take about 2g to 3g of calcium oxide (also called quick lime) in a glass beaker. Pour water over it very slowly. What will you observe ?

The reaction will be highly vigorous as well as exothermic. It will be accompanied by hissing noise and bubbles. In fact, solution will initially start boiling. In this reaction, calcium hydroxide (also known as slaked lime) will be formed as a result of combination between two compounds.

$$\underset{\textbf{Quick lime}}{\mathbf{CaO(s)}} + \mathbf{H_2O(\ell)} \longrightarrow \underset{\textbf{Slaked lime /Calcium hydroxide}}{\mathbf{Ca(OH)_2(s)}}$$

Slaked lime is used for white wash. Slaked lime or calcium hydroxide formed in the above reaction will be in the form of a white suspension. It is filtered and solution containing soluble calcium hydroxide is applied on the wall with a brush. Carbon dioxide present in air will come into its contact and as a result, a thin layer of calcium carbonate (white) will be deposited on the wall. This is known as white wash.

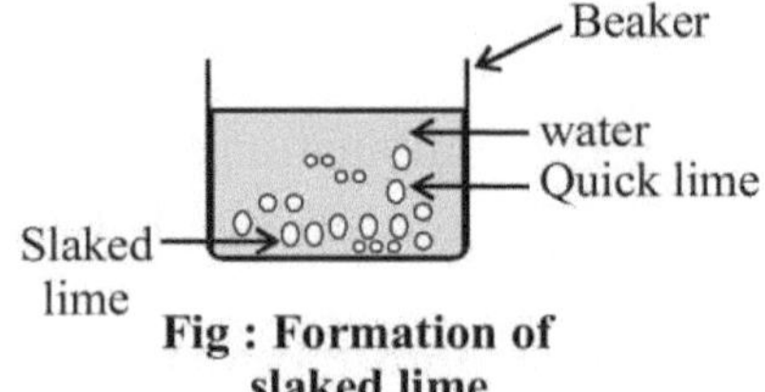

Fig : Formation of slaked lime

Quick lime (CaO) reacts with water to form calcium hydroxide (slaked lime)

$$\underset{\textbf{(Calcium hydroxide)}}{\mathbf{Ca(OH)_2(aq)}} + \underset{\textbf{(from air)}}{\mathbf{CO_2(g)}} \longrightarrow \underset{\textbf{(Calcium carbonate)}}{\mathbf{CaCO_3(s)}} + \mathbf{H_2O(\ell)}$$

Some more Examples of combination reactions :

1. **Combination between hydrogen and chlorine :**

   Hydrogen and chlorine gases combine in the presence of sun light to form hydrogen chloride gas.

   $$H_2(g) + Cl_2(g) \xrightarrow{\text{Sun light}} 2HCl\,(g)$$

   Hydrogen chloride gas is highly soluble in water and forms hydrochloric acid.

2. **Formation of iron sulphide :**

   Iron sulphide is formed, when fine pieces of iron are heated with sulphur powder (yellow in colour). It is in the form of a black mass.

   $$Fe(s) + S(s) \xrightarrow{\text{Heat}} FeS(s)$$

3. **Formation of ferric chloride :**

   When vapours of dry chlorine gas are passed through iron in the form of a fine wool, a chemical reaction takes place.

   A brown mass of ferric chloride or iron (III) chloride is formed as a result of the combination reaction.

   $$2Fe(s) + 3Cl_2(g) \longrightarrow 2FeCl_3(s)$$

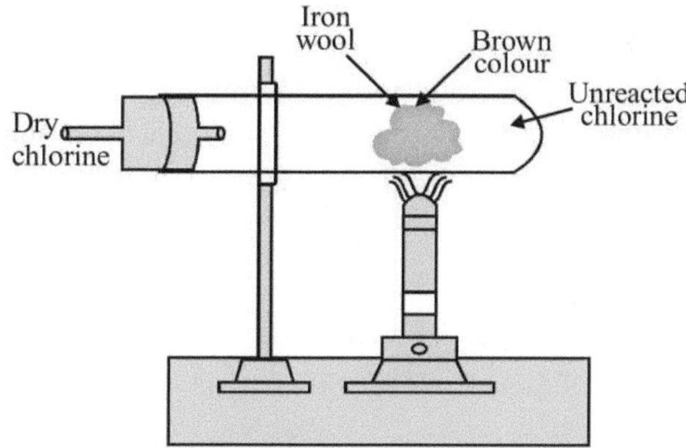

Figure : Formation of Ferric Chloride

Knowledge Enhancer

Exothermic and Endothermic Reactions :

Exothermic Reactions: The chemical reactions in which formation of products is accompanied by evolution of heat are known as **exothermic reactions.**

Some examples of exothermic reactions are :

(i) Burning of coal :

$$C(s) + O_2(g) \rightarrow CO_2(g) + \text{Heat}$$

(ii) Burning of natural gas :

$$CH_4(g) + 2O_2(g) \rightarrow CO_2(g) + 2H_2O(l) + \text{Heat}$$

(iii) Formation of slaked lime from quick lime :

$$\underset{\text{Quicklime}}{CaO(s)} + H_2O(l) \rightarrow \underset{\text{Slaked lime}}{Ca(OH)_2\,(aq)} + \text{Heat}$$

(iv) Respiration

This energy is generally supplied by food we eat. Bread, potatoes and rice etc. which we eat all contains carbohydrates.

$$C_6H_{12}O_6\,(aq) + 6O_2(aq) \rightarrow 6CO_2(aq) + 6H_2O(l) + \text{Energy}$$

The reaction is known by a special name **respiration**.

(v) Decomposition of vegetable matter on a compost heap is also an example of exothermic reaction.

Endothermic Reactions: The chemical reactions in which formation of products is accompanied by the absorption of heat are known as **endothermic reactions.**

Some examples of endothermic reactions are :

(i) $N_2(g) + O_2(g) \rightleftharpoons 2NO(g) - \text{Heat}$

(ii) $H_2(g) + I_2(g) \rightleftharpoons 2HI(g) - \text{Heat}$

(iii) $C(s) + 2S(g) \longrightarrow CS_2(l) - \text{Heat}$

(iv) $C(s) + H_2O(g) \longrightarrow CO(g) + H_2(g) - \text{Heat}$

➤ Decomposition Reactions :

(i) Those chemical reactions in which a compound breaks down to produce two or more simpler substances are known **as decomposition reactions**.

(ii) These reactions take place when the energy is supplied in the form of heat, light or electricity.

(iii) It may be noted that decomposition reactions are just the reverse of combination reactions.

(a) **Thermal Decomposition Reactions:** Chemical reactions in which the decomposition is achieved by supplying heat energy are called thermal decomposition reactions.

(i) Decomposition of ferrous sulphate. Ferrous sulphate on heating decomposes as given below:

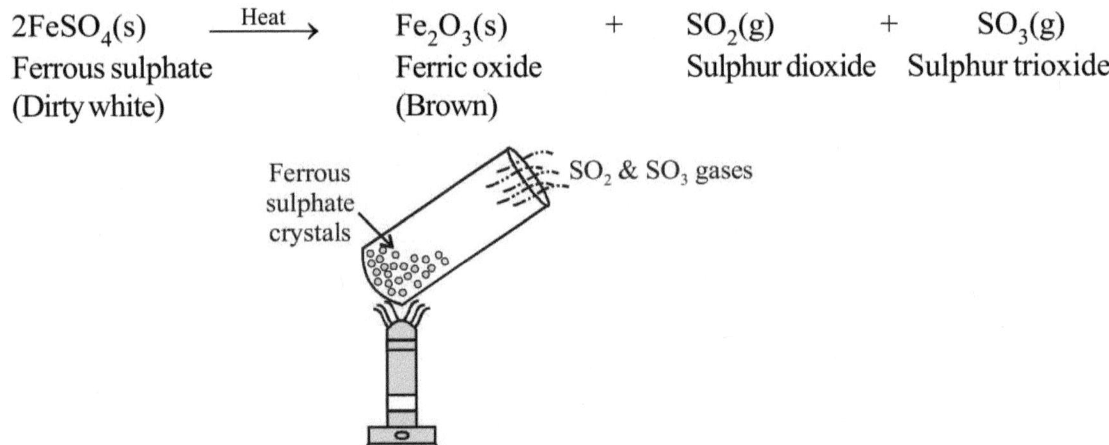

Figure : Decomposition of Ferrous sulphate crystals

(ii) Decomposition of lead nitrate

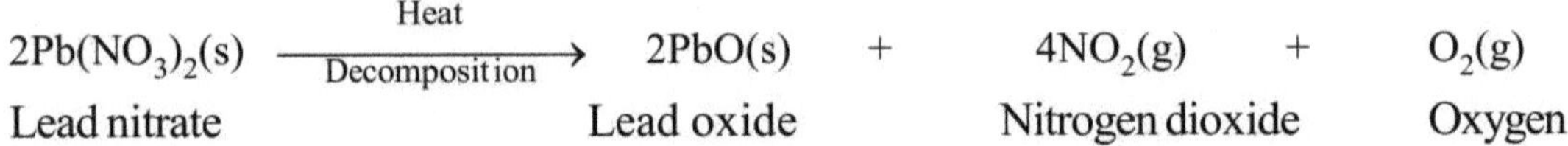

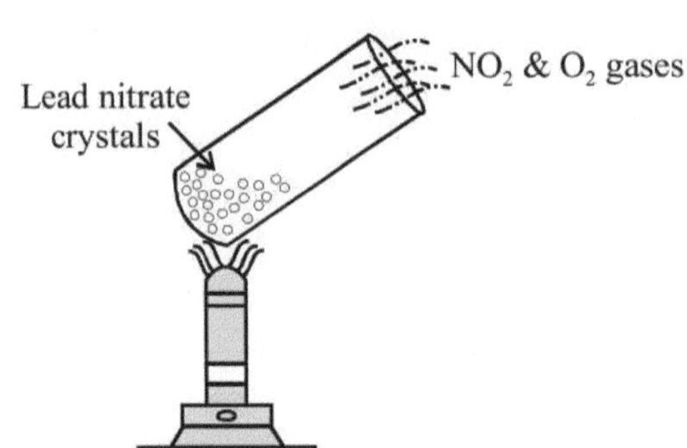

Figure : Decomposition of Lead nitrate crystals

(iii) Decomposition of calcium carbonate

$$CaCO_3(s) \xrightarrow[\text{Decomposition}]{\text{Heat}} CaO(s) + CO_2(g)$$

(Calcium carbonate) **(Calcium oxide)** **(Carbon dioxide)**

Calcium oxide obtained in this process is called lime or quick lime, it has many uses. The most important is in the manufacture of cement.

(b) **Electrolytic Decomposition Reactions :** Chemical reactions in which decomposition is achieved by passing electric current are called electrolytic decomposition reactions. This process of electrolytic decomposition of a substance is also known as electrolysis.

Note : In electrolysis, electro refer to electricity and lysis refers to break down.

Electrolytic decomposition of water → When electric current is passed through acidulated water, it decomposes to give hydrogen gas and oxygen gas.

⇨ Activity :

The electrolysis of water resulting in hydrogen and oxygen gases is a common example of decomposition reaction carried by passing electric current. Water as such is a poor conductor of electricity but water containing a few drops of sulphuric acid (acidulated water) is a good conductor.

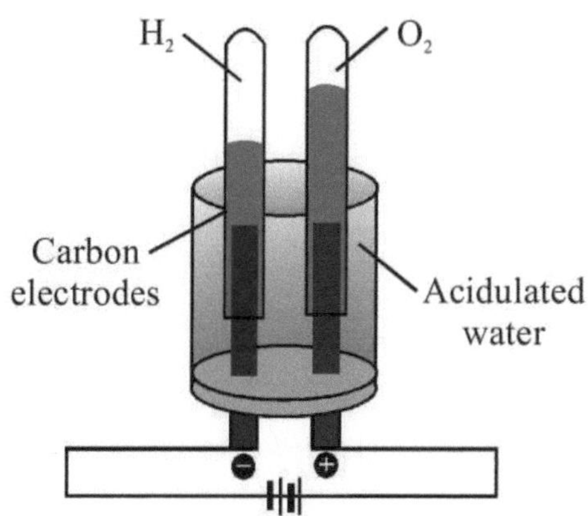

Electrolysis of Acidulated Water

In a plastic mug, drill two holes at the base and insert graphite (carbon) electrodes into these holes. Connect these electrodes to a 6 volts battery. The plastic mug will act as voltameter. Fill the mug with water to nearly half and add a few drops of dilute sulphuric acid. Invert graduated test tubes containing water on both the electrodes as shown in the figure. Pass current slowly through the voltameter. Bubbles of gases will appear above the electrodes in both the tubes. As a result, water level will be pushed downwards.

The gases are hydrogen and oxygen and are formed by the decomposition of water on passing electric current.

$$\underset{\text{Water}}{2H_2O(l)} \xrightarrow{\text{Electric current}} \underset{\text{Hydrogen}}{2H_2(g)} + \underset{\text{Oxygen}}{O_2(g)}$$

The volume of hydrogen collected will be double than that of oxygen. This is quite expected as well according to the chemical equation. These gases can be tested later on.

(c) Decomposition in the presence of sun light: Some compounds decompose when placed in sun light.

$$2AgCl\,(s) \xrightarrow{\text{Sunlight}} \underset{\text{(Grey)}}{2Ag(s)} + \underset{\text{(Chlorine)}}{Cl_2\,(g)}$$

(Decomposition reactions are generally endothermic in nature.)

(i) If we take silver bromide in place of silver chloride, it is also converted into grey coloured silver.

$$\underset{\substack{\text{Silver bromide}\\\text{(Yellow)}}}{2AgBr} \xrightarrow{\text{Sunlight}} \underset{\substack{\text{Silver metal}\\\text{(Grey)}}}{2Ag} + \underset{\text{Bromine}}{Br_2}$$

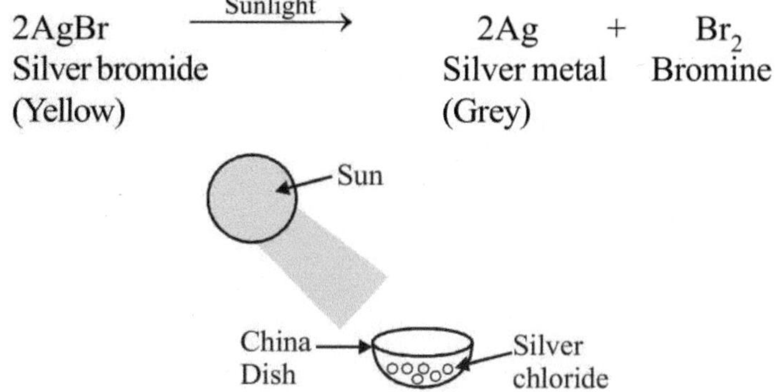

Figure : Action of sun light on silver chloride crystals

(ii) Photolytic decomposition of hydrogen peroxide.

$$\underset{\text{Hydrogen peroxide}}{2H_2O_2} \xrightarrow{\text{Light}} \underset{\text{Water}}{2H_2O} + \underset{\text{Oxygen}}{O_2 \uparrow}$$

Silver halides are sensitive to sunlight and are decomposed by it. This forms the basis of black & white photography. Silver halides are generally kept in coloured bottles.

Photolysis of AgBr is used in black and white photography.

During photosynthesis liberations of O_2 takes place because of photolysis of water.
Hydrogen peroxide is kept in coloured bottles so as to cut off light.

➤ Advantages of Decomposition Reactions :

Decomposition reactions find a large number of its advantages in industry and our daily life. Some important advantages of decomposition reactions are :

(i) **Extraction of metals :** Metals like sodium, potassium, aluminium, calcium, magnesium, etc. can be extracted by the electrolytic decomposition of their molten salts. When fused (molten) metal chloride or oxide is decomposed by passing electricity, the metal is produced at the cathode (negative electrode).

(ii) **Isolation of some non-metals :** Some non-metals like hydrogen, oxygen and chlorine etc. can be obtained on large scale by the electrolytic decomposition of their respective compounds. For example, hydrogen and oxygen can be obtained by the electrolysis of acidulated water.

(iii) **Digestion of food in our body :** For example, starch which we take in the form of food like rice, wheat, potatoes, etc. decomposes in our bodies to produce simple sugars like glucose. Similarly, proteins consumed by us in different forms decompose to form amino acids.

➤ Displacement Reactions :

Those reactions in which a more active element displaces or removes another less active element from a compound are called **displacement reactions**.

Relative reactivity of metals :

Different metals possess different reactivities. The arrangement of metals in a vertical column in order of their decreasing reactivity from top to bottom is called reactivity series or activity series of metals.

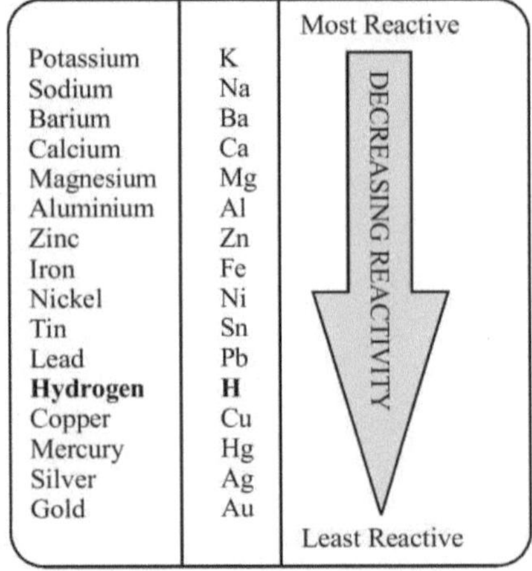

Activity series of some metals

(i) **Displacement of copper by iron :** When a piece of iron metal is dipped in a solution of copper sulphate, deep blue colour of copper sulphate starts fading and starts converting into green colour. This is due to displacement of copper from copper sulphate solution by more reactive iron metal which results in the formation of green coloured ferrous sulphate solution along with the deposition of reddish brown copper metal on the surface of iron metal.

$$Fe(s) + CuSO_4(aq) \longrightarrow FeSO_4(aq) + Cu(s)$$

Iron, Copper sulphate (Blue) → Iron (II) sulphate (Green), Copper

(ii) **Displacement of copper by zinc :** If we dip a strip of zinc metal in copper sulphate solution, zinc displaces copper from copper sulphate forming zinc sulphate and copper metal

$$Zn(s) + CuSO_4(aq) \longrightarrow ZnSO_4(aq) + Cu(s)$$

Zinc, Copper sulphate solution (Blue) → Zinc sulphate (Colourless), Copper

As zinc sulphate solution is colourless, therefore, the blue colour of copper sulphate solution goes on fading with the passage of time. At the same time, a reddish brown deposit of copper metal is formed on the zinc strip.

One more example of displacement of copper from its salt solution is given below :

$$Pb(s) + CuCl_2(aq) \longrightarrow PbCl_2(aq) + Cu(s)$$

Lead, Copper chloride → Lead chloride, Copper

Let us now consider a reaction in which more reactive copper displaces less reactive metal from its salt solution.

(iii) **Displacement of less reactive non metal by more reactive metal :**
Like metals a more reactive non-metal also displaces a less reactive non-metal from its compound. For example, more reactive chlorine gas when bubbled through a colourless solution of potassium iodide, displaces iodine from it as violet vapours.

$$2KI(aq) + Cl_2(g) \longrightarrow 2KCl(aq) + I_2(g)$$

Potassium iodide (Colourless), Chlorine → Potassium chloride (Violet), Iodine

➤ Double Displacement Reactions :

Double Displacement Reactions are also known as METATHESIS REACTIONS.

The reaction in which two different atoms or groups of atoms are displaced by other atoms or groups of atoms or in which two compounds react by an exchange or displacement of ions to form new compounds are called **double displacement reactions**.

The double decomposition reactions can be further classified in two types :

(a) Precipitation reactions **(b) Neutralisation reactions**

Let us discuss these double decomposition reactions, individually.

(a) **Precipitation reaction :** Those reactions in which two clear and transparent solutions on mixing result in the formation of an insoluble product are known as precipitation reactions and the insoluble product is known as precipitate.

$$Na_2SO_4(aq) + BaCl_2(aq) \longrightarrow 2NaCl(aq) + BaSO_4(s)\downarrow$$

Sodium sulphate, Barium chloride → Sodium chloride, Barium sulphate (White ppt.)

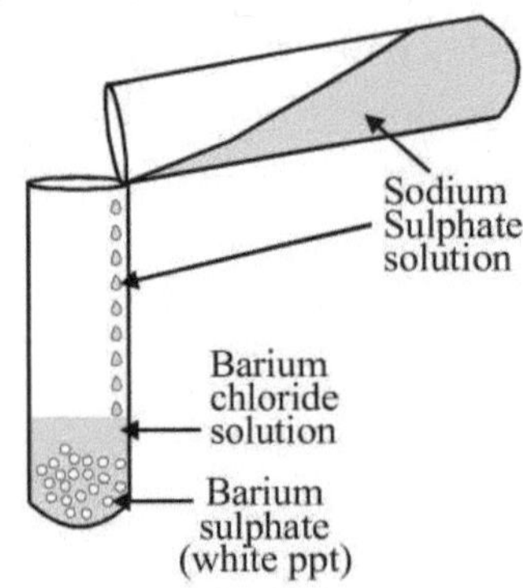

Figure : Formation of $BaSO_4$ by double displacement reaction

In this reaction, SO_4^{2-} ions displace Cl^- ions and Cl^- ions displace SO_4^{2-} ions. Since the reactions involves the displacement of two chemical species, therefore, it is known as **double displacement reaction**.

$$\underset{\text{Silver nitrate}}{AgNO_3(aq)} + \underset{\text{Sodium chloride}}{NaCl(aq)} \longrightarrow \underset{\substack{\text{Silver chloride} \\ \text{(white ppt)}}}{AgCl(s)\downarrow} + \underset{\text{Sodium nitrate}}{NaNO_3(aq)}$$

These reactions usually occur in ionic compounds.

(b) Neutralisation Reactions :

Reactions in which an acid and a base react with each other to produce salt and water are known as **neutralisation reactions.**

When an aqueous solution of hydrochloric acid is mixed with an aqueous solution of sodium hydroxide in equivalent amounts, a reaction takes place to form sodium chloride and water

(i) $$\underset{\substack{\text{Hydrochloric acid} \\ \text{(Acid)}}}{HCl(aq)} + \underset{\substack{\text{Sodium hydroxide} \\ \text{(Base)}}}{NaOH(aq)} \longrightarrow \underset{\substack{\text{Sodium chloride} \\ \text{(Salt)}}}{NaCl(aq)} + \underset{\text{(Water)}}{H_2O(l)}$$

(ii) $$\underset{\text{(Base)}}{KOH(aq)} + \underset{\text{(Acid)}}{HNO_3(aq)} \longrightarrow \underset{\text{(Salt)}}{KNO_3(aq)} + \underset{\text{(Water)}}{H_2O(\ell)}$$

(iii) $$\underset{\text{(Base)}}{Ba(OH)_2(aq)} + \underset{\text{(Acid)}}{2HCl(aq)} \longrightarrow \underset{\text{(Salt)}}{BaCl_2(aq)} + \underset{\text{(Water)}}{2H_2O(\ell)}$$

(iv) $$\underset{\text{(Base)}}{2NaOH(aq)} + \underset{\text{(Acid)}}{H_2SO_4(aq)} \longrightarrow \underset{\text{(Salt)}}{Na_2SO_4(aq)} + \underset{\text{(Water)}}{2H_2O(\ell)}$$

Such a reaction is termed as a **neutralisation reaction.** The hydrogen (H^+) ions which were responsible for the acidic properties of HCl have reacted with hydroxyl (OH^-) ions which were responsible for the basic properties of NaOH to produce neutral water. The Na^+ and Cl^- ions have undergone no chemical change and appear in the form of crystalline sodium chloride on evaporation.

Since HCl, NaOH and NaCl are all soluble strong electrolytes, therefore, the above equation can also be written in an ionic form as under:

$$H^+(aq) + Cl^-(aq) + Na^+(aq) + OH^-(aq) \longrightarrow Na^+(ag) + Cl^-(aq) + H_2O(l)$$

Cancelling the common ions on both sides, the net ionic equation is :

$$H^+(aq) + OH^-(aq) \longrightarrow H_2O(l)$$

Neutralisation reaction is infact a combination of H^+ ions of the acid and OH^- ions of the base to produce H_2O.

➤ Application of neutralization reaction in daily life :

(i) The most important use of neutralization reaction is in the form of antacids. The substances which remove excess acid in our stomach are called antacids.

(ii) In other words, antacids are simple bases that neutralize digestive acids. Their ability to neutralize acids is due to the hydroxide, carbonate or bicarbonate they contain.

Illustration 3 : ***Identify the type of chemical reaction***

(a) $2KNO_3 \longrightarrow 2KNO_2 + O_2$

(b) $N_2 + 3H_2 \longrightarrow 2NH_3$

(c) $CuSO_4 + Fe \longrightarrow FeSO_4 + Cu$

(d) $AgNO_3\ (aq) + NaCl\ (aq) \longrightarrow AgCl\ (s) + NaNO_3\ (aq)$

Solution : (a) Decomposition (b) Combination

(c) Displacement (d) Double displacement reaction

Illustration 4 : ***What are condition required for decomposition reaction.***

Solution : Heat, light and electricity.

➤ Oxidation and reduction reactions :

Oxidation : (i) The addition of oxygen to a substance is called **oxidation.**

(ii) The removal of hydrogen from a substance is also called **oxidation.**

Reduction : (i) The addition of hydrogen to a substance is called **reduction.**

(ii) The removal of oxygen from a substance is also called **reduction.**

The process of **reduction** is just the opposite of oxidation. Moreover, oxidation and reduction occur together.

Oxidising agent : (i) The substance which gives oxygen for oxidation is called an oxidising agent.

(ii) The substance which removes hydrogen is also called an oxidising agent.

Reducing agent : (i) The substance which gives hydrogen for reduction is called a reducing agent.

(ii) The substance which removes oxygen is also called a reducing agent.

The oxidation and reduction reactions are also called redox reactions (In the name 'redox', the term 'red' stands for 'reduction' and 'ox' stands for oxidation). We will now give some examples of oxidation and reduction reactions.

Example 1 : When copper reacts with oxygen, copper oxide is obtained.

Sol. : Heat a china dish containing about 1 g copper powder.

It is observed that the brown copper powder gets coated with black copper (II) oxide.

Conclusion

Copper (brown in colour) on heating combines with oxygen to form black copper (II) oxide.

$$\underset{\text{Copper (Brown)}}{2Cu(s)} + \underset{\text{Oxygen}}{O_2(g)} \longrightarrow \underset{\text{Copper (II) oxide (Black)}}{2CuO(s)}$$

Here, we can say that copper is being oxidised, as it is gaining oxygen. In the above activity if hydrogen gas is passed over product (CuO) and the black coating on the surface becomes brown because reverse reaction take place.

$$CuO(s) + H_2(g) \xrightarrow{\text{Heat}} Cu(s) + H_2O(\ell)$$

Here, we can say that copper oxide is being reducing, as it is loosing oxygen and hydrogen is being oxidised.

Or

One reactant (H_2) gets oxidised and other (CuO) gets reduced during the reaction.

Oxidation

$$CuO + H_2 \xrightarrow{Heat} Cu + H_2O$$

Reduction

Such reactions where both oxidation and reduction reactions takes place are called **oxidation reduction reactions or redox reactions.**

Example 2 : When zinc oxide is heated with carbon, then zinc metal and carbon monoxide are formed:

Oxidation

$$ZnO + C \xrightarrow{Heat} Zn + CO$$

Reduction

In this reaction,

(i) zinc oxide (ZnO) is losing oxygen, so it is being reduced to zinc (Zn).

(ii) carbon (C) is gaining oxygen, so it is being oxidised to carbon monoxide (CO). In this reaction, zinc oxide is the oxidising agent whereas carbon is the reducing agent. Carbon is used in the form of coke for the extraction of zinc metal.

Example 3 : When manganese dioxide reacts with hydrochloric acid, then manganese dichloride, chlorine and water are formed :

Oxidation

$$MnO_2 + 4HCl \xrightarrow{Heat} MnCl_2 + Cl_2 + 2H_2O$$

Reduction

In this reaction, MnO_2 is losing oxygen to form $MnCl_2$ so manganese dioxide (MnO_2) is being reduced to manganese dichloride ($MnCl_2$). On the other hand, HC1 is losing hydrogen to form Cl_2, so hydrochloric acid (HC1) is being oxidised to chlorine (Cl_2). In this reaction, manganese dioxide (MnO_2) is the oxidising agent whereas hydrochloric acid (HCl) is the reducing agent.

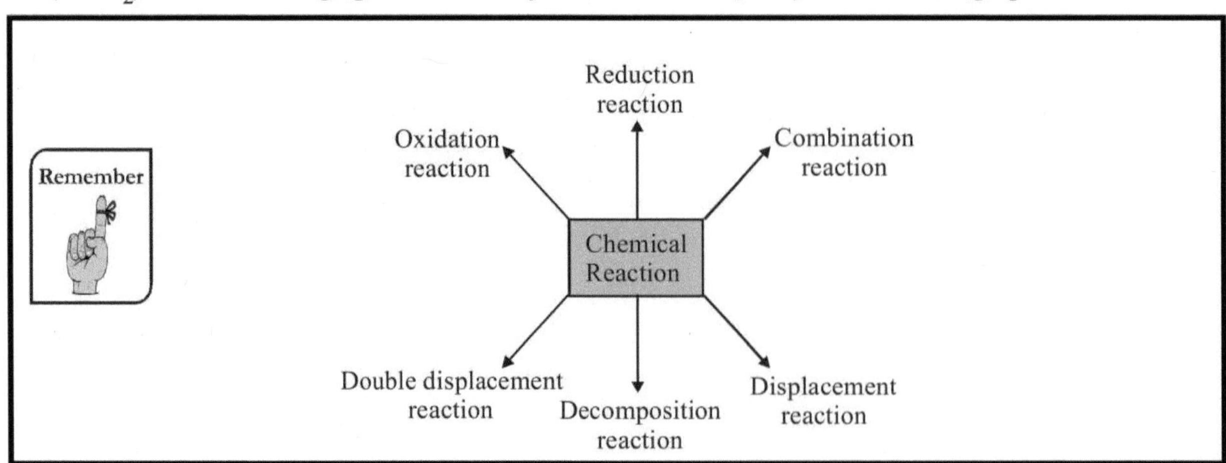

1.6 MODERN CONCEPT OF OXIDATION AND REDUCTION :

Electronic concept : This concept is applicable when reactants are ionic in nature.

Oxidation is defined as a process in which an atom, ion or molecule looses one or more eletrons.

$$Mg \longrightarrow Mg^{2+} + 2e^{\ominus}$$
$$Na \longrightarrow Na^{+} + e^{\ominus}$$
$$Cu \longrightarrow Cu^{2+} + 2e^{\ominus}$$

Reduction is defined as a process in which atom, ion or molecule gains one or more electrons.

$$Cl + e^{\ominus} \longrightarrow Cl^{-}$$
$$Zn^{2+} + 2e^{\ominus} \longrightarrow Zn$$
$$Sn^{4+} + 2e^{\ominus} \longrightarrow Sn^{2+}$$

Oxidising agent : A substance i.e. atom, ion or molecule that oxidises other one and in return gets reduced itself by gain of electron is called Oxidising agent.

Examples of Oxidising agent

(i) Non-metals such as halogens and oxygen, ozone are good oxidising agents. Among halogens fluorine is the strongest oxidising agent.

(ii) Oxides of elements such as CaO, MgO, CuO, P_4O_{10}, Na_2O etc.

(iii) Acidified $K_2Cr_2O_7$

$$Cr_2O_7^{2-} + 14H^{+} + 6e^{\ominus} \longrightarrow 2Cr^{3+} + 7H_2O$$

(iv) Hydrogen peroxide H_2O_2

$$H_2O_2 + 2H^{+} + 2e^{\ominus} \longrightarrow 2H_2O$$

(v) Potassium permangnate $KMnO_4$

(a) In acidic medium

$$MnO_4^{-} + 8H^{+} + 5e^{\ominus} \longrightarrow Mn^{2+} + 4H_2O$$

i.e. $Mn^{7+} + 5e^{\ominus} \longrightarrow Mn^{2+}$

(b) In alkaline medium

$$MnO_4^{-} + e^{\ominus} \longrightarrow MnO_4^{2-}$$

i.e. $Mn^{7+} + e^{\ominus} \longrightarrow Mn^{6+}$

(c) In neutral medium

$$MnO_4^{-} + 2H_2O + 3e^{\ominus} \longrightarrow MnO_2 + 4OH^{-}$$

i.e. $Mn^{7+} + 3e^{\ominus} \longrightarrow Mn^{4+}$

Reducing agent : A substance i.e., atom, ion or molecule which reduces the other one and gets oxidised it self by loss of electrons is called a reducing agent.

Example :

(i) All the metals are strong reducing agents. For e.g. , Na, K, Zn, Al, V, Cr, Fe etc.

(ii) Metallic hydrides such as, CaH_2, NaH, LiH etc.

(iii) Strongest reducing power is shown by Lithium in its solution state.

(iv) Compounds such as $FeSO_4$, HI, HCl, HBr, H_2S, $SnCl_2$, O_3 and H_2O_2 etc. also show strong reducing power.

(v) In the reaction of stannous chloride and mercuric chloride, stannous chloride acts as a reducing agents as it oxidation state is increased from +2 to +4

Oxidation

$$SnCl_2 + 2HgCl_2 \longrightarrow SnCl_4 + Hg_2Cl_2$$

Reduction

$$Sn^{2+} \longrightarrow Sn^{4+} + 2e^- \text{(Oxidation)}$$

$$2Hg^{2+} + 2e^- \longrightarrow 2Hg^{1+} \text{(Reduction)}$$

The overall reaction can be written as

$$Sn^{2+} + 2Hg^{2+} \longrightarrow 2Hg^{1+} + Sn^{4+}$$

(vi) Oxalic acid $\begin{bmatrix} COOH \\ | \\ COOH \end{bmatrix} \longrightarrow C_2O_4^{2-} + 2H^{\oplus}$

$$C_2O_4^{2-} \longrightarrow 2CO_2 + 2e^-$$

The substance which act as both oxidising and reducing agents are O_3, H_2O_2, H_2SO_3, HNO_2, $NaNO_2$, SO_2, $Na_2S_2O_3$ etc.

1.7 VALENCY, OXIDATION STATE AND OXIDATION NUMBER

Valency of an element is defined as number indicating its combining capacity.
For example,

(i) It represents the number of hydrogen atoms which can combine with a given atom.
(ii) It also represents the number of single bonds which an atom can form.
(iii) It is also defined as a number of electrons its atom is able to lend, borrow or share.
(iv) In any case valency is a pure number and has no plus or minus sign associated with it.
In ionic compounds the hereby oxidation state of an element is the same as the charge on the ion formed from an atom of the element. For example, in potassium bromide potassium is said to be in the + 1 oxidation state and bromine in – 1 oxidation state. It ionizes as
$KBr \longrightarrow K^+ + Br^-$
(v) Oxidation state of aluminium in Al_2O_3 is +3 and the total oxidation number of two aluminium atoms is +6.
(vi) Thus oxidation state of an element is its oxidation number per atom.

Difference between the magnitude of valency and the oxidation number :

For example, consider the following compounds of carbon:

CH_4	CH_3Cl	CH_2Cl_2
Methane	Methyl chloride	Methylene chloride
$CHCl_3$	CCl_4	
Chloroform	Carbon tetrachloride	

In each case one atom of carbon shares a total of 4 pairs of electrons with other atoms. Carbon atom is, therefore, tetravalent in each case.
Oxidation number for carbon in CH_4, CH_3Cl, CH_2Cl_2, $CHCl_3$ and CCl_4 is –4, –2, 0, +2 and +4 respectively.

Difference between oxidation number and valency :

Thus while valency of carbon remains constant (=4) in each one of the five compounds, its oxidation number varies from –4 to +4.

➤ **Oxidation and Reduction in terms of Oxidation Number :**

The term oxidation refers to any chemical change involving increase in oxidation number whereas the term reduction applies to any chemical change involving decrease in oxidation number

Consider the following chemical changes :

(i) $2H_2 + O_2 \longrightarrow 2H_2O$

Here in oxidation number of hydrogen changes from 0 (in H_2) to + 1 (in H_2O). It is, therefore, a case of oxidation of hydrogen.

(ii) Sugar ($C_{12}H_{22}O_{11}$) burns to give CO_2 and water. In this oxidation number of carbon increases from 0 (in $C_{12}H_{22}O_{11}$) to +4 in CO_2. The sugar is, therefore, said to have undergone oxidation.

(iii) When oxygen reacts with hydrogen to give water [example (i)] the oxidation number of oxygen decreases from 0 (in O_2) to –2 (in H_2O). It is, therefore, a case of reduction of oxygen.

In the same reaction, oxidation number of hydrogen increases, and that of oxygen decreases, i.e., hydrogen undergoes oxidation while oxygen undergoes reduction. Thus oxidation and reduction occur together.

An oxidising agent is a substance which brings about oxidation. It contains an atom which undergoes a decrease in oxidation number. It can also be defined as a substance which picks up electrons and thus brings about de-electronation.

➤ Oxidation Number or Oxidation State :

Definition of Oxidation Number : The oxidation number is defined as a positive or negative number that represents a charge that an atom appears to have in a given species when the bonding electrons are counted as per the certain prescribed set of rules.

Rules for assigning oxidation number : Oxidation number for atoms & ions can be assigned using the following set of rules.

■ **Rule 1 :** The oxidation number of an atom in an element in its free uncombined state is zero, regardless of whether the element exists as monoatomic or polyatomic molecule. For example, each fluorine atom in F_2, each phosphorus atom in P_4 & the silver atom in Ag, is assigned as oxidation number of zero.

■ **Rule 2 :** The oxidation number of a monoatomic ion is same as the charge on the ion. For example, the oxidation number of calcium ion is +2, in sulphur S^{-2} ion has oxidation number of –2.

■ **Rule 3 :** Oxidation numbers conventionally assigned to atoms in their chemical compounds are as follows :

(a) Oxygen = –2 (except in peroxides where it is –1). For example, the oxidation state of oxygen in SO_2, $KClO_3$ and $KMnO_4$ is –2. In Na_2O_2 & H_2O_2, the oxidation number of oxygen is –1. In the very rare instance when oxygen is bound to an element that is more electronegative than itself, such as in OF_2, Oxygen exhibits an oxidation number of +2 and in O_2F_2, oxygen shows +1 oxidation number.

(b) Hydrogen = +1 (except in metallic hydrides where it is –1). For example the oxidation number of hydrogen atom in H_2O, $H_2O_2NH_3$, CH_3COOH is +1. In LiH, it is –1.

(c) Group IA elements (alkali metals) = +1.

(d) Group IIA elements (alkaline earth elements) = +2.

(e) Halogen atoms in binary ionic compounds (halides) = –1. The halogen atom in Na^+, KBr, CsI has an oxidation number of –1.

■ **Rule 4 : The algebric sum of the positive & negative oxidation numbers in a compound is zero.**

The oxidation number of a specified atom in a compound can therefore be determined as illustrated below.

Oxidation number of Mn in $KMnO_4$

Let oxidation number of Mn be x

Oxidation number of oxygen is –2

& Oxidation number of K is +1

$\therefore$ $+1 + x + 4(-2) = 0$

$\therefore$ $x = +7$

Therefore, the oxidation number of Mn in $KMnO_4$ is +7

■ **Rule 5 :** The algebraic sum of the positive and negative oxidation states or numbers of the atoms in a polyatomic ion is equal to charge on the ion.

(i) Let us find out the oxidation number of chromium in $Cr_2O_7^{-2}$

Let the oxidation number of chromium be x and oxygen as –2,

Sum of oxidation numbers = $2x + 7(-2) = -2$

$2x - 14 = -2$

$x = +6$

Thus the oxidation number of chromium in $Cr_2O_7^{-2}$ ion is +6.

(ii) Oxidation number of S in H_2SO_4 is as,

Let oxidation number of S be x.

Sum of oxidation numbers of various atoms in $H_2SO_4 = 2x(+1) + x + 4x(-2)$

$= 2 + x - 8 = x - 6$

This sum must be zero. Hence

$x - 6 = 0$

when $x = 6$

or oxidation number of S in $H_2SO_4 = +6$

Putting oxidation number of S in $Na_2S_2O_3$

$2 + 2x - 6 = 0$

$2x - 4 = 0$, we have

$x = +2$

$\therefore$ Oxidation number of S in $Na_2S_2O_3 = +2$

(iii) Oxidation state of Mn in Mn_2O_7 is as,

Let the oxidation state of manganese be x.

Sum of oxidation numbers of various atoms in Mn_2O_7 is as,

$2(x) + 7(-2) = 0$

$\therefore$ $2x = +14$

$x = +7$

■ **Rule 6 :** The oxidation numbers of atoms in covalent compounds can be derived by assigning the electrons of each bond to the more electromagnetic atom of the bonded atoms.

(i) Oxidation state of S in per monosulphuric acid (H_2SO_5).

Let the oxidation number S be x, oxygen –2, hydrogen +1 and the oxidation state of oxygen in peroxylinkage is – 1.

Sum of oxidation number of various atoms is,

$+2 + x + 3(-2) - 2 = 0$

$+2 + x - 6 - 2 = 0$

$x = +6$

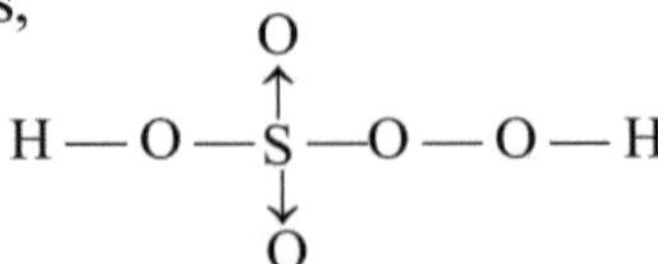

➤ Distinction between valency and oxidation state / oxidation number :

(i) Valency is always a whole number, on the other hand the oxidation number of the element may be a whole number or fractional.

(ii) Valency of the element is never zero except of noble gases but the oxidation number of the element may be zero.

(iii) Valency is the combining power of an element with no plus or minus sign. On the other hand oxidation number is the charge present on the atom of the element while being in combination. It may have plus or minus sign.

Note : The oxidation number changes with the following cases.

Oxidation → Oxidation number increases

Reduction → Oxidation number decreases

Oxidizing agent → Oxidation number decreases

Reducing agent → Oxidation number increases

➤ Oxidation State / Oxidation number in Complex molecules :

(i) Carbon in Glucose ($C_6H_{12}O_6$)

Let the oxidation number of carbon be x, hydrogen +1 and oxygen –2

Sum of oxidation number of various atoms in $C_6H_{12}O_6$ is

$$6x + 12(+1) + 6(-2) = 0$$
$$6x + 12 - 12 = 0$$
$$6x = 0$$
$$x = 0$$

In glucose the oxidation state of carbon is zero.

(ii) Ni in $[Ni(CO)_4]$

The oxidation state of CO is zero, hence the oxidation state of nickel will also be zero.

(iii) Sulphur in $(CH_3)_2$ SO i.e., dimethyl sulphoxide.

Let the oxidation state of S be x, oxygen –2, and each methyl group is +1

Sum of oxidation numbers of various atoms in $(CH_3)_2SO$ is

$$+2 + x - 2 = 0$$
$$x = 0$$

Thus the oxidation state of sulphur in $(CH_3)_2SO$ is zero.

(iv) Boron in Li BH_4

In metal hydrides, the oxidation state of hydrogen is –1 and the metal Lithium is +1

Sum of oxidation number of various atoms in $LiBH_4$ is,

$$+1 + x - 4 = 0$$
$$x = +3$$

Thus the oxidation state of B in $LiBH_4$ is +3

➤ **Fractional values of Oxidation numbers are possible with the following components :**

(i) Hydrazoic acid N_3H

Let the oxidation no. of nitrogen be x and hydrogen +1.

$$3x + 1 = 0$$
$$3x = -1$$
$$x = -\frac{1}{3}$$
$$x = -0.333$$

The oxidation number of N in N_3H is –1/3.

(ii) $Na_2S_4O_6$

Let the oxidation no. of sulphur be x, sodium +1 and oxygen –2,

$$2 + 4x + 6(-2) = 0$$
$$2 + 4x - 12 = 0$$
$$4x = +10$$
$$x = 10/4 = 2.5$$

The oxidation number of S in $Na_2S_4O_6$ is 2½

Try your self :

Find out the oxidation number / oxidation state of :

(a) S in $H_2S_2O_7$ (b) S in $Na_2S_2O_3$ (c) Cr in $Cr(CO)_6$

(d) Fe in $Fe_2(CO)_9$ (e) Fe in Fe_3O_4 (f) Mn in MnO_4^-

1.8 BALANCING OF REDOX REACTIONS

The redox reactions can be balanced by following methods

(i) Oxidation number method

(ii) Ion-electron method

Balancing by oxidation number method : The various steps involved in balancing a redox equation by oxidation number method are:

(i) Write the skeleton equation.

(ii) Indicate the oxidation numbers of all the atoms involved in the equation above their symbols.

(iii) Identify the elements which undergo change in oxidation number.

(iv) Calculate the increase and decrease in oxidation number per atom with respect to the reactants. If more than one atom is involved, then multiply with the number of the atoms undergoing the change to calculate the total change in oxidation number.

(v) Equate the increase and decrease in oxidation number on the reactant side by multiplying the formulae of the oxidising and reducing agents suitably.

(vi) Balance the equation with respect to all the atoms except hydrogen and oxygen.

(vii) Finally balance hydrogen and oxygen atoms also.

(viii) In the reactions taking place in the acidic medium, balance the O atoms by adding required number of H_2O molecules to the side deficient in O atoms. Then balance the H atoms by adding H^+ to the side deficient in H atoms.

(ix) In the basic medium, first balance the number of negative charges by adding required number of OH^- ions to the side deficient in the magnitude of the charges. Then add H_2O molecules on the other side in order to balance the OH^- ions added.

Let us try to balance a few chemical equations by oxidation number method.

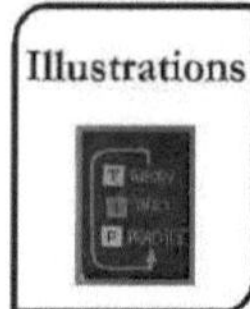

Illustration 5 : Balance the following chemical equations by the oxidation number method

$$CuO + NH_3 \longrightarrow Cu + N_2 + H_2O$$

Solution : The balancing is done in the following steps:

1. Write the O.N. of each atom in the skeleton equation

$$\overset{+2}{Cu}\ \overset{-2}{O} + \overset{-3}{N}\ \overset{+1}{H_3} \longrightarrow \overset{0}{Cu} + \overset{0}{N_2} + \overset{+1}{H_2}\ \overset{-2}{O}$$

2. Identify the atoms which undergo change in O.N.

$$\overset{+2}{Cu}O + \overset{-3}{N}H_3 \longrightarrow \overset{0}{Cu} + \overset{0}{N_2} + H_2O$$

3. Calculate the increase and decrease in O.N. w.r.t. reactant atoms

Increase in O.N. = 3

$$\overset{+2}{Cu}O + \overset{-3}{N}H_3 \longrightarrow \overset{0}{Cu} + \overset{0}{N_2} + H_2O$$

Decrease in O.N. = 2

4. Equate the increase and decrease in O.N. on the reactant side.

$$3CuO + 2NH_3 \longrightarrow Cu + N_2 + H_2O$$

5. Balance the number of Cu and N atoms on both sides of the equation.

$$3CuO + 2NH_3 \longrightarrow 3Cu + N_2 + H_2O$$

6. Now balance H and O atoms by hit and trial method

$$3CuO + 2NH_3 \longrightarrow 3Cu + N_2 + 3H_2O$$

Try your self :

(i) $Cu + NO_3^- \longrightarrow NO_2 + Cu^{2+}$ **(Acidic medium)**

(ii) $C_6H_6 + O_2 \longrightarrow CO_2 + H_2O$

(iii) $SnO_2 + C \longrightarrow Sn + CO$

Balancing by Ion-electron method (or half reaction method) :

Balancing can also be done by another method known as ion-electron method. **It is based on the principle that the electrons lost during oxidation half reaction in a particular redox reaction is equal to the electrons gained in the reduction half reaction.** The method is, therefore, called **half** reaction **method**. The balancing is completed in the following steps :

(i) Write the redox reaction in ionic form.

(ii) Find out species which are getting oxidised and also which are getting reduced.

(iii) Split the whole equation into two half reactions i.e. oxidation half reaction and reduction half reaction.

(iv) While balancing each half reaction add electrons for the number of atoms of each element.

(v) In the acidic medium, and neutral medium add water molecules to the side dificient in O and H^+ to the side deficient in hydrogen.

(vi) In the basic medium, for each excess of oxygen, add one water molecule to the same side and two OH^+ ions to the other side. If hydrogen is still unbalanced, add on OH^- ion for each excess hydrogen on the same side and one water molecule to the other side.

(vii) Multiply one or both half reactions by suitable number so that the number of e^-s become equal in both the equation.

(viii) Add the two balanced half reactions and cancel any term common to both sides.

Illustration 6 : Balance the following chemical equation by ion-electron method.

$$Cr_2O_7^{2-} + Fe^{2+} + H^+ \longrightarrow Cr^{3+} + Fe^{3+} + H_2O$$

Solution : **Step I. Separation of the equation in two half reactions**

(i) Write the O.N. of all the atoms involved in the skeleton equation

$$(\overset{+6}{Cr_2}\ \overset{-2}{O_7})^{2-} + (\overset{+2}{Fe})^{2+} + (\overset{+1}{H})^{+} \longrightarrow (\overset{+3}{Cr})^{3+} + (\overset{+3}{Fe})^{3+} + \overset{+1}{H_2}\ \overset{-2}{O}$$

(ii) Identify the atoms which undergo change in O.N.

$$(\overset{+6}{Cr_2}\ O_7)^{2-} + (\overset{+2}{Fe})^{2+} + (\overset{+1}{H})^{+} \longrightarrow (\overset{+3}{Cr})^{3+} + (\overset{+3}{Fe})^{3+} + H_2O$$

(iii) Find out the species involved in the oxidation and reduction half reactions.

Increase in O.N. (oxidation)

$$(\overset{+6}{Cr_2}O_7)^{2-} + (\overset{+2}{Fe})^{2+} + H^+ \longrightarrow (\overset{+3}{Cr})^{3+} + (\overset{+3}{Fe})^{3+} + H_2O$$

Decrease in O.N. (reduction)

Thus, the two half reactions are:

Oxidation half reaction: $Fe^{2+} \longrightarrow Fe^{3+}$

Reduction half reaction: $(Cr_2O_7)^{2-} \longrightarrow Cr^{3+}$

Step II. Balancing of oxidation half reaction:

The oxidation half reaction is: $Fe^{2+} \longrightarrow Fe^{3+}$

(i) As the increase in O.N. as a result of oxidation is 1, add one e^- on the product side to balance change in O.N.

$Fe^{2+} \longrightarrow Fe^{3+} + e^-$

(ii) The charge is already balanced, and thus the equation is alo balanced

$Fe^{2+} \longrightarrow Fe^{3+} + e^-$ .....(i)

Step III. Balancing of reduction half reaction :

The reduction half reaction is: $(\overset{+6}{Cr_2}\ O_7)^{2-} \longrightarrow (\overset{+3}{Cr})^{3+}$

(i) The decrease in O.N. per Cr atom is 3 and the total decrease in O.N. for two Cr atoms is 6. Therefore, add $6e^-$ on the reactant side

$(Cr_2O_7)^{2-} + 6e^- \longrightarrow Cr^{3+}$

(ii) Balance Cr atoms on both sides of the equation

$(Cr_2O_7)^{2-} + 6e^- \longrightarrow 2Cr^{3+}$

(iii) In order to balance O atoms add seven H_2O molecules on the product side and then to balance H atoms add 14 H^+ on the reactant side.

$(Cr_2O_7)^{2-} + 6e^- + 14H^+ \longrightarrow 2Cr^{3+} + 7H_2O$ .....(ii)

Step IV. Adding the two half reactions :

In order two equate the electrons, multiply the equation (i) by 6 and then add to equation (ii) in order to get the final equation.

$$[Fe^{2+} \rightarrow Fe^{3+} + e^-] \times 6$$
$$(Cr_2O_7)^{2-} + 14H^+ + 6e^- \rightarrow 2Cr^{3+} + 7H_2O$$
$$6Fe^{2+} + Cr_2O_7^{2-} + 14H^+ \rightarrow 6Fe^{3} + 2Cr^{3+} + 7H_2O$$

Try your self :

Q.1 $Pb(NO_3)_2\ (s) \xrightarrow{\Delta} PbO\ (s) + NO_2\ (g) + O_2\ (g)$

Q.2 $MnO_2 + C_2O_4^{2-} \longrightarrow Mn^{2+} + CO_2$

Q.3 $MnO_2 + Al \longrightarrow Mn + Al_2O_3$

Q.4 $Fe_2O_3 + CO \longrightarrow Fe + CO_2$

Q.5 $Al + CuCl_2 \longrightarrow AlCl_3 + Cu$

Q.6 $C_2H_6 + O_2 \longrightarrow CO_2 + H_2O$

Q.7 $NH_3 + O_2 \longrightarrow NO + H_2O$

Q.8 $K_2Cr_2O_7 + KOH \longrightarrow H_2O + K_2CrO_4$

Q.9 $Na_2CO_3 + HCl \longrightarrow NaCl + H_2O + CO_2$

Q.10 $As_2O_3 + H_2S \longrightarrow As_2S_3 + H_2O$

Q.11 $KI + H_2O_2 \longrightarrow KOH + I_2$

Q.12 $Zn(NO_3)_2 \longrightarrow ZnO + NO_2 + O_2$

Q.13 $NaOH + H_2SO_4 \longrightarrow Na_2SO_4 + H_2O$

Q.14 $NH_3 + O_2 \longrightarrow N_2 + H_2O$

Q.15 $SO_2 + H_2S \longrightarrow H_2O + S$

Q.16 $H_2S + O_2 \longrightarrow SO_2 + H_2O$

Q.17 $Al(OH)_3 \xrightarrow{\Delta} Al_2O_3 + H_2O$

Q.18 $Al_2(SO_4)_3 + NaOH \longrightarrow Al(OH)_3 + Na_2SO_4$

Q.19 $NH_3 + O_2 \longrightarrow NO + H_2O$

Q.20 Peramanganate (VII) ion, MnO_4^- in basic solution oxidises iodide ion, I^- to produce molecular iodine (I_2) and manganese (IV) oxide (MnO_2). Write a balanced ionic equation to represent this redox reaction.

1.9 EFFECTS OF OXIDATION REACTIONS IN EVERYDAY LIFE :

We are all aware of the fact that oxygen is the most essential for sustaining life. One can live without food or even water for a number of days but not without oxygen. It is involved in variety of reactions which have wide range of effects on our daily life. Most of them are quite useful while a few may be harmful in nature. Some of these effects are briefly discussed.

➤ **Respiration :**

Respiration is the most important biochemical reaction which releases energy in the cells. When we breathe in air, oxygen enters our lungs and passes into thousands of small air sacs (alveoli). These air sacs occupy a large area of membranes and oxygen diffuses from the membranes into blood. It binds itself to haemoglobin present in red blood cells and is carries to millions of cells in the body. Respiration occurs in these cells and is accompanied by the combustion of glucose producing carbon dioxide and water. Since the reaction is of exothermic nature, the energy released during respiration carries many cell reactions and keeps our heart and muscles working. It also provides the desired warmth to the body. Both carbon dioxide and water pass back into the blood and we ultimately breathe them our. Please note that respiration takes place in the cells of all living beings.

$$\underset{\text{Glucose}}{C_6H_{10}H_6(s)} + 6O_2(g) \longrightarrow 6CO_2(g) + 6H_2O(\ell) + \text{energy}$$

➤ Combustion Reactions :

A chemical reaction in which a substance burns or gets oxidised in the presence of air or oxygen is called combustion reaction. For example, kerosene, coal, charcoal, wood etc. burn in air and thus, undergo combustion. Methane (CH_4), a major constituent of natural gas, undergoes combustion in excess of oxygen upon heating.

$$\underset{\text{Methane}}{CH_4(g)} + 2O_2(g) \longrightarrow CO_2(g) + 2H_2O(\ell)$$

Similarly, butane (C_4H_{10}), the main constituent of L.P.G. also undergoes combustion.

$$\underset{\text{Butane}}{C_4H_{10}(g)} + \frac{13}{2}O_2(g) \longrightarrow 4CO_2(g) + 5H_2O(\ell)$$

Remember that all the combustion reactions are oxidation reactions in nature.
The human body may be regarded as a furnace or machine in which various food stuff that we eat undergo combustion or oxidation or oxidation. The heat energy evolved keeps our body working. Carbohydrates such as glucose, fructose, starch etc. are the major source of energy to the human body. They undergo combustion with the help of oxygen that we inhale to form carbon dioxide and water. For example,

$$\underset{\text{Glucose}}{C_6H_{10}H_6(s)} + 6O_2(g) \longrightarrow 6CO_2(g) + 6H_2O(\ell) + \text{energy}$$

➤ Harmful Effects of Combustion :

We have discussed the utility of combustion in releasing energy which our body needs to keep it warm and working. However, combustion has harmful effect also. The environmental pollution is basically due to combustion. Poisonous gases like carbon monoxide (CO), sulphur dioxide (SO_2), sulphur trioxide (SO_3) and nitrogen dioxide (NO_2) etc. are being released into the atmosphere as a result of variety of combustion reaction which are taking place. They pollute the atmosphere and make our lives miserable. In addition to these, other harmful effect of combustion are through corrosion and rancidity. These are briefly discussed.

1.10 CORROSION & RANCIDITY :

Oxidation has damaging effect on metals as well as on food. The damaging effect of oxidation on metals is studied as corrosion and that on food is studied as rancidity. Thus, there are two common effects of oxidation reactions which we observe in daily life. These are :
1. Corrosion of metals , and 2. Rancidity of food.
Corrosion : Corrosion is the process in which metals are eaten up gradually by the action of air, moisture or a chemical (such as an acid) on their surface. Corrosion is caused mainly by the oxidation of metals by the oxygen of air. Rusting of iron metal is the most common form of corrosion. When an iron object is left in damp air for a considerable time, it gets covered with a red-brown flaky substance called '**rust**'. This is called **rusting of iron.**

$$2Fe + \frac{3}{2}O_2 + xH_2O \longrightarrow \underset{\text{Hydrated ferric oxide (rust)}}{Fe_2O_3.xH_2O}$$

Rusting involves unwanted oxidation of iron metal which occurs in nature on its own.

Rust is a soft and porous substance which gradually falls off from the surface of an iron object, and then the iron below starts rusting. Thus, rusting of iron (or corrosion of iron) is a continuous process which, if not prevented in time, eats up the whole iron object. **Corrosion weakens the iron and steel objects and structures such as railings, car bodies, bridges and ships, etc., and cuts short their life.** A lot of money has to be spent every year to prevent the corrosion of iron and steel objects, and to replace the damaged iron and steel structures.The black coating on silver and the green coating on copper are other examples of corrosion.

Rancidity : When the fats and oils present in food materials get oxidised by the oxygen (of air), their oxidation products have unpleasant smell and taste. **The condition produced by aerial oxidation of fats and oils in foods marked by unpleasant smell and taste is called rancidity**. Rancidity spoils the food materials prepared fats and oils which have been kept for a considerable time and makes them unfit for eating.

(i) **Rancidity can be prevented by adding anti-oxidants to foods containing fats and oils.** Anti-oxidant is a substance (or chemical) which prevents oxidation. The two common anti-oxidants used in foods to prevent the development of rancidity are BHA (Butylated Hydroxy Anisole) and BHT (Butylated Hydroxy Toluene).

Common antioxidants are :

(a) BHA (Butylated Hydroxy Anisole)

(b) BHT (Butylated Hydroxy Toluene)

Vitamin-E and vitamin-C (ascorbic acid) are the two antioxidants occuring in natural fats.

(ii) **Rancidity can be prevented by packaging fat and oil containing foods in nitrogen gas**. When the packed food is surrounded by an unreactive gas nitrogen, there is no oxygen (of air) to cause its oxidation and make it rancid. The manufacturers of potato chips (and other similar food products) fill the plastic bags containing chips with nitrogen gas to prevent the chips from being oxidised and turn rancid.

(iii) **Rancidity can be retarded by keeping food in a refrigerator**. The refrigerator has a low temperature inside it. When the food is kept in a refrigerator, the oxidation of fats and oils in it is slowed down due to low temperature. So, the development of rancidity due to oxidation is retarded.

(iv) **Rancidity can be retarded by storing food in air-tight containers**. When food is stored in air-tight containers, then there is little exposure to oxygen of air. Due to reduced exposure to oxygen, the oxidation of fats and oils present in food is slowed down and hence the development of rancidity is retarded.

(v) **Rancidity can be retarded by storing foods away from light**. In the absence of light, the oxidation of fats and oils present in food is slowed down and hence the development of rancidity is retarded.

Knowledge Enhancer

No doubt, there is a huge loss of lives and materials that is taking place every year on account of corrosion and rusting. However, there are some cases where corrosion plays a useful role. We all know that aluminium is placed high in the activity series and is expected to be quite reactive. It combines with oxygen present in air to form its oxide called aluminium oxide (Al_2O_3) and this is a case of corrosion. The metal oxide formed slowly gets deposited on the surface of aluminium. It forms a protective coating on the surface. This coating makes the metal passive to the attack by water, air, acids and alkalies etc. As a result, aluminium articles and containers are not corroded. Aluminium foils are commonly used for packing food preparations, cigarettes etc.

Food industry has picked up very fast throughout the world and also in India. The manufactures are adding certain substances called anti-oxidants to the food materials. As the name suggests, these check their oxidation. When anti-oxidants are added to foods, the fats and oils present in them do not get oxidised easily and thus, do not get rancid. This means that the role of anti-oxidants is to act as reducing agents. Two commonly used anti-oxidants are BHA (Butylated hydroxyanisole) and BHT (Butylated hydroxytoluene). These are both organic compounds and it is not possible to give more information about these at the present level of the students.

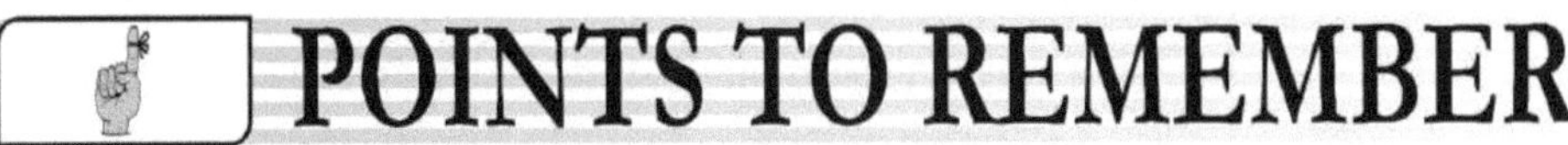

POINTS TO REMEMBER

1. A chemical reaction involves a chemical change in which substances react to form new substances with entirely new properties.Substances that react or take part in the reaction are known as **reactants** and the substances formed are known as **products.**

2. During a chemical reaction, there is a breaking of bonds between atoms of the reacting molecules to give products.

3. A chemical reaction can be observed with the help of any of the following observations:
   a. Evolution of a gas b. Change in temperature
   c. Formation of a precipitate d. Change in colour e. Change of state

4. **Physical change :** If a change involves change in colour or state but no new substance is formed, then it is a physical change.

5. **Chemical change :** If a change involves formation of new substances, it is a chemical change.

6. **Exothermic and endothermic reactions :** If heat is evolved during a reaction, then such a reaction is known as Exothermic reaction. If heat is absorbed from the surroundings, then such a reaction is known as endothermic reaction.

7. **Chemical equation :** The symbolic representation of a chemical reaction is called a chemical equation.

8. **Features of a chemical equation :**
   a. The reactants are written on the left hand side with a plus sign between them.
   b. The products are written on the right hand side with a plus sign between them.
   c. An arrow separates the reactants from the products.

9. **Skeletal chemical equation :** A chemical equation which simply represents the symbols and formulae of reactants and products taking part in the reaction is known as skeletal chemical equation for a reaction.
   For example : For the burning of Magnesium in the air, $Mg + O_2 \rightarrow MgO$ is the skeletal equation.

10. Balanced chemical equation: A balanced equation is a chemical equation in which number of atoms of each element is equal on both sides of the equation i.e. number of atoms of an element on reactant side = number of atoms of that element on the product side.

11. As per the law of conservation of mass, the total mass of element in the products of a chemical reaction is equal to the total mass of the elements present in the reactants.

12. The process of equating the number of atoms on both the sides of a chemical equation is known as balancing of a chemical equation.
    a. The first step in balancing a chemical equation is to write the number of atoms of each element present on the left hand side and right hand side.
    b. We should always start balancing with the compound that contains maximum number of atoms. It can be reactant or a product. Then in that compound select the element which has the maximum number of atoms.
    c. While balancing a chemical equation, the molecular formulae of the reactants and products should not change. The molec ular formulae are simply multiplied by suitable coefficients.
    d. To make a chemical equation more informative, the reaction conditions such as temperature, pressure or catalyst are written on the arrow separating the reactants and products.
    e. The evolution of gas is indicated by an upward arrow.
    f. The formation of precipitate is indicated by a downward arrow.
    g. Heat evolved during the reaction is written as + Heat on the product side.
    h. Heat absorbed during the reaction is written as + Heat on the reactant side.

13. **Types of chemical reactions :**
    a. Combination reaction
    b. Decomposition reaction
    c. Displacement reaction
    d. Redox reaction
    e. Double displacement reaction

14. **Combination reaction** is a reaction in which 2 or more substances combine to give a single product. Combination reaction can be between 2 elements, between an element and a compound or between 2 compounds.

15. **Decomposition reaction:** In a decomposition reaction, a single reactant decomposes to give 2 or more products. Decomposition reactions require energy in the form of heat, light or electricity

16. **Types of decomposition reactions :**
    a. Decomposition reactions which require heat are known as thermolytic decomposition reactions.
    b. Decomposition reactions which require light are known as photolyticdecomposition reactions.
    c. Decomposition reactions which require electricity are known as electrolytic decomposition reactions.

17. **Displacement reaction:** A reaction in which a more active element displaces less active element from its salt solution.

18. The reactivity series is a list of metals arranged in the order of decreasing reactivity. The most reactive metal is placed at the top and the least reactive metal is placed at the bottom.

19. **Double displacement reaction:** A chemical reaction in which there is an exchange of ions between the reactants to give new substances is called double displacement reaction.

20. **Precipitation reaction:** An insoluble solid known as precipitate is formed during a double displacement reaction. Such reactions are also known as precipitation reactions.

21. **Redox reaction:** A reaction in which oxidation and reduction take place simultaneously in a reaction, is known as a redox reaction.

22. Oxidation is a chemical process in which a substance gains oxygen or loses hydrogen.

23. Reduction is a chemical process in which a substance gains hydrogen or loses oxygen.

24. If a substance gains oxygen or loses hydrogen during a reaction, it is said to be oxidised.

25. If a substance gains hydrogen or loses oxygen during a reaction, it is said to be reduced.

26. A substance that loses oxygen or gains hydrogen is known as an oxidising agent.

27. A substance that loses hydrogen or gains oxygen is known as a reducing agent.

28. An oxidising agent gets reduced whereas a reducing agent gets oxidised.

29. In terms of electronic concept, Oxidation is defined as a loss of electrons while reduction is defined as a gain of electrons.

30. Corrosion is the slow eating up of metals by the action of air and moisture on their surfaces. Corrosion in case of Iron is known as Rusting.

31. Chemically, rust is hydrated ferric oxide ($Fe_2O_3.xH_2O$)

32. **Advantages of corrosion:** Though corrosion is undesirable, it can be advantageous in case of aluminium which on exposure to air, gets coated with a protective layer of aluminium oxide. This protects the metal underneath from further corrosion and damage.

33. **Rancidity:** When oils and fats or foods containing oils and fats are exposed to air, they get oxidised due to which the food becomes stale and gives a bad taste or smell. This is called Rancidity.

34. **Rancidity can be prevented by :**
    a. Adding antioxidants i.e. the substances which prevent oxidation.
    b. Refrigeration.
    c. Storing the food in air-tight containers

CONCEPT APPLICATION LEVEL - I [NCERT Questions]

Q.1 Why should a magnesium ribbon be cleaned before burning in air?

Ans. Magnesium is very reactive metal. When stored it reacts with oxygen to form a layer of magnesium oxide on its surface. This layer of magnesium oxide is quite stable and prevents further reaction of magnesium with oxygen. The magnesium ribbon is cleaned by sand paper to remove this layer so that the underlying metal can be exposed to air.

Q.2 Write the balanced equation for the following chemical reactions.

(i) Hydrogen + Chlorine $\longrightarrow$ Hydrogen chloride

(ii) Barium chloride + Aluminium sulphate $\longrightarrow$ Barium sulphate + Aluminium chloride

(iii) Sodium + Water $\longrightarrow$ Sodium hydroxide + Hydrogen

Ans. (i) $H_2(g) + Cl_2(g) \longrightarrow 2HCl(g)$

(ii) $3BaCl_2(aq) + Al_2(SO_4)_3(aq) \longrightarrow 3BaSO_4(s) + 2AlCl_3(aq)$

(iii) $2Na(s) + 2H_2O(\ell) \longrightarrow 2NaOH(aq) + H_2(g)$

Q.3 Write a balanced chemical equation with state symbols for the following reactions.

(i) Solutions of barium chloride and sodium sulphate in water react to give insoluble barium sulphate and the solution of sodium chloride.

(ii) Sodium hydroxide solution (in water) reacts with hydrochloric acid solution (in water) to produce sodium chloride solution and water.

Ans. (i) $BaCl_2(aq) + Na_2SO_4(aq) \longrightarrow BaSO_4(s) + 2NaCl(aq)$

(ii) $NaOH(aq) + HCl(aq) \longrightarrow NaCl(aq) + H_2O(\ell)$

Q.4 A solution of a substance 'X' is used for white washing.

(i) Name the substance 'X' and write its formula.

(ii) Write the reaction of the substance 'X' named in (i) above with water.

Ans. (i) The substance 'X' is calcium oxide. Its chemical formula is CaO.

(ii) Calcium oxide reacts vigorously with water to form calcium hydroxide (slaked lime).

$CaO(s)$	+	$H_2O(\ell)$	$\longrightarrow$	$Ca(OH)_2(aq)$
Calcium oxide (Quick lime)		Water		Calcium hydroxide (Slaked lime)

Q.5 Why is the amount of gas collected in one of the test tubes on electrolysis of H_2O, double of the amount collected in the other? Name this gas.

Ans. Water (H_2O) contains two parts of hydrogen and one part of oxygen. Therefore, the amount of hydrogen and oxygen produced during electrolysis of water is in a 2 : 1 ratio. During electrolysis, since hydrogen goes to one test tube and oxygen goes to another, the amount of gas collected in one of the test tubes is double of the amount collected in the other.

Q.6 Why does the colour of copper sulphate solution change when an iron nail is dipped in it?

Ans. When an iron nail is placed in a copper sulphate solution, iron displaces copper from copper sulphate solution forming iron sulphate, which is green in colour.

$Fe(s)$	+ $CuSO_4(aq)$	$\longrightarrow$	$FeSO_4(aq)$	+	$Cu(s)$
Iron	Copper sulphate (Blue colour)		Iron sulphate (Green colour)		Copper

Therefore, the blue colour of copper sulphate solution fades and green colour appears.

Q.7 Give an example of a double displacement reaction.

Ans. Sodium carbonate reacts with calcium chloride to form calcium carbonate and sodium chloride.

$Na_2CO_3(aq)$	+	$CaCl_2(aq)$	$\longrightarrow$	$CaCO_3(s)$	+	$2NaCl(aq)$
Sodium carbonate		Calcium chloride		Calcium carbonate		Sodium chloride

In this reaction, sodium carbonate and calcium chloride exchange ions to form two new compounds. Hence, it is a double displacement reaction.

Q.8 Identify the substances that are oxidised and the substances that are reduced in the following reactions.

(i) $4Na(s) + O_2(g) \longrightarrow 2Na_2O(s)$

(ii) $CuO(s) + H_2(g) \longrightarrow Cu(s) + H_2O(\ell)$

Ans. (i) Sodium (Na) is oxidised as it gains oxygen and oxygen gets reduced.

(ii) Copper oxide (CuO) is reduced to copper (Cu) while hydrogen (H_2) gets oxidised to water (H_2O).

Q.9 Which of the statements about the reaction below are incorrect?

$$2PbO(s) + C(s) \longrightarrow 2Pb(s) + CO_2(g)$$

(a) Lead is getting reduced.
(b) Carbon dioxide is getting oxidised.
(c) Carbon is getting oxidised.
(d) Lead oxide is getting reduced.

(A) (a) and (b) (B) (a) and (c) (C) (a), (b) and (c) (D) all

Ans. (A) (a) and (b)

Q.10 $Fe_2O_3 + 2Al \longrightarrow Al_2O_3 + 2Fe$

The above reaction is an example of a

(A) combination reaction. (B) double displacement reaction.
(C) decomposition reaction. (D) displacement reaction.

Ans. (D) The given reaction is an example of a displacement reaction.

Q.11 What happens when dilute hydrochloric acid is added to iron filings? Tick the correct answer.

(A) Hydrogen gas and iron chloride are produced.
(B) Chlorine gas and iron hydroxide are produced.
(C) No reaction takes place.
(D) Iron salt and water are produced.

Ans. (A) Hydrogen gas and iron chloride are produced. The reaction is as follows:

$$Fe(s) + 2HCl(aq) \longrightarrow FeCl_2(aq) + H_2(g)\uparrow$$

Q.12 What is a balanced chemical equation? Why should chemical equations be balanced?

Ans. A reaction which has an equal number of atoms of all the elements on both sides of the chemical equation is called a balanced chemical equation. The law of conservation of mass states that mass can neither be created nor destroyed. Hence, in a chemical reaction, the total mass of reactants should be equal to the total mass of the products. It means that the total number of atoms of each element should be equal on both sides of a chemical equation. Hence, it is for this reason the chemical equations should be balanced.

Q.13 Translate the following statements into chemical equations and then balance them.

(a) Hydrogen gas combines with nitrogen to form ammonia.

(b) Hydrogen sulphide gas burns in air to give water and sulphur dioxide.

(c) Barium chloride reacts with aluminium sulphate to give aluminium chloride and a precipitate of barium sulphate.

(d) Potassium metal reacts with water to give potassium hydroxide and hydrogen gas.

Ans. (a) $3H_2(g) + N_2(g) \longrightarrow 2NH_3(g)$

(b) $2H_2S(g) + 3O_2(g) \longrightarrow 2H_2O(\ell) + 2SO_2(g)$

(c) $3BaCl_2(aq) + Al_2(SO_4)_3(aq) \longrightarrow 2AlCl_3(aq) + 3BaSO_4(s)$

(d) $2K(s) + 2H_2O(\ell) \longrightarrow 2KOH(aq) + H_2(g)$

Q.14 Balance the following chemical equations.

(a) $HNO_3 + Ca(OH)_2 \longrightarrow Ca(NO_3)_2 + H_2O$

(b) $NaOH + H_2SO_4 \longrightarrow Na_2SO_4 + H_2O$

(c) $NaCl + AgNO_3 \longrightarrow AgCl + NaNO_3$

(d) $BaCl_2 + H_2SO_4 \longrightarrow BaSO_4 + HCl$

Ans. (a) $2HNO_3 + Ca(OH)_2 \longrightarrow Ca(NO_3)_2 + 2H_2O$

(b) $2NaOH + H_2SO_4 \longrightarrow Na_2SO_4 + 2H_2O$

(c) $NaCl + AgNO_3 \longrightarrow AgCl + NaNO_3$

(d) $BaCl_2 + H_2SO_4 \longrightarrow BaSO_4 + 2HCl$

Q.15 Write the balanced chemical equations for the following reactions.

(a) Calcium hydroxide + Carbon dioxide ⟶ Calcium carbonate + Water

(b) Zinc + Silver nitrate ⟶ Zinc nitrate + Silver

(c) Aluminium + Copper chloride ⟶ Aluminium chloride + Copper

(d) Barium chloride + Potassium sulphate ⟶ Barium sulphate + Potassium chloride

Ans. (a) $Ca(OH)_2 + CO_2 \longrightarrow CaCO_3 + H_2O$

(b) $Zn + 2AgNO_3 \longrightarrow Zn(NO_3)_2 + 2Ag$

(c) $2Al + 3CuCl_2 \longrightarrow 2AlCl_3 + 3Cu$

(d) $BaCl_2 + K_2SO_4 \longrightarrow BaSO_4 + 2KCl$

Q.16 Write the balanced chemical equation for the following and identify the type of reaction in each case.

(a) Potassium bromide(aq) + Barium iodide(aq) $\longrightarrow$ Potassium iodide(aq) + Barium bromide(s)

(b) Zinc carbonate(s) $\longrightarrow$ Zinc oxide(s) + Carbon dioxide(g)

(c) Hydrogen(g) + Chlorine(g) $\longrightarrow$ Hydrogen chloride(g)

(d) Magnesium(s) + Hydrochloric acid(aq) $\longrightarrow$ Magnesium chloride(aq) + Hydrogen(g)

Ans. (a) $2KBr(aq) + BaI_2(aq) \longrightarrow 2KI(aq) + BaBr_2(s)$; Double displacement reaction

(b) $ZnCO_3(s) \longrightarrow ZnO(s) + CO_2(g)$; Decomposition reaction

(c) $H_2(g) + Cl_2(g) \longrightarrow 2HCl(g)$; Combination reaction

(d) $Mg(s) + 2HCl(aq) \longrightarrow MgCl_2(aq) + H_2(g)$; Displacement reaction

Q.17 What does one mean by exothermic and endothermic reactions? Give examples.

Ans. Chemical reactions that release energy in the form of heat, light, or sound are called exothermic reactions.

Example: Mixture of sodium and chlorine to yield table salt

$$Na(s) + \frac{1}{2}Cl_2(g) \longrightarrow NaCl(s) + 411 \text{ kJ of energy}$$

In other words, combination reactions are exothermic.

Reactions that absorb energy or require energy in order to proceed are called endothermic reactions. For example: In the process of photosynthesis, plants use the energy from the sun to convert carbon dioxide and water to glucose and oxygen.

$$6CO_2(g) + 6H_2O(\ell) \xrightarrow{\text{Sunlight}} \underset{\text{Glucose}}{C_6H_{12}O_6(aq)} + 6O_2(g)$$

Q.18 Why is respiration considered as an exothermic reaction? Explain.

Ans. Energy is required to support life. Energy in our body is obtained from the food we eat. During digestion, large molecules of food are broken down into simpler substances such as glucose. Glucose combines with oxygen in the cells and provides energy. The special name of this combustion reaction is respiration. Since energy is released in the whole process, it is an exothermic process.

$$\underset{\text{Glucose}}{C_6H_{12}O_6(aq)} + \underset{\text{Oxygen}}{6O_2(g)} \longrightarrow \underset{\text{Carbon dioxide}}{6CO_2(g)} + \underset{\text{Water}}{6H_2O(\ell)} + \text{Energy}$$

Q.19 Why are decomposition reactions called the opposite of combination reactions? Write equations for these reactions.

Ans. Decomposition reactions are those in which a compound breaks down to form two or more substances. These reactions require a source of energy to proceed. Thus, they are the exact opposite of combination reactions in which two or more substances combine to give a new substance with the release of energy.

Decomposition reaction : $AB + \text{Energy} \longrightarrow A + B$

$$2H_2O(\ell) \xrightarrow{\text{Electrolysis}} 2H_2(g) + O_2(g)$$

Combination reaction : $A + B \longrightarrow AB + \text{Energy}$

$$2H_2(g) + O_2(g) \longrightarrow 2H_2O(\ell) + \text{Energy}$$

Q.20 Write one equation each for decomposition reactions where energy is supplied in the form of heat, light or electricity.

Ans. **(a) Thermal decomposition :**

$$2FeSO_4(s) \xrightarrow{\Delta} Fe_2O_3(s) + SO_2(g) + SO_3(g)$$

Ferrous sulphate — Ferric oxide — Sulphur ioxide — Sulphur trioxide

(b) Decomposition by light :

$$2AgCl(s) \xrightarrow{Light} 2\,Ag(s) + Cl_2(g)$$

Silver chloride — Silver — Chlorine

(c) Decomposition by electricity :

$$2Al_2O_3(aq) \xrightarrow{Electricity} 4\,Al(s) + 3O_2(g)$$

Aluminium oxide — Aluminium — Oxygen

Q.21 What is the difference between displacement and double displacement reactions? Write equations for these reactions.

Ans. In a displacement reaction, a more reactive element displaces a less reactive element from a compound.

$$A + BX \longrightarrow AX + B;\ \text{where A is more reactive than B}$$

In a double displacement reaction, two atoms or a group of atoms switch places to form new compounds.

$$AB + CD \longrightarrow AD + CB$$

For example:

Displacement reaction :

$$CuSO_4(aq) + Zn(s) \longrightarrow ZnSO_4(aq) + Cu(s)$$

Double displacement reaction:

$$HCl(aq) + NaOH(aq) \longrightarrow NaCl(aq) + H_2O(\ell)$$

Q.22 In the refining of silver, the recovery of silver from silver nitrate solution involved displacement by copper metal. Write down the reaction involved.

Ans.

$$2AgNO_3(aq) + Cu(s) \longrightarrow Cu(NO_3)_2(aq) + 2Ag(s)$$

Silver nitrate — Copper — Copper nitrate — Silver

Q.23 What do you mean by a precipitation reaction? Explain by giving examples.

Ans. A reaction in which an insoluble solid (called precipitate) is formed is called a precipitation reaction. For example:

$$Na_2CO_3(aq) + CaCl_2(aq) \longrightarrow CaCO_3(s) + 2NaCl(aq)$$

Sodium carbonate — Calium chloride — Calcium carbonate — Sodium chloride

In this reaction, calcium carbonate is obtained as a precipitate. Hence, it is a precipitation reaction. Another example of precipitation reaction is :

$$Na_2SO_4(aq) + BaCl_2(aq) \longrightarrow BaSO_4(s) + 2NaCl(aq)$$

Sodium sulphate — Barium chloride — Barium sulphate — Sodium chloride

In this reaction, barium sulphate is obtained as a precipitate.

Q.24 Explain the following in terms of gain or loss of oxygen with two examples each.
(a) Oxidation (b) Reduction

Ans. (a) Oxidation is the gain of oxygen.
For example :

(i) $CO_2 + H_2 \longrightarrow CO + H_2O$
Addition of oxygen – oxidation

(ii) $2Cu + O_2 \longrightarrow 2CuO$
Gain of oxygen-oxidation

In equation (i), H_2 is oxidized to H_2O and in equation (ii), Cu is oxidised to CuO.

(b) Reduction is the loss of oxygen.
For example :

(i) $CO_2 + H_2 \longrightarrow CO + H_2O$
Removal of oxygen – reduction

(ii) $CuO + H_2 \xrightarrow{\Delta} Cu + H_2O$
Loss of oxygen - reduction

In equation (i), CO_2 is reduced to CO and in equation (ii), CuO is reduced to Cu.

Q.25 A shiny brown-coloured element 'X' on heating in air becomes black in colour. Name the element 'X' and the black coloured compound formed.

Ans. 'X' is copper (Cu) and the black-coloured compound formed is copper oxide (CuO). The equation of the reaction involved on heating copper is given below.

$$\underset{\text{(Shiny brown in colour)}}{2Cu} + O_2 \xrightarrow{\text{Heat}} \underset{\text{(Black in colour)}}{2CuO}$$

Q.26 Why do we apply paint on iron articles?

Ans. Iron articles are painted because it prevents them from rusting. When painted, the contact of iron articles from moisture and air is cut off. Hence, rusting is prevented.

Q.27 Oil and fat containing food items are flushed with nitrogen. Why?

Ans. Nitrogen is an inert gas and does not easily react with these substances. On the other hand, oxygen reacts with food substances and makes them rancid. Thus, bags used in packing food items are flushed with nitrogen gas to remove oxygen inside the pack. When oxygen is not present inside the pack, rancidity of oil and fat containing food items is avoided.

Q.28 Explain the following terms with one example each.
(a) Corrosion (b) Rancidity

Ans. **(a) Corrosion :** Corrosion is defined as a process where materials usually metals deteriorate as a result of a chemical reaction with air, moisture, chemicals, etc.
For example, iron in the presence of moisture reacts with oxygen to form hydrated Ferric oxide.

$$4Fe + 3O_2 + nH_2O \longrightarrow \underset{\text{Hydrated Ferric oxide}}{2Fe_2O_3.nH_2O}$$

This hydrated iron oxide is rust.

(b) Rancidity : The process of oxidation of fats and oils that can be easily noticed by the change in taste and smell is known as rancidity.
For example, the taste and smell of butter changes when kept for long. Rancidity can be avoided by :
1. Storing food in air tight containers
2. Storing food in refrigerators
3. Adding antioxidants
4. Storing food in an environment of nitrogen

CONCEPT APPLICATION LEVEL - II

SECTION-A

(OBJECTIVE QUESTIONS)

Q.1 When quick lime is reacted with water, calcium hydroxide is formed, it is a
(A) combination reaction (B) displacement reaction
(C) double displacement reaction (D) decomposition reaction

Q.2 When water is added in a vessel containing lumps of quick lime, it is observed that
(A) the vessel becomes hot
(B) a hissing sound is produced
(C) lump of quick lime breaks and dissolves partially in water
(D) All the above.

Q.3 In a beaker 5 g of calcium oxide (quick lime) is mixed with some water, it is observed that
(A) it dissolves completely (B) it does not dissolve at all
(C) it is sparingly soluble (D) it forms a transparent mixture

Q.4 Quick lime is a
(A) red coloured solid (B) green coloured solid
(C) blue coloured solid (D) colourless or white coloured solid

Q.5 Calcium oxide (CaO) is also known as
(A) quick lime (B) slaked lime (C) milk of lime (D) lime water

Q.6 The products of reaction between water and quick lime are
(A) calcium, hydrogen and oxygen (B) calcium and hydrogen
(C) calcium hydroxide (D) calcium hydroxide and oxygen

Q.7 When Quick lime reacts with water
(A) heat is absorbed (B) heat is released.
(C) no change of temperature takes place (D) none of these

Q.8 When we heat ferrous sulphate crystals we observe that
(A) no gas is evolved
(B) a brown coloured gas is evolved
(C) a gas having smell of burning sulphur is evolved
(D) no residue is left after heating.

Q.9 When crystals of ferrous sulphate are heated strongly red coloured residue is obtained. It is an example of:
(A) combination reaction (B) decomposition reaction
(C) displacement reaction (D) double displacement reaction

Q.10 The colour of ferrous sulphate crystals is
(A) Blue (B) Yellow (C) Green (D) Brown

Q.11 When we heat crystals of ferrous sulphate in a test tube which one of the following is NOT obtained ?
(A) Brown solid is formed (B) A gas having smell of burning sulphur is evolved
(C) A brown gas is evolved (D) Oxides of sulphur are produced

Q.12 A student while heating some ferrous sulphate crystals in a dry boiling tube will observe:
(A) water droplets near the mouth of boiling tube (B) colour change of the crystals
(C) smell of burning sulphur (D) All of the above

Q.13 When we heat ferrous sulphate crystals a gas evolves which has a smell of:
(A) rotten eggs (B) pleasant smell
(C) irritating smell (D) burning smell

Q.14 The colour changes observed when the ferrous sulphate crystals are heated in a dry boiling tube is
(A) green → orange → brown (B) green → white → brown
(C) blue → green → white (D) green → brown → black

Q.15 A student heated small amount of ferrous sulphate in a test tube. She made the following observations:
(i) Ferrous sulphate colour changes to brown
(ii) A gas having a smell of burning sulphur is evolved
(iii) Water droplets collect on the upper side of the test tube
(iv) Brown coloured gas is evolved.
The correct set of observation is
(A) (i), (ii), (iv) (B) (i), (ii), (iii) (C) (i), (iii), (iv) (D) (ii), (iii), (iv)

Q.16 To a solution of copper sulphate in a beaker, some iron filings are dropped.
After a few minutes it is observed that
(A) a white precipitate is formed
(B) the colour of the solution becomes darker
(C) a reddish brown coating starts appearing on the iron filings
(D) the solution becomes colourless.

Q.17 When an iron nail rubbed with sand paper is dipped in copper sulphate solution, we observe that copper gets deposited.
(A) first on the lower part of the nail and proceeds to the upper part
(B) first on the upper part of the nail and proceeds to the lower part
(C) on the entire surface of the nail
(D) on the nail in small patches

Q.18 Reaction of iron nails with copper sulphate solution is an example of
(A) combination reaction (B) decomposition reaction
(C) displacement reaction (D) double displacement reaction

Q.19 Iron filings were added to an aqueous solution of copper sulphate solution. After sometime on observation it was found that the colour of the solution has changed from :
(A) blue to pale green (B) blue to dark green
(C) blue to colourless (D) blue to reddish brown

Q.20 Four groups of the students were assigned separately the experiment of interaction of iron nail with a solution of copper sulphate. Each group recorded the observations as given below in the table. Which group of students recorded all the observations correctly?

Group of Students	Initial colour of solution	Final colour of solution	Change in the iron nail
(A)	Blue	Colourless	Grey coat
(B)	Green	Green	Brown coat
(C)	Blue	Blue	Brown coat
(D)	Blue	Light green	Brown coat

Q.21 To show that iron is more reactive than copper, the correct procedure is to :
(A) prepare ferrous sulphate solution and dip copper strip in it
(B) prepare copper sulphate solution and dip iron strip in it
(C) add dil. nitric acid on both strips
(D) heat iron and copper strips both

Q.22 Four students were asked to study the reaction between aqueous solutions of barium chloride and sodium sulphate. They reported that their experiment as follows. On mixing the solutions of the two salts in a test tube
(i) the colour of the mixture becomes brown
(ii) the solutions form separate layer
(iii) a colourless mixture is obtained
(iv) a white substance settles at the bottom.
The correct report is
(A) (i) (B) (ii) (C) (iii) (D) (iv)

Q.23 White ppt obtained when aqueous solutions of $BaCl_2$ and Na_2SO_4 are mixed, is that of
(A) NaCl (B) $BaSO_4$ (C) Both (A) and (B) (D) None of these

Q.24 Reaction between a solution of sodium sulphate in water and barium chloride in water is an example of
(A) combination reaction (B) decomposition reaction
(C) displacement reaction (D) double displacement reaction

Q.25 Barium sulphate is
(A) colourless and soluble in water (B) colourless and insoluble in water
(C) green colour and soluble in water (D) None of these

Q.26 The insoluble product (precipitate) formed when barium chloride is mixed with sodium sulphate solution is
(A) barium (B) barium sulphate (C) sodium chloride (D) barium sulphide

Q.27 To study the reaction between barium chloride and sodium sulphate, the two compounds are mixed in the form of:
(A) dry powders (B) molten liquids (C) aqueous solutions (D) None of these

Q.28 A solution of barium chloride in water is
(A) colourless (B) sky blue incolour (C) pale green in colour (D) reddish brown in colour

Q.29 A solution of sodium sulphate in water is-
(A) sky blue in colour (B) pale green in colour
(C) yellow in colour (D) colourless

Q.30 When a solution of barium chloride in water is added to an aqueous solution of sodium sulphate, the following happens:
(A) a white precipitate is formed (B) a red precipitate is formed
(C) the colour of the solution turns blue (D) a pungent smelling gas is evolved

SECTION-B

(VERY SHORT ANSWER TYPE QUESTIONS) [1 MARKS]

Q.1 What is the colour of fresh crystals of ferrous sulphate?
Ans. It is light green coloured.

Q.2 Name the type of reaction when ferrous sulphate is heated.
Ans. Decomposition.

Q.3 What is the formula of crystalline ferrous sulphate?
Ans. $FeSO_4.7H_2O$.

Q.4 Name the gases evolved when ferrous sulphate crystals are heated strongly.
Ans. Sulphur dioxide (SO_2) and sulphur trioxide (SO_3).

Q.5 What is the colour of the residue obtained when crystals of ferrous sulphate are heated strongly in air? What is its chemical composition?
Ans. The residue is red in colour. Chemically it is iron (III) oxide, Fe_2O_3.

Q.6 What are thermal decomposition reactions?
Ans. When a decomposition reaction is carried out by heating, it is called thermal decomposition reaction.

Q.7 Give an example of thermal decomposition reaction.
Ans. Decomposition of ferrous sulphate on heating is an example of thermal decomposition.

$$2FeSO_4 \xrightarrow{\Delta} Fe_2O_3 + SO_2 + SO_3$$

Q.8 Can the heating of ferrous sulphate be classified as redox reaction?
Ans. Yes, it is a type of redox reaction.

Q.9 What is the smell of the gases evolved when crystals of ferrous sulphate are heated strongly?
Ans. The mixture of gases so produced has a pungent suffocating smell of burning sulphur.

Q.10 What happens when crystals of ferrous sulphate are kept exposed to atmosphere for a long time ?
Ans. Ferrous sulphate is oxidised to ferric sulphate by atmospheric oxygen.

Q.11 State an example of each an endothermic and exothermic reaction. **[SAI-2013,14,15]**

Sol. (a) $N_2(g) + O_2(g) + \text{Heat} \longrightarrow 2NO(g)$
(Nitrogen) (Oxygen) (Nitric oxide)

(b) $2Mg\,(s) + O_2(g) \xrightarrow{\text{Heat}} 2MgO\,(s) + \text{Energy}$

Q.12 To prevent rancidity of foods containing fats and oils, some substances are added to them. What are these substances called. **[SAI-2012,15]**

Sol. Substances which are added to prevent rancidity are called antioxidants as they prevent oxidation of fats and oils.

Common antioxidants are :

(a) BHA (Butylated Hydroxy Anisole)

(b) BHT (Butylated Hydroxy Toluene)

Vitamin-E and vitamin-C (ascorbic acid) are the two antioxidants occuring in natural fats.

Q.13 Why burning of a candle wax is considered a chemical change? **[SAI-2015]**

Ans. Because when candle burns new products are formed, i.e., hydrocarbons combine

Q.14 Give reason that moist air and acidic gases are not good for some metals. **[SAI-2015]**

Ans. Moist air causes corrosion of iron while acidic gases cause corrosion of copper and silver.

Q.15 Why does white coloured silver chloride turn grey when kept in sunlight ? **[SAI-2015]**

Ans. This is due to the decomposition of silver chloride into silver and chlorine by light.

Q.16 Give one industrial application of reduction. **[SAI-2015]**

Ans. It is used in metallurgical processes of refining metals.

(SHORT ANSWER TYPE QUESTIONS) [2 MARKS]

Q.17 Identify the type of chemical reaction and also write the chemical equation for the reaction that takes place when a solution of potassium chloride is mixed with silver nitrate solution. Write the chemical name of one of the products obtained. **[SAI-2013, 2015]**

Ans. $AgNO_3(aq) + KCl(aq) \longrightarrow AgCl(s) + KNO_3(aq)$

It is double displacement reaction. Silver chloride/Potassium nitrate.

Q.18 Identify the type of each of the following reactions. Also write balanced chemical equation for each.

(a) The reaction mixture becomes warm. **[SAI-2015]**

(b) An insoluble substance is formed.

Sol. (a) It is a combination reaction.

$CaO(s) + H_2O(l) \longrightarrow Ca(OH)_2(aq) + \text{Heat}$

(b) It is a double displacement reaction.

$Na_2SO_4(aq) + BaCl_2(aq) \longrightarrow BaSO_4(s) + 2NaCl(aq)$

Q.19 Write the balanced chemical equation for the following reaction and identify the type of reaction and define it.
'Iron(III) oxide reacts with aluminium and gives molten iron and aluminium oxide.' **[SAI-2014, 2015]**

Sol. $Fe_2O_3 + 2Al \longrightarrow Al_2O_3 + 2Fe$
Displacement reaction -One element displaces another element.

Q.20 Write two observations that you will make when an iron nail is kept in an aqueous solution of copper sulphate. Write the chemical equation for this reaction. **[SAI-2012, 2015]**

Ans. Blue colour changes to light green. Reddish-brown deposit on the iron nail.
$Fe(s) + CuSO_4(aq) \rightarrow FeSO_4(aq) + Cu(s)$

Q.21 Identify the type of each of the following reactions : **[SAI-2012]**
(a) A reaction in which a single product is formed from two or more reactants.
(b) The reaction mixture becomes warm.
(c) An insoluble substance is formed.
(d) External surface of the container in which reaction takes place becomes freezing/cold.

Sol. (a) Combination reaction
(b) Exothermic reaction
(c) Precipitation reaction
(d) Endothermic reaction

Q.22 Explain giving chemical equation any two uses of chemical decomposition reaction in industry. **[SAI-2013,2015]**

Sol. In manufacturing cement, quicklime is used and it is obtained by thermal decomposition of limestone.
$CaCO_3(s) \longrightarrow CaO(s) + CO_2(g)$
In manufacturing photochromic glass, silver chloride/bromide is used which turns grey in sunlight.

$$2AgCl(s) \xrightarrow{\text{Sunlight}} 2Ag(s) + Cl_2(g)$$
$$2AgBr(s) \xrightarrow{\text{Sunlight}} 2Ag(s) + Br_2(g)$$

Q.23 Classify the following as exothermic and endothermic reactions:
(a) Photosynthesis (b) Respiration
(c) Burning of natural gas (d) Electrolysis of water. **[SAI-2015]**

Sol. (a) Photosynthesis -Endothermic reaction.
(b) Respiration - Exothermic reaction.
(c) Burning of natural gas -Exothermic reaction.
(d) Electrolysis of water -Endothermic reaction.

Q.24 Write two examples of everyday life, where redox reactions are taking place. **[SAI-2015]**

Sol. (i) Silver jewellery tarnishes due to reaction of H_2S gas of the air and silver is oxidised to silver sulphide.
(ii) In rusting of iron, iron is oxidised to iron oxide.

Q.25 (i) When a metal 'X' is added to salt solution of a metal 'Y', following chemical reaction takes place :
Metal X + Salt solution of 'Y' $\longrightarrow$ Salt solution of 'X' + Metal 'Y'
(ii) Mention the inference you draw regarding the reactivity of metal 'X' and 'Y' and also about the type of reaction. State the reason of your conclusions. **[SAI-2012, 2013, 2015]**

Sol. It is a displacement reaction.
(i) Metal X is more reactive than metal Y.
(ii) Metal X is displacing metal Y from its salt solution. A more reactive metal displaces less reactive one from its salt solution, hence X is more reactive than Y.

Q.26 On heating blue coloured powder of copper (II) nitrate in a boiling tube, copper oxide (black), oxygen gas and a brown gas X is formed. **[SAI-2015]**
(a) Write a balanced chemical equation of the reaction.
(b) Identify the brown gas X evolved.
(c) Identify the type of reaction.
(d) What could be the pH range of aqueous solution of the gas X ?

Sol. (a) Balanced chemical equation :
$2Cu(NO_3)_2(s) \xrightarrow{\text{Heat}} 2CuO(s) + O_2(g) + 4NO_2(g)$
(b) The brown gas X evolved is nitrogen dioxide (NO_2).
(c) This is a decomposition reaction.
(d) Nitrogen.dioxide dissolves in water to form acidic solution because it is an oxide of non-metal. Therefore, pH of this solution is less than 7.

Q.27 $MnO_2 + 4HCl \longrightarrow MnCl_2 + 2H_2O + Cl_2$ Identify the substance in the above reaction which is :
(i) Oxidised (ii) reduced (iii) oxidising agent (iv) reducing agent **[SAI-2013]**

Sol. (i) HCl (ii) MnO_2 (iii) MnO_2 (iv) HCl.

(LONG ANSWER TYPE QUESTIONS) [3 MARKS]

Q.28 What is meant by balanced chemical equation ? Why chemical equations are balanced? Balance the chemical equation given below :
$Al_2O_3 + NaOH \longrightarrow NaAlO_2 + H_2O$ **[SAI-2012, 2013, 2015]**

Ans.
- A chemical equation in which the numbers of atoms of each type involved in it are the same on the reactants and products is called balanced chemical equation.
- To follow the law of conservation of mass in a reaction, we need to balance a chemical equation.
- $Al_2O_3 + 2NaOH \rightarrow 2NaAlO_2 + H_2O$

Q.29 What is meant by a skeletal chemical equation? **[SAI-2010, 2011]**
What does it represent? Using the equation for electrolytic decomposition of water, differentiate between a skeletal chemical equation and a balanced chemical equation.
- Skeletal chemical equation is an unbalanced chemical equation.
- It represents a chemical reaction.

$H_2O \xrightarrow{\text{Electricity}} H_2 + O_2 \rightarrow$ Skeletal
$2H_2O \xrightarrow{\text{Electricity}} 2H_2 + O_2 \rightarrow$ Balanced

Q.30 Write two observations each for the following chemical reactions : **[SAI-2015]**
(a) Dilute sulphuric acid is poured over zinc granules.
(b) Potassium iodide solution is added to lead nitrate solution
(c) Lead nitrate is strongly heated in a hard glass test tube.

Ans. (a) $Zn(s) + \text{dil. } H_2SO_4(aq) \rightarrow ZnSO_4(aq) + H_2\uparrow$
(i) The container of the reaction mixture becomes hot as it is an exothermic reaction.
(ii) Bubbles are seen with the evolution of H_2 gas, which is combustible gas.
(b) $2KI(aq) + Pb(NO_3)_2(aq) \rightarrow \underset{\text{Yellow}}{PbI_2(s)\downarrow} + 2KNO_3(aq)$
(i) Yellow colour of potassium iodide solution disappears.
(ii) Yellow precipitate of lead iodide is formed.

(c) $2Pb(NO_3)_2 \xrightarrow{\text{Strongly heated}} 2PbO(s) + 4NO_2(g) + O_2(g)$

(i) Yellow fumes of NO_2 gas are observed.

(ii) Light yellow residue of lead oxide is left.

Q.31 Consider the following reaction :

$Pb(NO_3)_2(s) \xrightarrow{\text{Heat}} PbO(s) + NO_2(g) + O_2(g)$ **[SAI-2015]**

(a) Name the gases produced in the above reaction.

(b) Balance the above chemical equation.

(c) Name the type of chemical reaction.

Ans. (a) Nitrogen dioxide and oxygen.

(b) $2Pb(NO_3)_2(s) \xrightarrow{\text{Heat}} 2PbO(s) + 4NO_2(g) + O_2(g)$

(c) Decomposition reaction.

Q.32 Give three examples to indicate the role of decompositon reactions in metal industries. **[SAI-2015]**

Ans. (i) CaO is obtained from $CaCO_3$ by thermal decompositon.

(ii)Sodium (Na) metal is obtained from NaCl (sodium chloride) by electrolytic decomposition.

(iii) Aluminium (Al) metal is obtained from Al_2O_3 by electrolytic decomposition.

Q.33 In the electrolysis of water : **[SAI-2012]**

(i) Name the gas collected at the cathode and anode respectively.

(ii) Why is the volume of one gas collected at one electrode double that at the other ? Name this gas

(iii) How will you test the evoled gases ?

Ans. (i) At cathode – Hydrogen gas (H_2) At anode-Oxygen gas (O_2)

(ii) Since $2H_2O \xrightarrow[\text{Current}]{\text{Electric}} 2H_2 + O_2$

Hydrogen gas is double of that of oxygen gas beause 2 molecules of hydrogen are liberated while only 1 molecule of oxygen is liberated.

(iii) When a burninng splinter is brought near the mouth of the liberated gases, the burning splinter extinguishes near H_2 gas while the burning splinter keeps burning more near the O_2 gas.

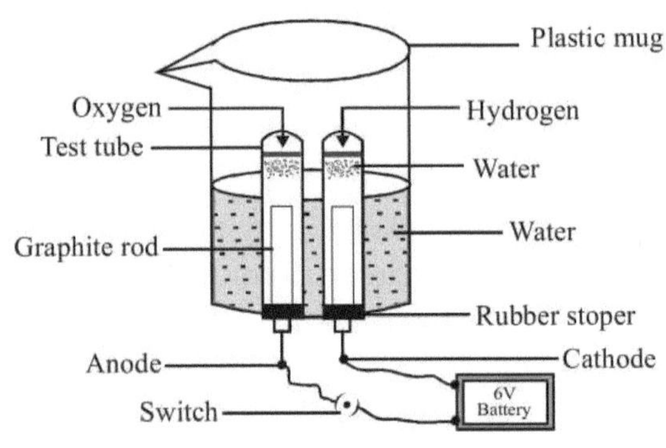

Q.34 A magnesium ribbon is burnt in oxygen to give a white compound X accompained by emission of light. If the burning ribbon is now placed in an atmosphere of nitrogen, it continues to burn and forms a compound Y. **[SAI-2012]**

(a) Write the chemical formulae of X and Y.

(b) Write a balanced chemical equation when X is dissolved in water.

Ans. $2Mg + O_2 \longrightarrow 2MgO$

$3Mg + N_2 \longrightarrow Mg_3N_2$

(a) X is MgO, Y is Mg_3N_2

(b) $MgO + H_2O \longrightarrow Mg(OH)_2$

Q.35 Point out the oxidising and reducing agents in the following reactions:

$$SO_2 + 2HNO_3 \longrightarrow H_2SO_4 + 2NO_2$$

Ans. (i)

$$\overset{+4\ -2}{SO_2} + 2\overset{+1\ +5\ -2}{HNO_3} \longrightarrow \overset{+1\ +6\ -2}{H_2SO_4} + 2\overset{+4\ -2}{NO_2}$$

Increase in O.N.

Decrease in O.N.

HNO_3 is an oxidising agent decrease in O.N. because N atom undergoes decrease in O.N.
SO_2 is a reducing agent, because S atom undergoes increase in O.N.

(ii)

Increase in O.N.

$$\overset{+4\ -4}{SO_2} + 2\overset{+1\ -2}{H_2S} \longrightarrow 2\overset{+1\ -2}{H_2O} + 3\overset{0}{S}$$

Decrease in O.N.

SO_2 is an oxidising agent because S atom undergoes decrease in O.N.
H_2S is a reducing agent, because S atom undergoes increase in O.N.

Q.36 "Oxidation and reduction processes occur simultaneously." Justify this statement with the help of an example. **[CBSE Sept. 2010]**

Ans. If a substance gains oxygen during a reaction, it is said to be oxidised. If a substance loses oxygen during a reaction, it is said to be reduced.

For example : Consider the following reaction :

$$\underset{\text{Copper(II) oxide (Black)}}{CuO} + \underset{\text{Hydrogen}}{H_2} \xrightarrow{\text{Heat}} \underset{\text{Copper metal (Reddish brown)}}{Cu} + H_2O$$

During this reaction, the copper (II) oxide is losing oxygen and is being reduced. The hydrogen is gaining oxygen and is being oxidised. In other words, one reactant gets oxidised while the other gets reduced during a reaction. Such reactions are called oxidation-reduction reactions or redox reactions. (It will act as reducing agent)

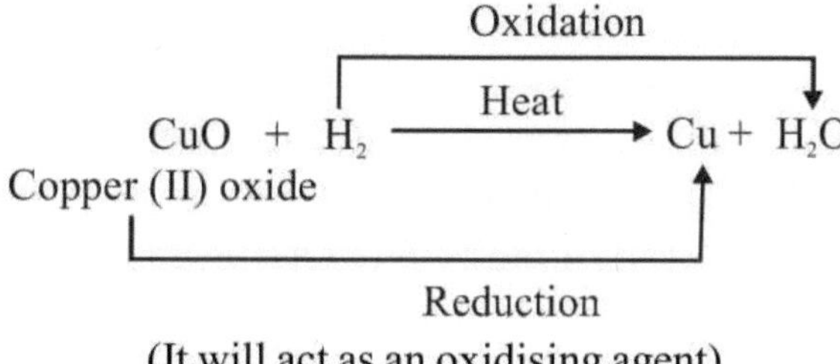

(It will act as an oxidising agent)

(VERY LONG QUESTIONS) [5 MARKS]

Q.37 Write the balanced chemical equations for the following reactions and identify the type of reaction in each case.

(a) Nitrogen gas is treated with hydrogen gas in the presence of a catalyst 773 K to form ammonia gas.

(b) Sodium hydroxide solution is treated with acetic acid to form sodium acetate and water.

(c) Ethanol is warmed with ethanoic acid to form ethyl acetate in the presence of concentrated H_2SO_4.

(d) Ethene is burnt in the presence of oxygen to form carbon dioxide, water and release heat and light.

(e) Thermit reaction, iron (III) oxide reacts with aluminium and gives molten iron and aluminium oxide.

[SAI-2014,15]

Ans. (a) $N_2(g) + 3H_2(g) \xrightarrow{\text{Catalyst}} 2NH_3(g)$
Combination reaction.
(b) $NaOH(aq) + CH_3COOH(aq) \longrightarrow CH_3COONa(aq) + H_2O(l)$
Double displacement reaction / Neutralisation reaction.
(c) $C_2H_5OH(l) + CH_3COOH(l) \longrightarrow CH_3COOC_2H_5(l) + H_2O(l)$
Double displacement reaction / Esterification reaction.
(d) $C_2H_4(g) + 3O_2(g) \longrightarrow 2CO_2(g) + 2H_2O(g) + \text{Heat} + \text{Light}$
Redox reaction / Combustion reaction
(e) $Fe_2O_3(s) + 2Al(s) \longrightarrow Al_2O_3(s) + 2Fe(l) + \text{Heat}$
Displacement reaction / Redox reaction.

Q.38 List three effects of oxidation in our daily life. Are these effects useful or harmful ? Justify. **[SAI-2012, 2015]**

Ans. (i) Corrosion :
It is harmful, as it loses shine of some metals such as copper and silver. Corrosion of iron called rusting is a serious problem as enormous amount of money is spent to replace damaged iron.
(ii) Rancidity :
It is also harmful because when fats and oils are oxidised, they become rancid and their smell and taste change.
(iii) Burning of fuels :
It is useful. As these are exothermic reactions, large amount of heat energy is evolved.

Q.39 What happens when zinc granules are treated with dilute solution of H_2SO_4, HCl, HNO_3, NaCl and NaOH, also write the chemical equations if reaction occurs. **[SAI-2015]**

Ans. The reaction of Zn granules with :
(a) Dilute H_2SO_4
$Zn(s) + H_2SO_4(aq) \rightarrow ZnSO_4(aq) + H_2(g)$
(b) Dilute HCl
$Zn(s) + 2HCl(aq) \rightarrow ZnCl_2(aq) + H_2(g)$
(c) Dilute HNO_3
Reaction with dilute HNO_3 is different as compared to other acids because nitric acid is an oxidising agent and it oxidises H_2 gas evolved to H_2O.
$4Zn(s) + 10HNO_3(aq) \longrightarrow 4Zn(NO_3)_2(aq) + 5H_2O(l) + N_2O(g)$
(d) NaCl solution
$Zn(s) + NaCl(aq) \longrightarrow \text{No reaction}$
(e) NaOH solution
$Zn(s) + 2NaOH(aq) \longrightarrow Na_2ZnO_2(aq) + H_2(g)$
Sodium zincate

Q.40 (i) Solid calcium oxide was taken in a container and water was added slowly to it :
(a) Write the observation.
(b) Write the chemical formula of the product formed.
(ii) What happens when carbon dioxide gas is bubbled through lime water:
(a) in small amount?
(b) in excess?
(iii) Why do you apply paint on iron articles? **[SAI-2014, 2015]**

Ans. (i) (a) Calcium oxide reacts vigorously with water and releases a large amount of heat.

(b) Calcium hydroxide (Slaked lime), i.e., $Ca(OH)_2$ is formed.

(ii) (a) In small amount, solution becomes milky due to the formation of calcium carbonate.

$$Ca(OH)_2 + CO_2 \rightarrow CaCO_3 + H_2O$$

(b) In excess, milkiness disappears because calcium carbonate changes to calcium hydrogen carbonate which is colourless in nature.

$$CaCO_3 + H_2O + CO_2 \rightarrow Ca(HCO_3)_2$$

(iii) Paint forms a protective coating on the surface of iron. Then oxygen and moisture present in the air cannot have a direct contact with paint.

Q.41 Balance the following chemical equations and identify the type of chemical reaction:

(a) $Mg(s) + Cl_2(g) \rightarrow MgCl_2(s)$

(b) $HgO(s) \xrightarrow{Heat} Hg(l) + O_2(g)$

(c) $Na(s) + S(s) \xrightarrow{Fuse} Na_2S(s)$

(d) $TiCl_4(l) + Mg(s) \longrightarrow Ti(s) + MgCl_2(s)$

(e) $H_2O_2(l) \xrightarrow{UV} H_2O(l) + O_2(g)$ **[SAI-2013]**

Ans. (a) Balanced ; Combination reaction.

(b) $2HgO(s) \xrightarrow{Heat} 2Hg(l) + O_2(g)$

Decomposition reaction.

(c) $2Na(s) + S(s) \xrightarrow{Fuse} Na_2S(s)$

Combination reaction.

(d) $TiCl_4(l) + 2Mg(s) \longrightarrow Ti\,(s) + 2MgCl_2(s)$

Displacement reaction.

(e) $2H_2O_2(l) \xrightarrow{UV} 2H_2O(l) + O_2(g)$

Decomposition reaction

CONCEPT APPLICATION LEVEL - III

Q.1 Dilute sulphuric acid is poured on zinc granules. Which of the following statements is false regarding this reaction ?
(A) Hydrogen gas is released
(B) It is an endothermic reaction
(C) It is a chemical reaction
(D) There will be rise in temperature

Q.2 Which of the following is false about chemical reaction ?
(A) A new substance with entirely different properties is formed.
(B) Old chemical bonds are broken while some new ones are formed.
(C) Atoms are rearranged to form new substance.
(D) Atoms of reactants are destroyed and products are formed with double the number of atoms of reactants.

Q.3 Which of the following pairs of reactions is not opposite to each other.
(A) Combination - decomposition
(B) Displacement - Double displacement
(C) Reduction - Oxidation
(D) Endothermic - Exothermic

Q.4 The metal which can displace copper from copper sulphate solution.
(A) Hg (B) Au (C) Fe (D) Ag

Q.5 Which of the following is an example of endothermic reaction ?
(A) burning of paper
(B) respiration
(C) decomposition of limestone
(D) slaking of lime

Q.6 Which of the following is not correct about the balanced chemical equation ?
(A) Short hand representation of a chemical reaction
(B) How much amount of reactants required to produce the given amount of products.
(C) How much amount of product will be obtained from given reactants.
(D) Rate of reactions can be known by chemical equation

Q.7 The CO_2 gas is produced during
(A) Complete combustion of fuel
(B) Incomplete respiration
(C) Complete combustion and respiration
(D) incomplete combustion and respiration

Q.8 The substance reduced in the $MnO_2 + 4HCl \longrightarrow MnCl_2 + 2H_2O + Cl_2$ reaction is :
(A) MnO_2 (B) HCl (C) $MnCl_2$ (D) H

Q.9 Which of the following on dissolution in water, will rise the temperature ?
(A) sodium chloride
(B) ammonium chloride
(C) glucose
(D) sodium hydroxide.

Q.10 During double displacement reaction :
(A) exchange of ions take place
(B) precipitate is formed
(C) colour change may take place
(D) all of these

Q.11 The rate of corrosion depends upon
(A) temperature
(B) presence of electroyte
(C) electropositive nature of the metal
(D) all of these

Q.12 In which of the following, heat energy is not released ?
(A) $C + O_2 \rightarrow CO_2$ (B) $CaO + H_2O \longrightarrow Ca(OH)_2$
(C) $C_6H_{12}O_6 + 6O_2 \rightarrow 6CO_2 + 6H_2O$ (D) $NH_4OH \longrightarrow NH_3 + H_2O$

Q.13 Digestion is the example of
(A) displacement reaction (B) Combination reaction
(C) neutralisation reaction (D) Decomposition reactions

Q.14 $2\,Na + Cl_2 \rightarrow 2NaCl$ this reaction is the example of
(A) Combination reaction (B) exothermic reaction
(C) redox reaction (D) all of these

Q.15 $2H_2S + SO_2 \rightarrow 3S + 2H_2O$, In this reaction the substance which gets reduced is :
(A) H_2O (B) S (C) SO_2 (D) H_2S

Q.16 When a black and white photographic film is exposed to light, the gray colour on the film appears due to the presence of
(A) Silver oxide (B) Bromine (C) Silver (D) All of these

Q.17 A metal 'M' produces white ash of 'N' and dazzling white light on burning in the presence of oxygen gas. The metal 'M' and ash 'N' would be
(A) magnesiumoxide,manganese respectively (B) manganese dioxide, magnesium respectively
(C) magnesium, magnesium oxide respectively (D) magnesium carbonate, magnesium respectively

Q.18 A student heated lead nitrate with an aqueous solution of potassium iodide. He would be getting
(A) white precipitate of lead (B) yellow precipitate of lead iodide.
(C) white precipitate of potassium (D) yellow coloured gas of lead.

Q.19 Green coating on copper utensils in rainy season is due to the presence of
(A) $CuCO_3$ (B) $CuCO_3.Cu(OH)_2$ (C) $Cu(OH)_2$ (D) CuS

Q.20 An acid which can decolourise purple colour of potassium permagnate solution is
(A) H_2SO_4 (B) KI (C) MnO_3 (D) $K_2Cr_2O_7$.

Q.21 In order to prevent the spoilage of potato chips, they are packed in pouches filled with
(A) nitrogen gas (B) oxygen gas (C) sulphur gas (D) none of these

Q.22 When we add common salt in $AgNO_3$ (silver nitrate) solution the precipitate formed will be
(A) black coloured (B) blue coloured (C) yellow coloured (D) white coloured

Q.23 Which of the following can be decomposed by the action of light ?
(A) AgCl (B) KCl (C) $CuCl_2$ (D) NaCl

Q.24 Give the number of molecules of carbon-dioxide formed upon complete oxidation of glucose.
(A) 1 (B) 3 (C) 6 (D) 4

Q.25 Chemical equation for the formation of hydrogen sulphide gas is $ZnS + xHCl \longrightarrow ZnCl_2 + H_2S\uparrow$.
What is the value of "x and y" in the equation, respectively ?
(A) 2 and 1 (B) 1 and 2 (C) 2 and 2 (D) 3 and 1

Q.26 Chemical equation for the combustion of methanol is as follows :
$xCH_3OH(g) + yO_2(g) \rightarrow zCO_2(g) + 4H_2O(g)$. What is the value of 'x, y and z" in the equation, respectively ?
(A) 1, 2 and 3 (B) 1, 2 and 4 (C) 2, 3 and 4 (D) 2, 3 and 2.

Q.27 The reaction between aqueous solutions of sodium chloride and silver nitrate is
(A) displacement reaction (B) synthesis reaction
(C) double displacement reaction (D) analysis reaction

Passage (Q.28 to Q.30)

In a double displacement reaction between aqueous potassium iodide and aqueous lead nitrate, a yellow precipitate of lead iodide is formed.

Q.28 While performing the activity if lead nitrate is not available, which of the following can be used in place of lead nitrate ?
(A) Lead sulphate (insoluble) (B) Lead acetate
(C) Ammonium nitrate (D) potassium sulphate

Q.29 Which of the following statements is true regarding precipitates ?
(A) Product formation after saturation point
(B) Product formation before saturation point
(C) Precipitation does not relate to saturation point of a solution
(D) Product with higher concentration in a reaction is precipitate.

Q.30 Which of the following is a double displacement reaction ?
(A) $2KI + Cl_2 \longrightarrow 2KCl + I_2$ (B) $Al + Fe_2O_3 \longrightarrow Al_2O_3 + 2Fe$
(C) $BaCl_2 + H_2SO_4 \longrightarrow BaSO_4 + 2HCl$ (D) $Mg + CuSO_4 \longrightarrow MgSO_4 + Cu$

Q.31 The reaction that releases energy is
(A) $2FeSO_4(s) \xrightarrow{\Delta} Fe_2O_3(s) + SO_2(g) + SO_3(g)$
(B) $3Pb(NO_3)_2(s) \xrightarrow{\Delta} 2PbO(s) + 4NO_2(g) + O_2(g)$
(C) $2AgBr(s) \xrightarrow{\text{Sunlight}} 2Ag(s) + Br_2(g)$
(D) $CH_4(g) + 2O_2(g) \longrightarrow CO_2(g) + 2H_2O(l)$

Q.32 $CH_4 + Cl_2 \longrightarrow CH_3Cl + HCl$ reaction is an example of
(A) synthetic (B) analytical (C) displacement (D) neutralisation

Q.33 A brown and bright element "x" when heated in presence of air turns into black substance "y". If hydrogen gas is passed over this heating material again "x" is obtained. "x" and "y" are
(A) Cu and CuO (B) S & SO_2 (C) C & CO_2 (D) Na and NaH

Q.34 Displacement reaction is :
(A) $CaO(s) + H_2O(l) \rightarrow Ca(OH)_2(aq)$
(B) $Pb(s) + CuCl_2(aq) \rightarrow PbCl_2(aq) + Cu(s)$
(C) $MnO_2(s) + 4HCl(l) \rightarrow MnCl_2(s) + 2H_2O + Cl_2(g)$
(D) $C_6H_{12}O_6 + 6O_2 \rightarrow 6CO_2 + 6H_2O$

Q.35 The Chemical reaction $HNO_3 + KOH \rightarrow KNO_3 + H_2O$ is an example of :
(A) neutralization (B) double displacement
(C) neutralization and double displacement (D) Combination

Q.36 Magnesium ribbon is rubbed with sand paper before making it to burn. The reason of rubbing the ribbon is to
(A) remove moisture condensed over the surface of ribbon.
(B) generate heat due to exothermic reaction.
(C) remove magnesium oxide formed over the surface of magnesium.
(D) Mix silicon from sand paper (silcon dioxide) with magnesium for lowering ignition temperature of the ribbon.

Q.37 The reaction that differs from the rest of the reactions given is :
(A) Formation of calcium oxide from limestone
(B) Formation of aluminium from aluminium oxide.
(C) Formation of sodium carbonate from sodium hydrogen carbonate
(D) Formation of mercury from mercuric oxide.

Q.38 **Statement 1 :** Calcium carbonate when heated decomposes to give calcium oxide and water.
Statement 2 : Calcium carbonate when heated decomposes to give calcium oxide and carbon dioxide.
(A) Statement-1 and Statement-2 are true and Statement-2 is the correct explanation of Statement-1.
(B) Statement-1 and Statement-2 are true but Statement-2 is NOT the correct explanation of Statement-1.
(C) Statement-1is true, Statement-2 False.
(D) Statement-1is False, Statement-2 True.

Q.39 **Statement 1 :** Brown fumes are produced when lead nitrate is heated because a displacement reaction takes place and lead is formed.
Statement 2 : Nitrogen dioxide gas is produced as a by product.
(A) Statement-1 and Statement-2 are true and Statement-2 is the correct explanation of Statement-1.
(B) Statement-1 and Statement-2 are true but Statement-2 is NOT the correct explanation of Statement-1.
(C) Statement-1is true, Statement-2 False.
(D) Statement-1is False, Statement-2 True.

Q.40 **Statement 1 :** Iodine can't displace bromine from a solution because the reactivity of bromine is higher as compared to iodine.
Statement 2 : Iodine is smaller than bromine and the outermost electrons are not influenced by the force of attraction exerted by the nucleus.
(A) Statement-1 and Statement-2 are true and Statement-2 is the correct explanation of Statement-1.
(B) Statement-1 and Statement-2 are true but Statement-2 is NOT the correct explanation of Statement-1.
(C) Statement-1is true, Statement-2 False.
(D) Statement-1is False, Statement-2 True.

Q.41 **Statement 1 :** Balance the following equation with the smallest whole number coefficients. Choose the answer that is the sum of the coefficients, in the balanced equation. Do not forget coefficients of "one".

$$Cr + H_2SO_4 \longrightarrow Cr_2(SO_4)_3 + H_2$$

The sum of the coefficients, representing the smallest whole number coefficient is 9.

Statement 2 : The equation can be balanced in many ways.

(A) Statement-1 and Statement-2 are true and Statement-2 is the correct explanation of Statement-1.
(B) Statement-1 and Statement-2 are true but Statement-2 is NOT the correct explanation of Statement-1.
(C) Statement-1is true, Statement-2 False.
(D) Statement-1is False, Statement-2 True.

Q.42 Match the following :

Column-I	Column-II
(A) Neutralisation	(1) $2Mg + O_2 \rightarrow 2MgO$
(B) Precipitation	(2) $H_2SO_4 + NaOH \rightarrow Na_2\ \ SO_4 + H_2O$
(C) Gas-formation	(3) $ZnS + 2HCl \longrightarrow ZnCl_2 + H_2S\uparrow$
(D) Oxidation	(4) $PbNO_3 + Na_2SO_4 \rightarrow PbSO_4 + 2NaNO_3$.

(A) A-1, B-2, C-3, D-4 (B) A-1, B-3, C-2, D-4
(C) A-3, B-4, C-2, D-1 (D) A-2, B-4, C-3, D-1

Q.43 Match the following :

Column-I	Column-II
(A) $AgNO_3 + NaCl \rightarrow AgCl + NaNO_3$	(1) Double displacement
(B) $2KI + Br_2 \rightarrow 2KBr + I_2$	(2) No reaction
(C) $Zn + 2NaCl \rightarrow 2Na + ZnCl_2$	(3) Single displacement.

(A) A-1, B-2, C-3 (B) A-1, B-3, C-2
(C) A-3, B-1, C-2 (D) A-2, B-1, C-3

Q.44 Column II gives type of reaction mention in column I, match them correctly.

Column-I	Column-II
(A) $C + O_2 \longrightarrow CO_2$	(1) Displacement
(B) $AgBr \xrightarrow{\text{light}} Ag + Br$	(2) Combination
(C) $Zn + CuSO_4 \longrightarrow ZnSO_4 + Cu$	(3) Decomposition
(D) $CH_3CH_2OH \xrightarrow{Cu} CH_3CHO + H_2$	(4) Oxidation

(A) A-2, B-3, C-1, D-4 (B) A-1, B-3, C-2, D-4
(C) A-3, B-4, C-2, D-1 (D) A-2, B-4, C-3, D-1

Q.45

Column I	Column II
(A) Double displacment	(1) $CuO + H_2 \xrightarrow{heat} Cu + H_2O$
(B) Decomposition	(2) $Na_2SO_4\,(aq) + BaCl_2\,(aq) \rightarrow BaSO_4\,(aq) + 2NaCl\,(aq)$
(C) Precipitation	(3) $CaCO_3 \xrightarrow{heat} CaO + CO_2$
(D) Redox	(4) $NaOH + HCl \rightarrow NaCl + H_2O$

(A) A-2, B-3, C-1, D-4 (B) A-1, B-3, C-2, D-4
(C) A-4, B-3, C-2, D-1 (D) A-2, B-4, C-3, D-1

CONCEPT APPLICATION LEVEL - II

SECTION-A

(OBJECTIVE QUESTIONS)

Q.1	A	Q.2	D	Q.3	C	Q.4	D	Q.5	A	Q.6	C	Q.7	B
Q.8	C	Q.9	B	Q.10	C	Q.11	C	Q.12	D	Q.13	C	Q.14	B
Q.15	B	Q.16	C	Q.17	C	Q.18	C	Q.19	A	Q.20	D	Q.21	B
Q.22	D	Q.23	B	Q.24	D	Q.25	B	Q.26	B	Q.27	C	Q.28	A
Q.29	D	Q.30	A										

CONCEPT APPLICATION LEVEL - III

Q.1	B	Q.2	D	Q.3	B	Q.4	C	Q.5	C	Q.6	D	Q.7	C
Q.8	A	Q.9	D	Q.10	D	Q.11	D	Q.12	D	Q.13	D	Q.14	D
Q.15	C	Q.16	C	Q.17	C	Q.18	B	Q.19	B	Q.20	B	Q.21	A
Q.22	D	Q.23	A	Q.24	C	Q.25	A	Q.26	D	Q.27	C	Q.28	B
Q.29	A	Q.30	C	Q.31	D	Q.32	C	Q.33	A	Q.34	B	Q.35	C
Q.36	C	Q.37	B	Q.38	D	Q.39	D	Q.40	C	Q.41	B	Q.42	D
Q.43	B	Q.44	A	Q.45	C								

2 ACIDS, BASES AND SALTS

CONCEPT TREE

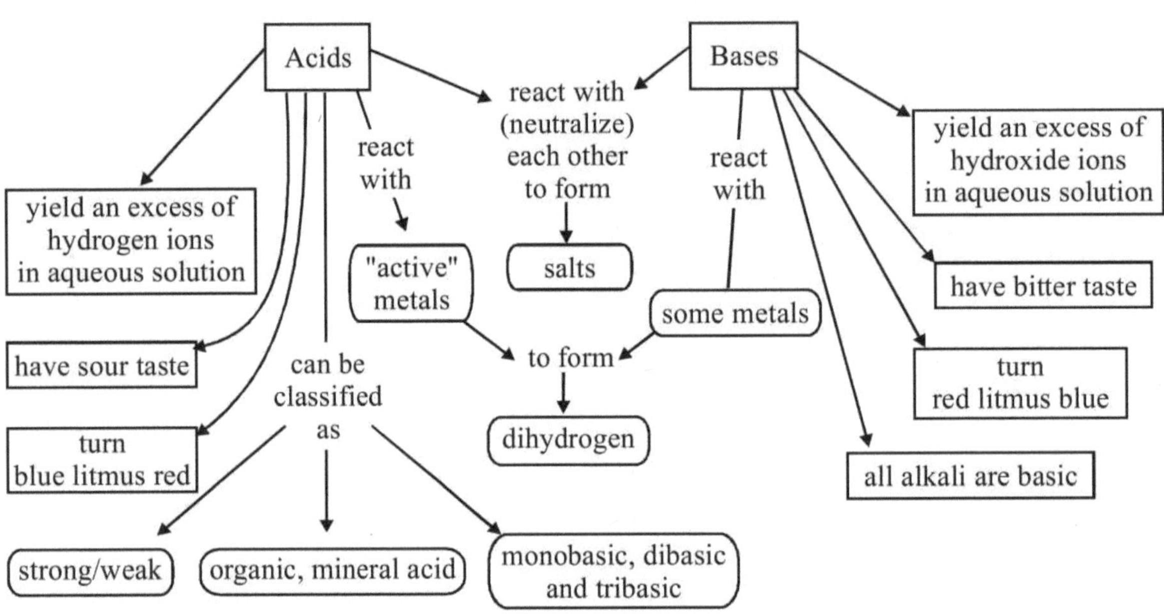

2.1 INTRODUCTION

The term acids and bases have become so common in routine and involve such a variety of substances that have been accepted as such without questions. Several definitions of acids and bases have been proposed from time to time. Going back to the historical development of the subject acids were earlier characterised by their sour taste, ability to dissolve substances in water, action on vegetable dyes etc. Modern definitions of acids and bases started with Arrhenius approach between 1880-1890. Latter on in 1923 Bronsted and Lowry independently defined acids and bases. But most advanced definition of acids and bases was given by Lewis.

Beside these, the strength of any solution can be determined from the concentration of H^+ or OH^- ions in the solution commonly described in terms of a parameter called pH. Further, salts are produced as a result of neutralization reaction between an acid and a base.

$$\text{Acid + Base} \longrightarrow \text{Salt + Water}$$

$$HCl(aq) + NaOH(aq) \longrightarrow NaCl(aq) + H_2O(aq)$$

We will study all these one by one in this chapter.

Before this, we should know the theories about acids and bases.

2.2 THEORIES OF ACIDS AND BASES

1. Arrhenius concept of acids and bases

The swedish chemist Svante Arrhenius in 1887 explained the ionisation of the strong and weak electrolytes (i.e. acids and bases) in water.

(i) According to Arrhenius an acid is defined as a substance containing hydrogen. [HA], which gives free hydrogen ions when dissolved in water.

$$HA\,(aq) \rightleftharpoons H^+\,(aq) + A^-\,(aq)$$

Strong acids like HCl, HNO_3, H_2SO_4 are almost completely ionised in water as shown below:

$$HCl\,(aq) \longrightarrow H^+\,(aq) + Cl^-\,(aq)$$

$$HNO_3\,(aq) \longrightarrow H^+\,(aq) + NO_3^-\,(aq)$$

Weak acids like CH_3COOH and H_3PO_4 are ionised to small extent. Therefore, there is a state of equilibrium between the unionised acid and ions formed in solution.

$$CH_3COOH\,(aq) \rightleftharpoons CH_3COO^-\,(aq) + H^+\,(aq)$$

$$H_3PO_4\,(aq) \rightleftharpoons 3H^+\,(aq) + PO_4^{3-}\,(aq)$$

Hence the common characteristics of acids are attributed to the presence of H^+ ions in aqueous solution.

(ii) According to Arrhenius a base is a hydroxyl group containing compound (BOH), which gives free hydroxyl ions when dissolved in water.

$$BOH\,(aq) \longrightarrow B^+\,(aq) + OH^-\,(aq)$$

Strong bases like NaOH, KOH are completely ionised.

$$NaOH\,(aq) \longrightarrow Na^+(aq) + OH^-\,(aq)$$

$$KOH\,(aq) \longrightarrow K^+\,(aq) + OH^-\,(aq)$$

Whereas weak bases like NH_4OH, are ionised to a smaller extent.

$$NH_4OH \rightleftharpoons NH_4^+\,(aq) + OH^-\,(aq)$$

Thus, hydroxyl ion is responsible for the basic properties exhibited by the bases in water.

According to this concept, neutralisation is the combination of H^+ ion of the acid with OH^- ion of the base to form molecules of H_2O, which are neutral.

$$H^+\,(aq) + OH^-\,(aq) \xrightarrow{\text{neutralisation}} H_2O\,(l)$$

2. Bronsted-lowry concept of acids and bases

In 1923, J.N. Bronsted and J.M. Lowry proposed more general definitions for acids and bases, simultaneously and independently. According to them, an acid is any substance which can donate a proton to any other substance. A base on the other hand, is any substance that can accept a proton.

In short, an acid is a proton donor, and a base is a proton acceptor

Conjugate acid and base pairs: In the ionisation of hydrogen chloride.

$$\underset{\text{(acid)}}{HCl\,(aq)} + \underset{\text{(base)}}{H_2O\,(l)} \longrightarrow H_3O^+(aq) + Cl^-(aq)$$

Hydrogen chloride donates a proton to water and hence is acid. Water on the other hand is accepting a proton from HCl and hence is acting as a base. Consider the reverse reaction. The hydronium ion, H_3O^+ donates a proton to chloride ion, hence it is an acid, chloride ion, is accepting a proton from hydronium ion, it is a base.

It is significant that according to Bronsted Lowry concept, not only neutral compounds, but ionic species can also act as acids or bases.

The acid hydrogen chloride, by losing a proton, forms the base, Chloride ion, which in turn, by gaining a proton, can form acid hydrogen chloride thus:

$$\underset{\text{(acid)}}{HCl} \underset{+H^+}{\overset{-H^+}{\rightleftharpoons}} \underset{\text{(base)}}{Cl^-}$$

Such an acid –base pair, the members of which can be formed from each other mutually by the gain or loss of proton is called a conjugate acid - base pair.

Similarly, the base water, accepts a proton to form the acid, hydronium ion, which in turn, forms water by loss of a proton.

$$\underset{\text{(base)}}{H_2O} \underset{-H^+}{\overset{+H^+}{\rightleftharpoons}} \underset{\text{(acid)}}{H_3O^+}$$

In general, we can represent any Bronsted - Lowry acid-base reaction as :

Conjugate acid pair (Loses Proton)

$$\text{acid I} + \text{base II} \rightleftharpoons \text{acid II} + \text{base I}$$

Conjugate base pair (Adds Proton)

Where acid I and base I represent one conjugate pair, whereas acid II and base II the other.

Some more examples :

$$HNO_3 + H_2O \rightleftharpoons H_3O^+ + NO_3^-$$

$$HCN + H_2O \rightleftharpoons H_3O^+ + CN^-$$

$$H_2SO_4 + H_2O \rightleftharpoons H_3O^+ + HSO_4^-$$

$$\underset{\text{(acid)}}{NH_4^+} + \underset{\text{(base)}}{H_2O} \rightleftharpoons H_3O^+(aq) + NH_3(aq)$$

$$\underset{\text{(acid)}}{H_2O\,(l)} + \underset{\text{(base)}}{NH_3(aq)} \rightleftharpoons NH_4^+(aq) + OH^-(aq)$$

$$\underset{\text{(acid)}}{H_2O\,(l)} + \underset{\text{(base)}}{CO_3^{2-}(aq)} \rightleftharpoons HCO_3^-(aq) + OH^-(aq)$$

3. Lewis concept of Acids and Bases

G. N. Lewis put forward a more general concept which does not require hydrogen to be an essential constituent of all acids. According to Lewis, an acid is a substance which can accept a pair of electrons, while a base is a substance which can donate a pair of electron to form a coordinate or dative bond. Hence, acid is an electron pair acceptor having empty orbitals to accommodate lone pair and base is an electron pair donar. This concept is also known as electronic–concept and is most fundamental of acids–bases concepts. In general :

$$A^+ \quad + \quad \ddot{B} \longrightarrow B{:} \longrightarrow A$$

Species with empty orbital   Species with lone pair of electron

For Examples,

$$H^+ + :\ddot{N}H_3 \longrightarrow [NH_4]^+$$

Lewis Acid   Lewis base

$$H_3N: + BF_3 \longrightarrow H_3N:BF_3$$

Lewis Base   Lewis Acid

$$:\ddot{Cl}^-: + AlCl_3 \longrightarrow [AlCl_4]^-$$

Lewis Base   Lewis Acid

Types of Lewis Acids: The Lewis acids are of following types :

(i) Molecules having the central atom with incomplete octet7. e.g. anhydrous BF_3, anhydrous $AlCl_3$, anhydrous $FeCl_3$.

(ii) Simple cation : all cations can be considered as Lewis acids, as they are deficient in electrons. e.g. Na^+, K^+, H^+, Ag^+.

(iii) Molecules in which the central atom has available vacant orbitals and may acquire more than 8 electrons i.e. molecules which can expand their octet. For example SiF_4, $SnCl_4$ etc.

(iv) Molecules in which atoms of different electronegativities are linked by multiple bonds. For example CO_2.

Types of Lewis Bases: Lewis bases are of following types :

(i) Neutral molecules with atleast one lone pair of electrons which can be donated easily. For example, $\ddot{N}H_3$ is a Lewis base.

(ii) Anions having negative charge acts as Lewis base. For example, F^-, Cl^-, Br^-, OH^-, etc.

(iii) Molecules having $>C=C<$ and $-C\equiv C-$ also acts as Lewis bases.

Illustration 1

Out of the following pairs, point out the stronger Lewis acid and assign reason.

(a) BF_3 ***or*** BH_3 ***(b)*** Sn^{2+} ***or*** Sn^{4+}

Solution

(a) BF_3 is stronger Lewis acid because B atom in BF_3 is more electron deficient than BH_3.

(b) Sn^{4+} is a stronger Lewis acid because it has greater number of vacant orbitals as compared to Sn^{2+} ion.

Illustration 2

What are amphoteric or amphiprotic species?

Solution

According to Bronsted Lowry concept, such species which can function both as acids as well as bases depending on the conditions are called amphoteric or amphiprotic species.

e.g. H_2O and NH_3 are amphoteric.

2.3 BASICS OF ACIDS, BASES AND SALTS

Substance with sour taste are regarded as acids. Lemon juice, vinegar, grape fruit juice and spoilt milk etc. taste sour since they are acidic. Similarly, substances with bitter taste and soapy touch are regarded as bases. Familiar examples of the bases are caustic soda, caustic potash, slaked lime etc.

➤ **Acids**

(i) The word acid was applied to the substances with 'sour taste'. Many substances can be identified as acids based on their taste. But this cannot be the sole criteria for the acidic character.

(ii) An acid may be defined as a substance which releases one or more H^+ ions in aqueous solution. Acids are mostly obtained from natural sources. Those obtained from rocks and minerals are called mineral acids while the acids present in animal and plant materials are known as organic acids.

➤ **Bases**

(i) They can be identified by their bitter taste and soapy touch. However, this cannot be the sole criteria in order to identify bases. Since many of them like sodium hydroxide and potassium hydroxide have corrosive action on the skin and can even harm the body.

(ii) A base may be defined as a substance capable of releasing one or more OH^- ions in aqueous solution. Some bases like sodium hydroxide and potassium hydroxide are water soluble. These known as alkalies.

1. The term "acid" is derived from the Latin word "acidus" meaning sour to taste.
2. Strength of an acid does not depend upon the concentration of an acid, but on the concentration of hydronium ion.
3. Bases which completely dissolves in water are called alkalis, example NaOH, KOH etc. "All alkalis are bases but all bases are not alkalis".
4. Acidity of a base is determined by the number of hydroxyl (OH^-) ions produced by per molecules of a base or alkali on complete dissociation in water.

(A) Classification of acids:

(a) On the basis of their source, acids are of two types.

(i) **Mineral acids/inorganic acids**

They are generally obtained from minerals or rocks. Examples,

Hydrochloric acid	(HCl)
Sulphuric acid	(H_2SO_4)
Nitric acid	(HNO_3)
Carbonic acid	(H_2CO_3)
Phosphoric acid	(H_3PO_4)

(ii) **Organic acids**

They are generally obtained from plants and animals. Examples,

Formic acid	($HCOOH$)
Acetic acid	(CH_3COOH)
Benzoic acid	(C_6H_5COOH)
Citric acid	($C_6H_8O_7$)

(b) On the basis of number of hydronium ions (H_3O^+) produced (Basicity) acids can be 3 types.

(i) **Monobasic acids**

One molecule of acid gives one hydronium ion. Examples, HCl, HBr, etc.

(ii) **Dibasic acids**

One molecule of acid gives two hydronium ion. Examples, H_2SO_4, H_2CO_3 etc.

(iii) **Tribasic acid**

One molecule of acid produces three hydronium ions. Examples, H_3PO_4, citric acid ($C_6H_8O_7$) etc.

(iv) **Tetrabasic acid**

One molecule of acid produce four hydronium ions. Example, H_4SiO_4, Silicic acid

(c) On the basis of their strength they can be of two types :

(i) **Strong acid**

They undergo complete ionisation in aqueous solution. Example, HCl, H_2SO_4 etc.

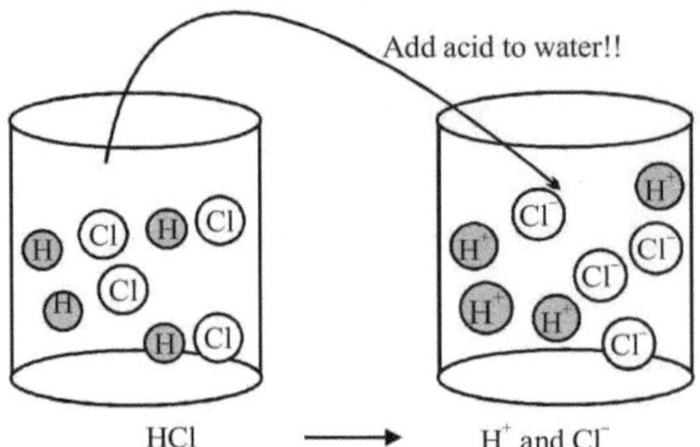

Fig. Strong acids completely dissociate in water

(ii) **Weak acid**

They undergo incomplete ionisation in aqueous solution Example, CH_3COOH, HCOOH, etc.

Fig. Organic acids are weak acids

(d) On the basis of concentration of the acid.

(i) **Concentrated acid :** They contain less amount of water and more amount of acid.

(ii) **Dilute acid:** They contain large volume of water and less amount of acid.

(B) Classification of bases

(a) On the basis of number of hydroxyl ion (OH^-) produced (acidity) bases are of three types.

(i) **Mono acidic bases**

Produce one hydroxyl (OH^-) ion per molecule. Examples: NaOH, KOH, LiOH, etc.

(ii) **Diacidic bases**

Examples: $Ca(OH)_2$, $Mg(OH)_2$, $Ba(OH)_2$ etc

(iii) **Triacidic bases**

Example: $Al(OH)_3$, $Fe(OH)_3$ etc.

(b) One the basis of strength, bases are of two types.

(i) **Strong bases**

They undergo complete ionisation in aqueous solution.

Examples, NaOH, KOH etc.

(ii) **Weak bases**

They undergo incomplete ionisation in aqueous solution.

Examples, $Ca(OH)_2$, $Mg(OH)_2$ etc.

(c) On the basis of concentration

(i) **Concentrated bases :** They contain less water.

(ii) **Dilute bases :** They contain excess of water.

Illustration 3

What are the characteristics of acids?

Solution:

1. Acids have sour taste.
2. Acids change the colour of litmus from blue to red.
3. Acids react with certain metals liberating hydrogen gas.
4. Acids decompose carbonates and hydrogen carbonates giving out carbon dioxide gas.
5. Acids neutralise bases to give salt and water.

Illustration 4

What are the characteristics of bases ?

Solution:

1. Bases have bitter taste.
2. Bases are slippery to touch.
3. Bases change the colour of litmus from red to blue.
4. Bases neutralise acids to form salt and water.

2.4 UNDERSTANDING THE CHEMICAL PROPERTIES OF ACIDS AND BASES

1. Action of Indicators

Indicator as the name suggests, indicates the nature of particular solution whether acidic, basic or neutral. Apart from this indicator also represents the change in nature of the solution from acidic to basic and vice versa. Indicators are basically coloured organic substances extracted from different plants. They can also be prepared in the laboratory.

A few common acid bases indicators are:

(i) **Litmus :** Litmus is a purple dye which is extracted from '*lichen*' a plant belonging to a variety *Thallophyta*. It can also be applied on paper in the form of strips and is available as blue and red strips. A blue litmus strip when dipped in an acid solution acquires red colour. Similarly, a red litmus strip when dipped in a base solution becomes blue. Litmus solution is a purple dye, which is extracted from lichen, a plant belonging to the division Thallophyta, and is commonly used as an indicator. When the litmus solution is neither acidic nor basic, its colour is purple. There are many other natural materials like red cabbage leaves, turmeric, coloured petals of some flowers such as Hydrangea, Petunia and Geranium, which indicate the presence of acid or base in a solution. These are called acid-base indicators or sometimes simply indicators.

(ii) **Phenolphthalein :** It is also an organic dye. In neutral or acidic solution, it is colourless while in the basis solution, the colour of indicator changes to pink.

(iii) **Methyl orange :** Methyl orange is an orange coloured dye and keeps this colour in the neutral medium. In the acidic medium, the colour of indicator becomes red and in the basic medium, it changes to yellow.

Both phenolphthalein and methyl orange are synthesised in laboratory by carrying certain chemical reactions. These are synthetic indicators. Litmus is a natural indicator extracted from plants.

➢ **Test of Distinguish Between Acids and Bases**

There are many substances which show one characteristic property (colour, odour etc.) in the acidic medium and a different property in the basic medium. **Such substances are called as acid–base indicators**. Depending upon the property of the indicator, we have the following two types of acid-base indicators.

(a) Indicators showing different colours in acidic and basic medium.

(b) Indicators giving different odours in acidic and basic medium (called olfactory indicators).

Now, we shall discuss each of these one by one.

(a) Indicators show different colours in acidic and basic medium:

Activity :

From the chemistry laboratory, collect the samples of a few acids like hydrochloric acid (HCl), nitric acid (HNO_3) and bases like sodium hydroxide (NaOH) and potassium hydroxide (KOH). Put a few drops of each of them on watch glass and then add one or two drops of the main acid base indicators on them. Note the observations i.e., change in colour if any in a tabular form.

Observation:

Sample	Blue litmus solution	Red litmus solution	Phenolphthalein	Methyl orange
HCl	Changes to red	No colour change	Colourless	Changes to red
HNO_3	Changes to red	No colour change	Colourless	Changes to red
NaOH	No colour change	Changes to blue	Changes to pink	No change in colour
KOH	No colour change	Changes to blue	Changes to pink	No change in colour

Conclusion:

Acids turn blue litmus red but have no effect on red litmus.

Bases turn red litmus blue but have no effect on blue litmus.

Phenolphthalein is colourless in acidic medium and turns pink in basic medium.

Methyl orange is yellow in basic medium and red in acidic medium.

(b) Indicators giving different odours in acidic and basic medium (Olfactory indicators):

There are some substance which give one type of odour in acidic and a different odour in the basic medium. Hence, they can be used to test whether the given substance is acidic or basic. Such indicators are called olfactory indicators. A few of these are briefly described below;

For example onion, vanilla and clove oil etc. all of them have characteristic odours and we are all quite familiar with them. These change when some acid or base solution is brought in their contact and can be identified. However, the results in this cases are not quite satisfactory. Only some guess can be made about the nature of the substance whether acid or bases.

Activity: Onion odoured cloth strips :

(i) Take some finely chopped onion in a plastic bag along with some strip of clean cloth. Tie up the bag tightly and leave overnight in the fridge. The cloth strips can now be used to test for acids and bases.

(ii) Take two of these cloth strips and check their odour.

(iii) Keep them on a clean surface and put a few drops of dilute HCl solution on one strip and a few drops of dilute NaOH solution on the other.

(iv) Rinse both cloth strips with water and again check their odour.

(v) Note your observations.

(vi) Now take some dilute vanilla essence and clove oil and check their odour.

(vii) Take some dilute HCl solution in one test tube and dilute NaOH solution in another. Add a few drops of dilute vanilla essence to both test tubes and shake well. Check the odour once again and record change in odour, if any.

(viii) Similarly, test the change in the odour of clove oil with dilute HCl and dilute NaOH solutions and record your observation.

Conclusion:

A substance which has one odour in acidic medium and different odour in basic medium can be used as an acid base indicator (called olfactory indicator).

- **Some other Indicators :** The acid base indicators mentioned above are very commonly used in the laboratory. Apart from these, red cabbage juice and turmeric juice can also act as acid base indicators.
  - **Red Cabbage juice :** It is purple in colour in neutral medium and turns red or pink in the acidic medium. In the basic or alkaline medium, its colour changes to green.
  - **Turmeric juice :** It is yellow in colour and remains as such both in the neutral and acidic medium. In the basic medium, its colour becomes reddish or deep brown.

Acids have been classified into two groups:

(i) Binary acids (ii) Oxy acids

Binary acids are those acids in which hydrogen atom combines with some other atom. These acids are also called hydroacids. Examples.

(i) Hydrochloric acid HCl

(ii) Hydrocyanic acid HCN

If an acid contains oxygen then it is called oxy acid.

Example : (I) Nitric acid HNO_3 (II) Sulphuric Acid H_2SO_4

2. How do Acids and Bases React with metals?

(i) How metals react with acids: Dilute acids like dilute HCl and dilute H_2SO_4 react with certain active metals to evolve hydrogen gas

$$\text{Metal} + \text{Dilute acid} \rightarrow \text{Metal salt} + \text{Hydrogen}$$
$$2Na\,(s) + 2\,HCl\,(dilute) \rightarrow 2NaCl\,(aq) + H_2\,(g)$$
$$Mg\,(s) + H_2SO_4\,(dilute) \rightarrow MgSO_4\,(aq) + H_2\,(g)$$

Metals which can displace hydrogen from acids are known as active metals e.g. Na, K, Zn, Fe, Ca, Mg. etc.

Activity:

In order to demonstrate the release of hydrogen when a metal reacts with dilute acid :

(i) Take a few pieces of granulated zinc in a conical flask.

(ii) Drop dilute sulphuric acid from a dropping funnel.

(iii) Pass the gas being evolved through the gas solution.

(iv) Now bring a burning candle near these bubbles. The gas will immediately catch fire and will burn more brightly accompanied by sound.

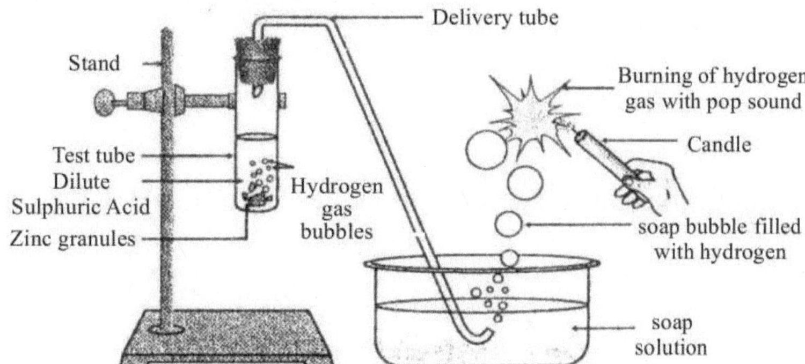

Reaction of zinc granules with dilute sulphuric acid and testing hydrogen gas by burning

Observation:

Bubbles are formed in the soap solution indicating that some gas is evolved during the reaction between the metal and the acid. The gas burns with a popping sound showing that the gas evolved is hydrogen. The same observation is found in all the cases. Reaction involved :

$$Zn(s) + \text{dil}\ H_2SO_4 \longrightarrow ZnSO_4(aq) + H_2(g)$$

Conclusion:

The active metal like zinc displaces hydrogen from all the acids and the remaining part of the acid combines with the metal to form the corresponding salt.

More examples,

$$\text{(i)}\ 2Na(s) + 2HCl\,(dil) \longrightarrow 2NaCl\,(aq) + H_2(g)$$
$$\text{(ii)}\ Fe(s) + H_2SO_4(dil) \longrightarrow FeSO_4\,(aq) + H_2(g)$$

(ii) How metals react with base?

Metals like zinc, tin and aluminium react with strong alkalies like NaOH (caustic soda) and KOH (caustic potash) to evolve hydrogen gas.

$$\underset{}{Zn(s) + 2NaOH(aq)} \longrightarrow \underset{\text{(sodium zincate)}}{Na_2ZnO_2(aq)} + H_2(g)\uparrow$$

$$Sn(s) + 2NaOH(aq) \longrightarrow \underset{\text{(sodium stannite)}}{Na_2SnO_2(aq)} + H_2(g)\uparrow$$

$$2Al(s) + 2NaOH + 2H_2O \longrightarrow \underset{\text{(sodium meta aluminate)}}{2NaAlO_2(aq)} + 2H_2(g)\uparrow$$

Activity:

(i) In a test tube, take few granules of zinc.

(ii) To this add a small amount of sodium hydroxide solution prepared in water.

(iii) Warm the tube and hydrogen gas will evolve. It will catch fire when a burning candle is brought in its contact.

Observation:

It is observed that metals like zinc react with strong base like NaOH, KOH etc., to liberate hydrogen gas and form the corresponding salt.

for example,

$$\underset{\text{(zinc)}}{Zn(s)} + \underset{\text{(sodium hydroxide)}}{2NaOH(aq)} \longrightarrow \underset{\text{(sodium zincate)}}{Na_2ZnO_2(aq)} + \underset{\text{(hydrogen)}}{H_2(g)}\uparrow$$

Conclusion:

Some metals react with bases to liberate hydrogen gas.

Some more example:

$$2Al(s) + 2NaOH\ (aq) + 2H_2O\ (\ell) \longrightarrow \underset{\text{(sodium meta aluminate)}}{2NaAlO_2(aq)} + 3H_2(g)$$

$$Sn(s) + 2NaOH\ (aq) \longrightarrow \underset{\text{(sodium stannite)}}{Na_2SnO_2(aq)} + H_2(g)$$

(iii) Action with Metal Oxides

Acids react with metal oxides to form salt and water. These reactions are mostly carried upon heating. For example,

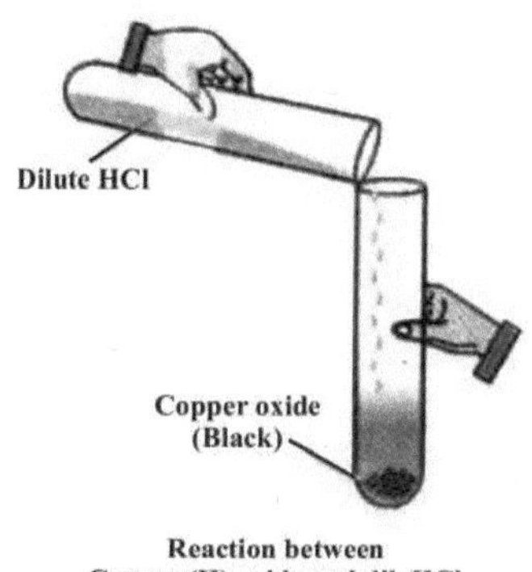

Reaction between Copper (II) oxide and dil. HCl

$$\text{Metal oxide} + \text{Acid} \longrightarrow \text{Salt} + \text{Water}$$

$$ZnO\,(s) + 2HCl \longrightarrow ZnCl_2\,(aq) + H_2O\,(l)$$

$$MgO(s) + H_2SO_4(aq) \longrightarrow MgSO_4\,(aq) + H_2O\,(l)$$

Activity:

(i) In a tube, take a small amount of copper (II) oxides also called cupric oxide.

(ii) To this add dilute HCl solution dropwise with slow stirring.

(iii) Note the colour of the solution.

Observation:

The black colour changes to bluish green due to the formation of copper (II) chloride also called cupric chloride.

$$\underset{\text{(black)}}{CuO\,(s)} + 2HCl\,(\text{dil.}) \longrightarrow \underset{\text{(bluish green)}}{CuCl_2\,(aq)} + H_2O\,(l)$$

Oxides of metals are generally basic in nature.

Conclusion:

Metal oxides react with the acids to form salt and water.

$$\text{Metal oxide} + \text{Acid} \longrightarrow \text{Salt} + \text{Water}$$

$$\underset{\text{(Copper (II) oxide)}}{CuO} + \underset{\text{(Hydrochloric Acid)}}{2HCl} \longrightarrow \underset{\substack{\text{(Copper (II) Chloride)}\\\text{(Blue green)}}}{CuCl_2} + \underset{\text{(water)}}{H_2O}$$

This shown the metal oxides are basic in nature.

Some more examples

$$CaO(s) + 2HCl(aq) \longrightarrow CaCl_2(aq) + H_2O(l)$$

$$MgO(s) + H_2SO_4(aq) \longrightarrow MgSO_4(aq) + H_2O(l)$$

(iv) Action with non-metallic oxides

Acids react with metal oxides but bases react with oxides of non-metals (e.g. CO_2 SO_2 SO_3 etc.) to form salt and water. For example,

$$\underset{\text{(sodium hydroxide)}}{2NaOH\,(aq)} + \underset{\text{(carbon dioxide)}}{CO_2(g)} \longrightarrow \underset{\text{(sodium carbonate)}}{Na_2CO_3\,(aq)} + \underset{\text{(water)}}{H_2O\,(l)}$$

We have already discussed under acids that CO_2 (g) turns lime water containing traces of $Ca(OH)_2$ milky due to the formation of insoluble calcium carbonate

$$CO_2(g) + \underset{\text{(lime water)}}{Ca(OH)_2} \longrightarrow \underset{\text{(white ppt)}}{CaCO_3(s)} + H_2O\,(1)$$

$$2KOH\,(aq) + CO_2\,(g) \rightarrow K_2CO_3\,(aq) + H_2O\,(l)$$

1. CO_2, SO_2, SO_3 are non metallic oxide. They are acidic in nature.
2. Copper, mercury and silver do not react with dil. HCl or H_2SO_4.

(v) Action with Metal carbonates and Metal bicarbonates

All metal carbonates and hydrogen carbonates react with acids to give a corresponding salt, carbon dioxide and water. Thus, the reaction can be summarised as –

Metal carbonate / metal hydrogencarbonate + Acid $\longrightarrow$ Salt + Carbon dioxide + Water.

Both metal carbonates and bicarbonates react with acids to evolve CO_2(g) and form salts. For example,

$$\underset{\text{(calcium carbonate)}}{CaCO_3(s)} + 2HCl \longrightarrow CaCl_2(aq) + H_2O\,(aq) + CO_2(g)$$

$$2NaHCO_3(s) + H_2SO_4(aq) \longrightarrow Na_2SO_4(aq) + 2H_2O(aq) + 2CO_2(g)$$

(A bicarbonate is also called hydrogen carbonate)

Let discuss the following activity:

Activity:

Take small amount of calcium carbonate in a test tube. To this add a little of dilute HCl.

(i) Take two test tubes. Label them as A and B.

(ii) Take about 0.5 g of sodium carbonate (Na_2CO_3) in test tube A and about 0.5 g of sodium hydrogen carbonate ($NaHCO_3$) in test tube B.

(iii) Add about 2 mL dilute H_2SO_4 to both the test tubes.

(iv) Pass the gas produced in each case through lime water (calcium hydroxide solution).

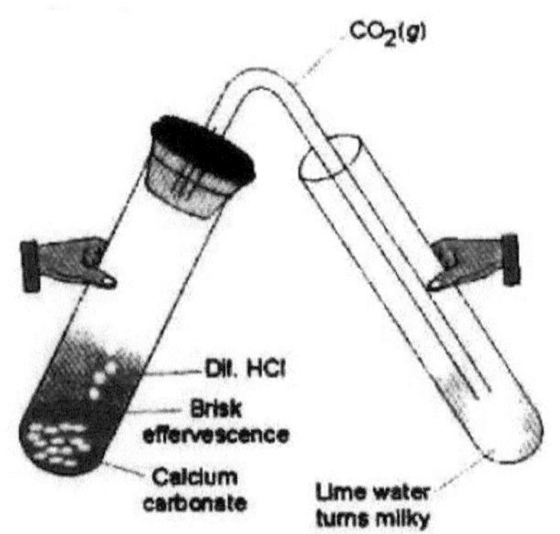

TO DEMONSTRATE THAT $CO_2(g)$ IS EVOLVED WHEN CALCIUM CARBONATE REACTS WITH dil. HCl.

Observation:

Reaction will immediately start and will be accompanied by brisk effervescence. This shows that a certain gas has been evolved. When the gas is bubbled through lime water, it immediately becomes milky. This shows that the gas evolved is CO_2 (g).

$$\underset{\text{(lime water)}}{Ca(OH)_2} + CO_2(g) \longrightarrow \underset{\text{(milky)}}{CaCO_3(s)} + H_2O\,(l)$$

The milkiness disappears when the gas is bubbled in excess through the same solution.

$$\underset{\text{(Milkiness)}}{CaCO_3(s)} + \underset{\text{(in excess)}}{CO_2(g)} + H_2O\,(l) \longrightarrow \underset{\text{(soluble)}}{Ca(HCO_3)_2\,(aq)}$$

[Calcium hydrogen bicarbonate]

$CaCO_3$ is insoluble in water while $Ca(HCO_3)_2$ is water soluble.

Carbon dioxide gas is involved in each case which turns lime water milky.

$$Na_2CO_3(s) + H_2SO_4(aq) \longrightarrow Na_2SO_4(aq) + H_2O(l) + CO_2\,(g)$$

$$2NaHCO_3 + H_2SO_4(aq) \longrightarrow Na_2SO_4(aq) + 2H_2O(aq) + 2CO_2(g)$$

Limestone, chalk and marble are different forms of calcium carbonate.

Conclusion:

All metal carbonates and hydrogen carbonates react with acids to give a corresponding salt, carbon dioxide and water.

$$CaCO_3(s) + 2HCl\,(dil.) \longrightarrow CaCl_2(aq) + H_2O(aq) + CO_2(g)$$

Egg – shell also contain calcium carbonate as the main constituent.

Hence, they react with the acids.

Illustration 5

What will happen when egg shell is placed in concentrated HNO_3?

Solution:

Egg shell contains carbonate as its main constituent. When dipped in concentrated HNO_3 calcium carbonate reacts to evolve CO_2. As a result egg shell slowly dissolves.

$$CaCO_3 + 2HNO_3\,(conc.) \longrightarrow Ca(NO_3)_2 + H_2O + CO_2$$

Note : Egg – shell also contain calcium carbonate as the main constituent.

Hence, they react with the acids.

Illustration 6

What will happen when magnesium carbonate react with nitric acid?

Solution

Magnesium nitrate and water will be formed and carbon dioxide gas will involved, when magnesium carbonate will react with nitric acid.

$$MgCO_3 + 2HNO_3 \longrightarrow Mg(NO_3)_2(aq) + H_2O\ (l) + CO_2\uparrow(g)$$

Illustration 7

What will happen when magnesium carbonate react with hydrochloric acid?

Solution

Magnesium chloride, water and carbon dioxide gas will be formed when magnesium carbonate will react with hydrochloric acid.

$$MgCO_3 + 2HCl \rightarrow MgCl_2(aq) + H_2O(l) + CO_2\uparrow(g)$$

---

3. Reaction of acid & base with each other

When a solution of acid is treated with a solution of base, salt and water are formed as the products. This reaction is called **neutralisation reaction**. In general, a neutralisation reaction can be written as

$$\text{Acid} + \text{Base} \longrightarrow \text{Salt} + \text{Water}$$

The reaction is called neutralisation because the salt which is formed is generally neutral towards litmus. Thus, neutralisation may be defined as:
The reaction between acid and base present in aqueous solution to form salt and water.

Activity:

Aim: To study the reaction between acids and bases i.e. neutralisation reaction.

Method:

(i) Take about 2 mL of dilute NaOH solution in a test tube and add two drops of phenolphthalein solution.

(ii) Note the colour of the solution.

(iii) Add dilute HCl solution to the above solution drop by drop.

(iv) Note the change in colour of the reaction mixture.

(v) Now add a few drops of NaOH solution to the above mixture.

Observation:

On adding phenolphthalein to NaOH solution, the colour becomes pink. On adding dilute HCl solution dropwise, finally the pink colour disappears and the solution again becomes colourless. On adding NaOH pink reappears because the medium becomes basic again.

Conclusion:

Acid and base react together to form salt and water.

$$\text{Acid} + \text{Base} \longrightarrow \text{Salt} + \text{Water}$$

The reaction is called neutralisation reaction.

Some more examples,

(i) $HNO_3(aq) + KOH\ (aq) \longrightarrow KNO_3(aq) + H_2O\ (l)$

(ii) $HCl\ (aq) + NH_4OH\ (aq) \longrightarrow NH_4Cl\ (aq) + H_2O\ (l)$

➤ **Practical Applications of Neutralisation**

(i) People particularly of old age suffer from acidity problems in the stomach which is caused mainly due to release of excessive gastric juices containing HCl. The acidity is neutralised by **antacid** tablets which contain sodium hydrogen carbonate (baking soda), magnesium hydroxide etc.

(ii) The stings of **bees** and **ants** contain formic acid. Its corrosive and poisonous effect can be neutralised by rubbing soap which contains NaOH (an alkali).

(iii) The stings of wasps contain an alkali and its poisonous effect can be neutralised by an acid like acetic acid (present in vinegar).

(iv) Farmers generally neutralise the effect of acidity in the soil caused by acid rain by adding slaked lime (calcium hydroxide) to the soil.

2.5 DISSOCIATION OF ACIDS & BASES

➤ **Dissociation of Acids**

When an acid is dissolved in water, it dissociates into ions and produces H^+ ions. The characteristic properties of acids are due to H^+ ions.

Hydrogen ion (H^+) is formed by loss of an electron by a hydrogen atom. It is simply a proton. It does not exist independently in aqueous solution, rather it combines with a water molecule to form H_3O^+ ion is known as **hydronium ion**. Thus H^+ ion in solution should be represented as H_3O^+ or H^+ (aq.)

$$H^+ + H_2O \longrightarrow H_3O^+$$

It may be noted that all compounds containing hydrogen do not behave as acids. Only those compounds can behave as acids which dissociate in solution to furnish hydrogen ions, H^+ (aq.).

For example, ethyl alcohol (C_2H_5OH) and glucose ($C_6H_{12}O_6$) do not behave as acids in solution because they do not produce H^+ ions in solutions.

Dissociation of some acids in aqueous solution, to form H_3O^+ ions is depicted as follows:

$$HCl + H_2O \longrightarrow H_3O^+ + Cl^-$$

$$H_2SO_4 + 2H_2O \longrightarrow 2H_3O^+ + SO_4^{2-}$$

When an acid such as hydrochloric acid (HCl) dissolves in water, almost all of it dissociates. Such acids are known as **strong acids**.

On the other hand, when acetic acid dissolves in water only a small fraction of the molecules ionizes. Such acids are called a **weak acids**.

$$HCl \longrightarrow H^+ + Cl^- \qquad \text{[Strong acid]}$$

$$CH_3COOH \rightleftharpoons H^+ + CH_3COO^- \qquad \text{[Weak acid]}$$

1. All acids produce hydrogen ions, H^+ (aq) in solution.
2. A strong acid is an acid that is almost completely dissociated in its aqueous solution.
3. A weak acid is an acid that is weakly dissociated in its aqueous solution.
4. All bases produce hydroxyl ions, OH^- (aq) in solution.

➢ Dissociation of Bases

A base when dissolved in water undergoes dissociation to produce hydroxyl ions (OH^-).

$$NaOH\,(s) \xrightarrow{H_2O} Na^+\,(aq) + OH^-\,(aq)$$

$$Ca(OH)_2\,(s) \xrightarrow{H_2O} Ca^{2+}\,(aq) + 2OH^-\,(aq)$$

The characteristic properties of bases are due to OH^- (aq) ions.

A base such as NaOH or KOH which is completely dissociated in aqueous solution is called a **strong base**. On the other hand, a base which is weakly dissociated in aqueous solution is called a **weak base. For** example: $Mg(OH)_2$ is a weak base.

When solution of some acid is mixed with solution of some base, the H^+ (aq) ion from acid combine with OH^- (aq) from base to form undissociated water (H_2O) molecules. Thus, during neutralization of an acid with a base the following reaction takes place:

$$\underset{\text{From acid}}{H^+\,(aq)} + \underset{\text{From base}}{OH^-} \longrightarrow H_2O\,(l)$$

➢ Strong and Weak Acids

Acids which are almost completely ionised in water, are known as strong acids. For example, hydrochloric acid (HCl), sulphuric acid (H_2SO_4), nitric acid (HNO_3) etc. are all strong acids.

$$HCl\,(l) \xrightarrow{(water)} H^+(aq) + Cl^-(aq)$$

$$H_2SO_4\,(l) \xrightarrow{(water)} 2H^+(aq) + SO_4^{2-}(aq)$$

Acids which are weakly ionised in water are known as weak acids. For example carbonic acid (H_2CO_3), phosphoric acid (H_3PO_4), formic acid (HCOOH), acetic acid (CH_3COOH) are weak acids.

$$CH_3COOH\,(l) \underset{}{\overset{(water)}{\rightleftharpoons}} CH_3COO^- + H^+\,(aq)$$

In general, **mineral acids are strong acids while organic acids are weak acids**.

➤ Classify the following acids into strong and weak acids.

H_2SO_4, H_2CO_3, H_3PO_4, HCl, HCOOH, HNO_3, CH_3COOH

Strong acids : H_2SO_4, HNO_3, HCl

Weak acids : H_2CO_3, H_3PO_4, HCOOH, CH_3COOH

Basicity of the acid:

As we have studied that acids on dissociation in water produce hydrogen ion.

The number of these replaceable hydrogen ions in an acid is known as the basicity of a acid. It is also one hydrogen ion or hydronium ion that can react with one hydroxyl ion (OH^-). Stated in another way, basicity is the number of hydroxyl ions, with which one molecule of an acid can combine. For example the basicity of HCl, H_2SO_4 and H_3PO_4 is one, two and three respectively as it on dissociation they produce one, two and three H^+ ions respectively.

$$HCl \rightleftharpoons H^+ + Cl^- \qquad \text{basicity} = 1$$

$$H_2SO_4 \rightleftharpoons 2H^+ + SO_4^{--} \qquad \text{basicity} = 2$$

$$H_3PO_4 \rightleftharpoons 3H^+ + PO_4^{---} \qquad \text{basicity} = 3$$

Reactions:

$$\underset{\text{(monobasic)}}{HCl\ (aq)} + NaOH\ (aq) \longrightarrow NaCl\ (aq) + H_2O\ (l)$$

$$\underset{\text{(dibasic)}}{H_2SO_4\ (aq)} + 2NaOH\ (aq) \longrightarrow Na_2SO_4\ (aq) + 2H_2O\ (l)$$

$$\underset{\text{(tribasic)}}{H_3PO_4\ (aq)} + 3KOH\ (aq) \longrightarrow K_3PO_4\ (aq) + 3H_2O\ (l)$$

➢ **Strong and Weak Bases**

We have learnt that a base contains in it one or more hydroxyl (OH) groups which releases in aqueous solution upon ionisation. Bases which are almost completely ionised in water, are known as strong bases. For example, sodium hydroxide (NaOH), potassium hydroxide (KOH), barium hydroxide $Ba(OH)_2$ are all strong bases.

$$NaOH\ (s) \xrightarrow{\text{(water)}} Na^+\ (aq) + OH^-\ (aq)$$

$$KOH\ (s) \xrightarrow{\text{(water)}} K^+\ (aq) + OH^-\ (aq)$$

Bases which are ionised to small extent in water are known as weak bases. For example, magnesium hydroxide $Mg(OH)_2$, ammonium hydroxide NH_4OH, copper hydroxide $Cu(OH)_2$ are weak bases.

$$NH_4OH\ (l) \xrightarrow{\text{(water)}} NH_4^+\ (aq) + OH^-\ (aq)$$

$$Mg(OH)_2\ (s) \xrightarrow{\text{(water)}} Mg^{2+}\ (aq) + 2OH^-\ (aq)$$

Both NaOH and KOH are deliquescent in nature which means that they absorb moisture from air and get liquefied.

Just like acids, relative strengths of bases can also be compared in terms of degree of ionisation also called degree of dissociation. It is denoted as α, Mathematically,

$$\alpha = \frac{\text{No. of molecules of base existing as ions}}{\text{Total number of molecules of base}}$$

For strong bases, α is close to one while for weak bases, it has small value.

Advance Learning

Acidity of base:

Acidity of a base may be defined as: The number of replaceable hydroxyl groups present in a base which it can release when dissolved in water or in aqueous solution as ions.

The acidity of a base is equal to the number of hydroxyl ions it has. It is also the number of hydrogen ions with which a base can combine as one hydrogen ion combines with one hydroxyl ion. Example the acidity of NaOH, $Ca(OH)_2$ and $Fe(OH)_3$ is one, two and three respectively as on dissociation they produce one, two and three OH^- ions respectively.

$NaOH \rightleftharpoons Na^+ + OH^-$ acidity = 1

$Ca(OH)_2 \rightleftharpoons Ca^{++} + 2OH^-$ acidity = 2

$Fe(OH)_3 \rightleftharpoons Fe^{+++} + 3OH^-$ acidity = 3

2.6 WHAT DO ALL ACIDS AND ALL BASES HAVE IN COMMON?

All acids and bases gives characteristic reactions. Both produce hydrogen gas when reacted with certain metals.

To know of it, let us perform the following example,

Activity:

Materials required: Dilute hydrochloric acid, Dilute sulphuric acid, Dilute solution of sodium hydroxide, Ethanol, Glucose solution

Apparatus required: Beaker (1), Carbon electrodes (2), Dry cells (2), Bulb 1.5 V (1) Key (1)

Procedure: Take a beaker and place two carbon electrodes into it. Connect the electrodes to a battery bulb through a key and a dry cell.

Pour dilute hydrochloric acid into the beaker and press the key. Did the bulb glow? Perform similar experiment with all the given solutions, and record your observations.

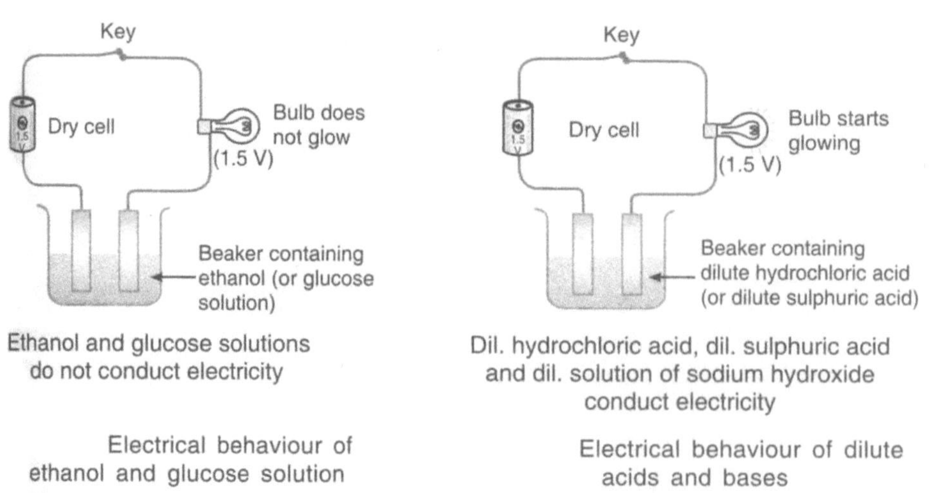

Electrical behaviour of ethanol and glucose solution

Electrical behaviour of dilute acids and bases

Observation:

Solution	Bulb glows	Bulb does not glow	Nature of the solution
Dil. Hydrochloric acid	✓	✗	Conducting
Dil. Sulphuric acid	✓	✗	Conducting
Dil. Sodium hydroxide solution	✓	✗	Conducting
Ethanol	✗	✓	Non conducting
Glucose solution	✗	✓	Non conducting

Conclusion:

The solutions of acids and bases are good conductors of electricity. The solution of glucose and ethanol are nonconductors of electricity.

Explanation:

Solutions conduct electricity due to the presence of ions in them. Therefore, acids and base/alkalis furnish ions in their solutions. Acids produce $H^+(aq)$ ions and bases/alkalis produce free $OH^-(aq)$ ions in their solutions in water.

Ethanol and the solution of glucose do not conduct electricity. Therefore, these compounds do not produce ions in their solutions.

Thus, the tendency to produce ions in their solutions in water is a common property of acids and bases/ alkalis.

2.7 WHAT HAPPENS TO AN ACID OR A BASE IN A WATER SOLUTION?

Activity :

Aim: To test that dry HCl gas is not acidic but its aqueous solution is acidic.

Method:

(i) Take about 1 g solid NaCl in a clean and dry test tube and set up the apparatus.

(ii) Add some concentrated sulphuric acid to the test tube.

(iii) Test the gas evolved successively with dry and wet blue litmus paper.

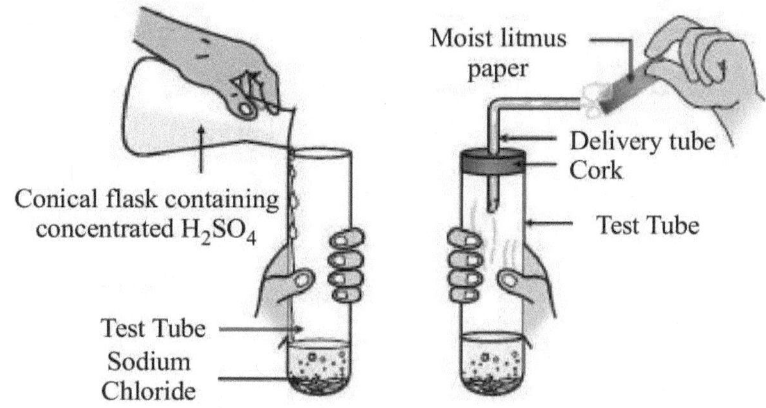

Preparation of HCl gas

Observation:

Dry blue litmus paper does not change colour but wet blue litmus paper changes its colour to red.

Conclusion:

Dry HCl gas is not acidic but HCl solution is acidic. This is because in the presence of water. HCl dissociates to give H^+ ions.

$$HCl\,(g) + H_2O\,(l) \longrightarrow \underset{(\text{hydronium ion})}{H_3O^+ \text{ or } H^+(aq)} + \underset{(\text{chloride ion})}{Cl^-(aq)}$$

Hydrogen ions cannot exist alone but they exist after combining with water molecules. Thus hydrogen ions must always be shown as H^+ (aq) or hydronium ion (H_3O^+).

$$H^+ + H_2O \longrightarrow H_3O^+$$

Similarly when a base is dissolved in water, it forms OH^- (aq) ion.

$$NaOH\,(s) \xrightarrow{H_2O} Na^+\,(aq) + OH^-\,(aq)$$

Bases generate hydroxide (OH^-) ions in water. Bases which are soluble in water are called **alkalis**. All bases do not dissolve in water.

Explanation:

According to Arrhenius theory, an acid when dissolved in water gives H^+ ions. Similarly a base when dissolved in water gives OH^- ions. Neutralisation is the combination between H^+ ions of the acid with OH^- ions of the base to form H_2O. For example,

$$\underbrace{H^+(aq) + Cl^-(aq)}_{HCl\,(aq)} + \underbrace{Na^+(aq) + OH^-(aq)}_{NaOH\,(aq)} \longrightarrow \underbrace{Na^+(aq) + Cl^-(aq)}_{NaCl\,(aq)} + H_2O$$

2.8 DILUTION OF ACID AND BASE WITH WATER

Acids and bases are mostly water soluble and can be diluted by adding the required amount of water. In fact, with the addition of water, the amount of acid or base per unit volume decreases and dilution occurs. The process is generally exothermic in nature. In some cases, so much heat is evolved that the acid or base immediately changes into vapour state. This will lead to the formation of dense fog which is likely to pollute the atmosphere.

CAUTION:

An acid should be diluted by adding acid to water and not water to the acid. If water is added to the acid, the heat produced may cause the mixture to splash out and cause burns. The glass container may also break due to excessive local heating.

➢ Precaution needed for dilution

Whenever a concentrated acid like sulphuric acid or nitric acid is to be diluted with water, care must be taken that acid should be added dropwise to water taken in the container with constant stirring. Heat evolved in this case will be quite slow. If water is added to the acid, it will have affinity for the entire quantity of the acid present . So much heat will be evolved that the glass container in which dilution is carried will crack. Moreover, the vapours released in the atmosphere as fog will cause pollution problem.

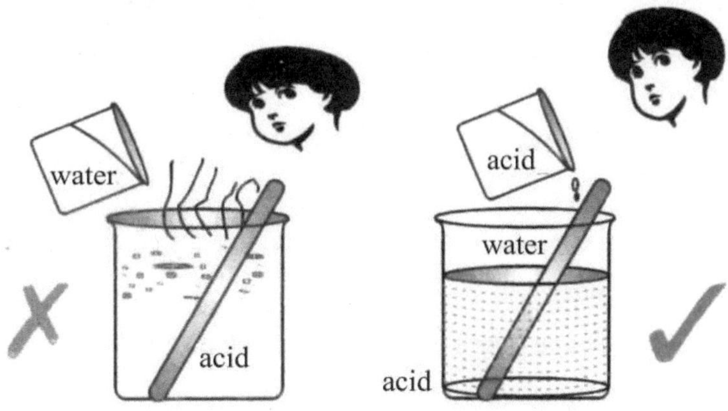

Diluting concentrated H_2SO_4 acid with water

Activity:

Aim: To see the nature of reaction.

Method:

(i) Take about 20 mL of water in a 100 mL beaker

(ii) Add 10 – 15 drops of concentrated H_2SO_4 to it. During addition, stir the solution with the help of a glass rod.

(iii) Touch the beaker from outside to feel the change in temperature.
(You may use a thermometer to note the change in temperature.)

Observation:

It is observed that on addition of concentrated sulphuric acid, the beaker becomes warm indicating that during the dissolution of sulphuric acid heat is given out. Thus, dissolution of sulphuric acid in water is an exothermic process.

Activity:

Aim: Dissolution of bases in water in an exothermic process.

Method:

(i) Take about 20 mL of water in a 100 mL beaker.

(ii) Add 4– 5 pallets of sodium hydroxide to it and stir the contents of the beaker with the help of a glass rod.

(iii) Touch the bottom of the beaker from outside to feel any change in temperature.

Observation:

It is observed that sodium hydroxide readily dissolves in water. As a result of dissolution the solution becomes warm indicating that the dissolution of sodium hydroxide in water is an exothermic process.

How strong are Acid and Base solution

We have studied that acids and bases may be either strong or weak and have compared their relative strengths on the basis of the Arrhenius theory. According to the theory, more the number of H^+ ions released by acid in water, stronger is the acid. Similarly, more the number of OH^- ions released by a base in water, stronger is the base.

Warning sign displayed on containers containing concentrated acids and bases

Illustrations

Illustration 8

Define alkalies, give examples also.

***Solution*:**

Base which are highly soluble in water are called alkalies. It means that an alkali is a water soluble bases.

All alkalies are bases but all bases are not alkalies.

Examples of alkalies are as:

NaOH: Sodium hydroxide or Caustic Soda. $Ca(OH)_2$: Calcium hydroxide or Slaked lime.

2.9 THE pH SCALE

An easier way to measure the strength of an acid or base solution was worked out by the Danish biochemist S. Sorensen. He was interested in checking the acidity of beer and introduced a scale known as **pH scale** (In German 'p' stands for 'potenz' meaning power). The scale runs from 0 to 14 and the characteristics of the scale are:

- Acids have pH less than 7
- The more acidic is a solution, lesser will be its pH
- Neutral solutions (e.g., water) have pH of 7
- Alkalies have pH more than 7
- The more alkaline is a solution, higher will be its pH.

A digital pH meter

Remember

All the pH values are calculated at room temperature i.e. 298 K.

In case, there is a change in temperature, the pH value of the solution also changes accordingly.

Mathematically pH is expressed as $pH = -\log [H^+]$.

The pH scale may be shown as follows:

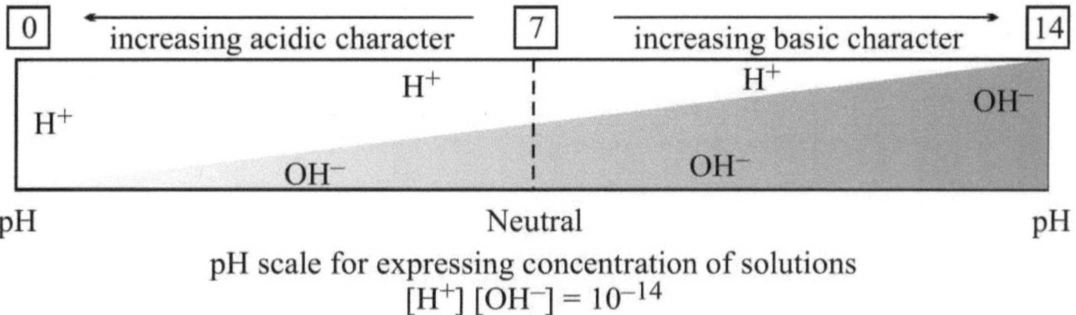

pH scale for expressing concentration of solutions

$[H^+][OH^-] = 10^{-14}$

➢ Universal indicator papers for pH values

We have seen the role of indicators like litmus, phenolphthalein and methyl orange in predicting the acidic and basic characters of the solutions. However, universal indicator papers have been developed to predict the pH of different solution. Such papers represent specific colours for different concentrations in terms of pH values.

➢ Ionic Product of water

Pure water is a very weak conductor of electricity i.e. it is a very weak electrolyte. Hence, it undergoes self ionisation to a very small extent. So that the following equilibrium is set up between water and its ions

$$H_2O\,(l) + H_2O\,(l) \rightleftharpoons H_3O^+\,(aq) + OH^-\,(aq)$$

Applying law of mass action, the dissociation constant K is written as :

$$K = \frac{\left[H_3O^+(aq)\right]\left[OH^-(aq)\right]}{\left[H_2O(l)\right]^2}$$

Since, water is ionised to a very small extent and its degree of ionisation is low, its ionisation does not appreciably change the concentration of water molecule. Therefore, $[H_2O(l)]$ may be supposed to remain constant, thus -

$$K\,[H_2O(l)]^2 = [H_3O^+(aq)][OH^-(aq)]$$

or $\quad K \times K' = [H_3O^+(aq)][OH^-(aq)]$

Where $\quad K' = [H_2O\,(l)]^2$

or $\quad Kw = k \times K' = [H_3O^+(aq)]\,[OH^-(aq)]$

Here, Kw is a constant, known as ionic product of water.

At room temperatures. (25°C or 298 K), the value of Kw of water is 1.0×10^{-14}.

➢ Relation between pH value and hydrogen ion concentration

According to Arrhenius theory, an acid releases H^+ ions in aqueous solution. The concentration of these ions is expressed by enclosing H^+ separately in square bracket i.e., as $[H^+]$. Thus, greater the $[H^+]$ ions, stronger will be the acid. However, according pH scale, lesser the pH value, stronger will be the acid. From the above discussion, we can conclude that:

pH value and H^+ ion concentration $[H^+]$ are inversely proportional to each other.

The relation between them can also be expressed:

$$pH = -\log [H^+] = \log \left[\frac{1}{H^+}\right]$$

For example, let the $[H^+]$ of an acid solution be 10^{-3} M. Its pH can be calculated as:

$$pH = -\log [H^+] = -\log [10^{-3}] = (-)(-3) \log 10 = 3$$

(Please remember that log 10 = 1)

For neutral solution : $pH = 7$, and $[H^+] = 10^{-7}$

For acidic solution : $pH < 7$ and $[H^+] > 10^{-7}$

For basic solution : $pH > 7$ and $[H^+] < 10^{-7}$

Note : Just as the $[H^+]$ of a solution can be expressed in term of pH value, the $[OH^-]$ can be expressed as pOH.

Mathematically, $pOH = -\log [OH^-] = \log \frac{1}{[OH^-]}$

Moreover, $pH + pOH = 14$

Thus, if pH value of solution is known, its pOH value can be calculated.

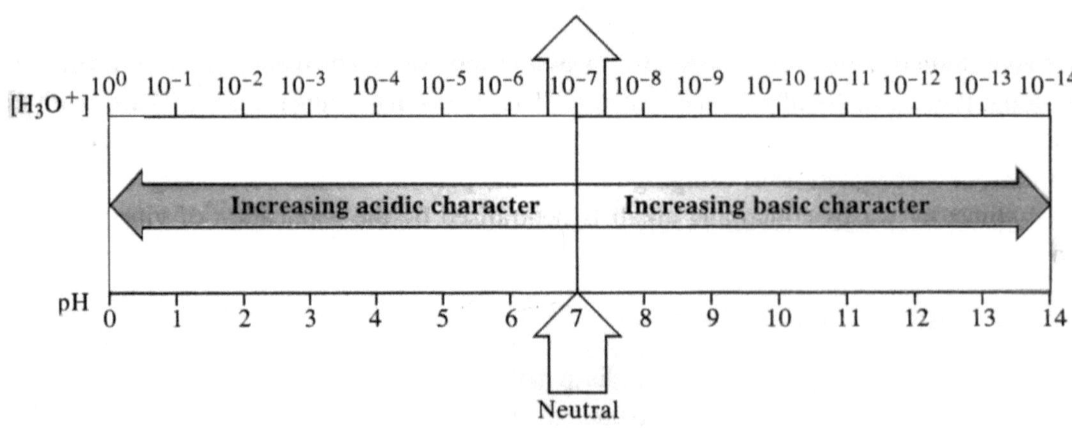

Relation between pH scale and $[H^+]$ or $[H_3O]^+$ at room temperature (298 K)

Illustration 9

Calculate the pH of (i) 0.0001 M HCl (ii) 0.001 M NaOH solutions.

Solution:

(i) **pH value of 0.0001 M HCl solution.** As HCl is a strong acid, it is completely dissociated and $[H^+]$ is the same as that of acid i.e., 0.0001 M.

$[H^+] = 0.0001\ M = 10^{-4}\ M$

$pH = -\log[H^+] = -\log[10^{-4}] = (-)(-4)\log 10 = 4$

(ii) **pH value of 0.001 M NaOH solution**

As NaOH is a strong base, it is completely dissociated and $[OH^-]$ is the same as that of base i.e., 0.001 M.

$[OH^-] = 0.001\ M$

$pOH = -\log[OH^-] = -\log[10^{-3}] = (-)(-3)\log 10 = 3$

$pH = 14 - pOH = 14 - 3 = 11$

Illustration 10

An aqueous solution has hydrogen ion concentration $[H^+] = 1.0 \times 10^{-7}\ mol\ L^{-1}$. Calculate its pH value.

Solution:

$[H^+] = 10^{-7}\ mol\ L^{-1} = 10^{-7}\ M$

$pH = -\log[H^+] = -\log[10^{-7}] = (-)(-7)\log 10 = 7$

The relation between $[H^+]$ and pH scale of expressing the nature of a solution.

Illustration 11

Calculate the pH of the solution when hydrogen ion concentration is 1.0×10^{-9} M.

Solution:

$[H_3O^+]$ or $[H^+] = 1.0 \times 10^{-9}\ mol\ L^{-1}$

$-pH = -\log[H^+] = -\log(1.0 \times 10^{-9}) = 9.0$

Illustration 12

What is the pH of 0.1 M solution of HCl?

Solution:

HCl is a strong acid. It is completely ionised in aqueous solution.

$HCl \longrightarrow H^+(aq) + Cl^-(aq)$

$[H^+] = [HCl] = 0.1\ M$ or $0.1\ mol\ L^{-1}$

$pH = -\log[H^+] = -\log(0.1) = -\log(10^{-1})$

$pH = 1$

➢ Importance of pH in everyday life

In general, lesser the pH of a solution, more will be its acidic strength.
Similarly, higher the pH of a solution, more will be its basic strength.

Are plants and animals pH sensitive?

Our body works within the pH range of 7.0 to 7.8. Living organisms can survive only in a narrow rang of pH change. When pH of rain water is less than 5.6, it is called acid rain. When acid rain flow into the rivers it lowers the pH of the river water. The survival of aquatic life in such river becomes difficult.

Acids in other planets

The atmosphere of venous is made up of thick white and yellowish clouds of sulphuric acid.

Some flowering plants carry their own built in pH 'indicators'.
For example, the flowers of a hydrangea bush are blue in colour when grown in an acidic soil. If it is alkaline in nature, the flowers become pink.

(i) pH of the soil

The growth of plants in a particular soil is also related to its pH. Actually, different plants prefer different pH range for their growth. It is therefore, quite important to provide the soil with proper pH for their healthy growth. Soils with high, pear content or iron minerals or with rotting vegetation tend to become acidic. The soil pH can reach as low as 4. The acidic effect can be neutralised by 'liming the soil' which is carried by adding calcium hydroxide, calcium oxide or powdered chalk (calcium carbonate). These all are basic in nature and have neutralising effect. Similarly, the soil with excess of lime stone or chalk is usually alkaline. Sometimes, its pH reaches as high as 8.3 and is quite harmful for the plant growth. In order to reduce the alkaline effect, it is better to add some decaying organic matter which is acidic in nature (compost or manure) or dig in some peat.

Plants	Preferred pH range
Potatoes	4.5 — 6.0
Carrot, Sweet Potato	5.5 — 6.5
Cauliflower, garlic, tomato	5.5 — 7.5
Onion, Cabbage	6.0 — 7.5

Plants require a specific pH range for their healthy growth. To find out the pH required for the healthy growth of a plant, we should collect the soil from various places and check the pH. Also, we should note down which plants are growing in the region from which you have collected the soil.

(ii) pH in our digestive system

Our stomach produces hydrochloric acid. It helps in the digestion of food without harming the stomach. During indigestion the stomach produces too much acid and this causes pain and irritation. To get rid of this pain, people use bases called antacids. These antacids neutralise the excess acid. Magnesium hydroxide (milk of magnesia), a mild base, is often used for this purpose.

The pH of human blood varies between 7.36 to 7.42. It is maintained by the soluble hydrogen carbonates and carbonic acid present in the blood. These are known as 'buffers'. In general, the role of different buffers is to help in controlling the pH of solutions. It is not possible to discuss mechanism of the buffer action at this level to the students.

(iii) pH change as the cause of tooth decay

Tooth decay starts when the pH of the mouth is lower than 5.5. Tooth enamel, made up of calcium phosphate is the hardest substance in the body. It does not dissolve in water, but is corroded when the pH in the mouth is below 5.5. Bacteria present in the mouth produce acids by degradation of sugar and food particles remaining in the mouth after eating. The best way to prevent this is to clean the mouth after eating food. Using toothpastes, which are generally basic, for cleaning the teeth, can neutralise the excess acid and prevent tooth decay.

The saliva produced in the mouth by salivary glands is of alkaline nature.
It is also partially neutralises the acid present in the mouth.

(iv) Self defence by animals and plants through chemical warfare

Bee-sting leaves an acid which causes pain and irritation. Use of a mild base like baking soda on the stung area gives relief. Stinging hair of nettle leaves inject methanoic acid causing burning pain. Nettle leaves have stinging hall which cause painful stings when touched accidentally. This is due to the methanoic acid secreted by them. A traditional remedy is rubbing the area with the leaf of the dock plant, which often grows beside the nettle in the wild.

Nettle plants are herbaceous in nature and grow in the wild. These have sharp hair which contain in them methanoic acid. If they happen to touch the body by accident, their stings are very painful because methanoic acid present gets injected in the body.

These are commonly known as **stinging nettles**. You will be surprised to note that the remedy for the same is provided by the nature itself. The stung area is rubbed by the leaves of 'dock plants' which often grow beside nettle plants. Most probably, these plants inject some base or alkali which neutralises the effect of acid and has soothing effect.

2.10 MORE ABOUT SALTS

Salts are the ionic compounds consisting of two parts, one part carrying a positive charge called positive ion or **cation** and the other part carrying a negative charge called a negative ion or **anion**.

➤ **Family of Salts**

Salts of a strong acid and a strong base are neutral with pH value of 7. On the other hand, salts of a strong acid and weak base are acidic with pH value less than 7 and those of a strong base and weak acid are basic in nature, with pH value more than 7.

Salts are generally formed by between an acid and base. Acid on the basis of kind of acid and base used they contain specific cation or anion. So we can divide salts in different families on the basis of cation or anion present.

The salts having the same positive radical (or cation) or negative radical (or anion) are said to belong to the same family. Or we can say, salts can be classified into different families based on the common ion present.

Activity:

Aim: Write the formulae of the salts and to identify their acids and bases and the families.

Method:

(i) Write down the formulae of the salts given below:

1. Potassium Sulphate 2. Sodium Sulphate 3. Calcium Sulphate
4. Magnesium Sulphate 5. Copper Sulphate 6. Sodium Chloride
7. Sodium Nitrate 8. Sodium Carbonate 9. Ammonium Chloride

(ii) Identify the acids and bases from which the above salts may be obtained.

(iii) Salts having the same positive or negative radicals are said to belong to a family. For example, NaCl and Na_2SO_4 belong to the family of sodium salts. Similarly, NaCl and KCl belong to the family of chloride salts.

How many families can you identify among the salts given in this activity?

Observation and Conclusion:

S.No.	Salt	Formula	Acid	Base
1	Potassium Sulphate	K_2SO_4	H_2SO_4	KOH
2	Sodium Sulphate	Na_2SO_4	H_2SO_4	NaOH
3	Calcium Sulphate	$CaSO_4$	H_2SO_4	$Ca(OH)_2$
4	Magnesium Sulphate	$MgSO_4$	H_2SO_4	$Mg(OH)_2$
5	Copper Sulphate	$CuSO_4$	H_2SO_4	$Cu(OH)_2$
6	Sodium Chloride	NaCl	HCl	NaOH
7	Sodium Nitrate	$NaNO_3$	HNO_3	NaOH
8	Sodium Carbonate	Na_2CO_3	H_2CO_3	NaOH
9	Ammonium Chloride	NH_4Cl	HCl	NH_4OH

Families:

(i) On the basis of common salts

Sulphates = K_2SO_4, Na_2SO_4, $CaSO_4$, $MgSO_4$, $CuSO_4$

Chlorides = NaCl, NH_4Cl

Carbonates = Na_2CO_3

(ii) On the basis of common bases

Sodium Salts = Na_2SO_4, NaCl, $NaNO_3$, Na_2CO_3

Potassium Salts = K_2SO_4

Calcium Salts = $CaSO_4$

Magnesium Salts = $MgSO_4$

Copper Salts = $CuSO_4$

Ammonium Salts = NH_4Cl

NaCl (sodium chloride) and Na_2SO_4 (sodium sulphate) belong to the family of sodium salts because both contain the same radical (or cation), that is Na^+. These may be called sodium salts.

Copper Sulphate ($CuSO_4$) and Sodium Sulphate (Na_2SO_4) belong to the family of sulphates because both contain the same acid radical (or anion) that is sulphate (SO_4^{2-}).

➢ **Formation of salts**

Salts can be prepared by many reactions some of these are

(i) By neutralisation of acids and bases.

E.g. $\underset{\text{(sodium hydroxide)}}{NaOH} + \underset{\text{(hydrochloric acid)}}{HCl} \longrightarrow \underset{\text{(sodium chloride)}}{NaCl} + \underset{\text{(water)}}{H_2O}$

(ii) By action of metals on acids.

E.g. $\underset{\text{(zinc)}}{Zn} + \underset{\text{(sulphuric acid)}}{H_2SO_4} \longrightarrow \underset{\text{(zinc sulphate)}}{ZnSO_4} + \underset{\text{(hydrogen)}}{H_2}$

(iii) By action of acids on metal carbonates and bicarbonates.

E.g. $\underset{\text{(calcium carbonate)}}{CaCO_3} + \underset{\text{(hydrochloric acid)}}{2HCl} \longrightarrow \underset{\text{(calcium chloride)}}{CaCl_2} + \underset{\text{(water)}}{H_2O} + \underset{\text{(carbon dioxide)}}{CO_2}$

(iv) By action of metal on alkalis.

E.g. $\underset{\text{(sodium hydroxide)}}{2NaOH} + \underset{\text{(zinc)}}{Zn} \longrightarrow \underset{\text{(sodium zincate)}}{Na_2ZnO_2} + \underset{\text{(hydrogen)}}{H_2}$

➢ pH of salts

Depending upon the nature of acid and base which react to form the salt.

OR

The nature of acid and base produced when salt reacts with water, the salts can be classified into the following four types.

(i) Salts of strong acid and strong base. E.g. NaCl

$$\underset{\text{(sodium chloride)}}{NaCl} + \underset{\text{(water)}}{H_2O} \longrightarrow \underset{\substack{\text{(sodium hydroxide)} \\ \text{strong base}}}{NaOH} + \underset{\substack{\text{(hydrochloric acid)} \\ \text{strong acid}}}{HCl}$$

Hence, the acid and the base produced neutralise each other completely.

So, pH = 7.

(ii) Salt of strong acid and weak base. E.g. NH_4Cl

$$\underset{\text{(ammonium chloride)}}{NH_4Cl} + \underset{\text{(water)}}{H_2O} \longrightarrow \underset{\substack{\text{(ammonium hydroxide)} \\ \text{weak base}}}{NH_4OH} + \underset{\substack{\text{(hydrochloric acid)} \\ \text{strong acid}}}{HCl}$$

Here, pH < 7.

(iii) Salt of weak acid and strong base. E.g. Na_2CO_3

$$\underset{\text{(sodium carbonate)}}{Na_2CO_3} + \underset{\text{(water)}}{2H_2O} \longrightarrow \underset{\substack{\text{(sodium hydroxide)} \\ \text{strong base}}}{2NaOH} + \underset{\substack{\text{(carbonic acid)} \\ \text{weak acid}}}{H_2CO_3}$$

Here, pH > 7

(iv) Salt of weak acid and weak base. E.g. CH_3COONH_4

$$\underset{\text{(ammonium acetate)}}{CH_3COONH_4} + \underset{\text{(water)}}{H_2O} \longrightarrow \underset{\text{(acetic acid)}}{CH_3COOH} + \underset{\text{(ammonium hydroxide)}}{NH_4OH}$$

Here pH ≈ 7

➢ Common salt: A raw material for chemical

The common salt thus obtained is an important raw material for materials of daily use, such as sodium hydroxide, baking soda, washing soda, bleaching powder and many more.

(i) **Sodium Chloride (NaCl):** By now we have learnt that the salt formed by the combination of hydrochloric acid and sodium hydroxide solution is called **sodium chloride**. This is the salt that we use in food it is a neutral salt.

Seawater contains many salts dissolved in it. Sodium chloride is separated from these salts. These large crystals are often brown due to impurities. This is called rock salt. Beds of **rock salt** were formed when seas of bygone ages dried up. Rock salt is mined like coal.

$$NaOH + HCl \longrightarrow NaCl + H_2O$$

(ii) Sodium Hydroxide (NaOH): When electricity is passed through an aqueous solution of sodium chloride (called brine), it decomposes to form sodium hydroxide process is called the chlor-alkali process because of the products chlor for chlorine and alkali for sodium hydroxide.

$$2NaCl\,(aq) + 2H_2O\,(l) \longrightarrow 2NaOH\,(aq) + Cl_2\uparrow(g) + H_2\uparrow(g)$$

Chlorine gas is given off at the anode, and hydrogen gas at the cathode Sodium hydroxide solution is formed near the cathode. The products produced in this process are all useful.

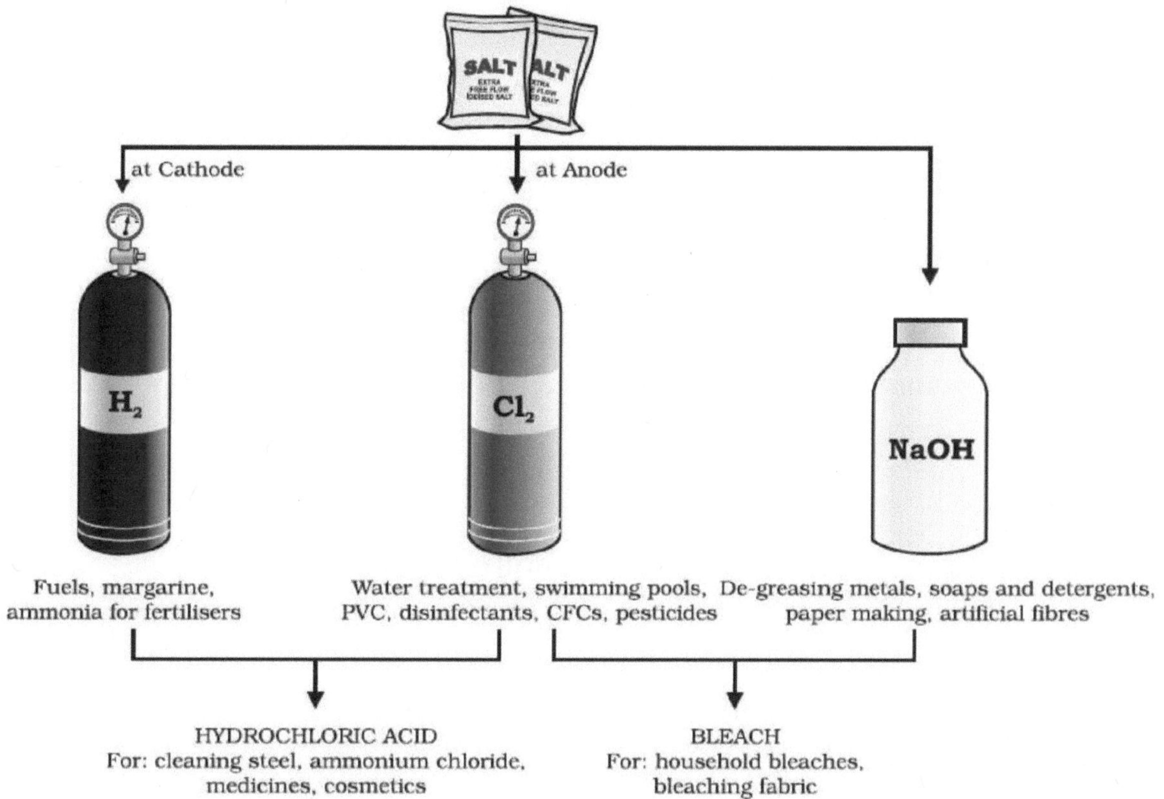

Important products from the chlor-alkali process

(iii) Bleaching Powder ($CaOCl_2$)

It is a calcium salt of hypochlorous acid. It may be represented by $CaOCl_2$ (Calcium Chlorohypochlorite, Chloride of lime).

Actually it is a mixture of $CaOCl_2.4H_2O$ and basic calcium chloride, $CaCl_2.Ca(OH)_2.H_2O$ chlorine is produced during electrolysis of aqueous sodium chloride (brine). This chlorine gas is use for the manufacture of bleaching powder. Bleaching powder is produced by the action of chlorine on dry slaked lime [$Ca(OH)_2$]. Bleaching power is represented as $CaOCl_2$, though the actual composition is complex.

$$Ca(OH)_2 + Cl_2 \longrightarrow CaOCl_2 + H_2O$$

Properties

1. Bleaching powder is a yellowish white powder which gives strong smell of chlorine.
2. It is soluble in water leaving behind a small residue of lime.
3. When exposed to air, bleaching powder deteriorates giving off chlorine. Decomposition of bleaching powder in air takes place due to its reaction with carbon dioxide gas.

$$CaOCl_2 + CO_2 \longrightarrow CaCO_3 + Cl_2 \uparrow$$

4. When bleaching powder is treated with excess dilute acid, chlorine gas is produced.

$$CaOCl_2 + H_2SO_4 \longrightarrow CaSO_4 + H_2O + Cl_2 \uparrow$$

$$CaOCl_2 + 2HCl \longrightarrow CaCl_2 + H_2O + Cl_2 \uparrow$$

Chlorine gas produced in this way is known as 'available chlorine'. It is this available chlorine which is responsible for the bleaching action of the bleaching powder.

Uses of Bleaching Powder.

1. Bleaching powder is chiefly used for bleaching cotton and linen textiles, wood and paper pulp. Delicate articles like silk, wool, straw etc are not bleached by it, as these are likely to be damaged.
2. It is strong disinfectant and is therefore, used for sterilization of water.
3. It is employed for making wool unshrinkable.
4. It is also used as an oxidizing agent in the manufacture of many chemicals.

➤ **Bleaching of Cloth by bleaching powder**

The cloth to be bleached is initially treated with a very dilute solution of sodium hydroxide which removes any greasy matter. It is then dipped in bleaching powder solution followed by dilute hydrochloric solution taken in a separate tank. The acid also reacts with bleaching powder to evolve chlorine which bleaches the cloth. In order to remove the unreacted chlorine, it is then dipped in a dilute solution of sodium thiosulphate called **antichlor**.

$$\underset{\text{(sodium thiosulphate)}}{Na_2S_2O_3} + Cl_2 + H_2O \longrightarrow Na_2SO_4 + 2HCl + S$$

An antichlor is a substance which removes the unreacted chlorine. The cloth is thoroughly washed with water and is then dried.

Illustration 13

How bleaching powder helps in disinfection of drinking water?

Solution:

Bleaching powder dissolves in water to generate hypochlorous acid.

$$Ca(OCl)_2 + 2H_2O \longrightarrow \underset{\text{(hypochlorous acid)}}{2HOCl} + Ca(OH)_2$$

Now, this hypochlorous acid have effective germicidal property which is responsible for disinfecting action of bleaching powder.

(iv) Baking Soda ($NaHCO_3$)

The soda commonly used in the kitchen for making tasty crispy pakoras is baking soda. Sometimes it is added for faster cooking. The chemical name of the compound is sodium hydrogencarbonate ($NaHCO_3$). **It is produced using sodium chloride as one of the raw materials.**

$$NaCl + H_2O + CO_2 + NH_3 \longrightarrow \underset{\text{(ammonium chloride)}}{NH_4Cl} + \underset{\text{(sodium hydrogen carbonate)}}{NaHCO_3}$$

It can be used to neutralise an acid It is a mild non-corrosive base. The following reaction takes place when it is heated.

Sodium hydrogen carbonate has got various uses in the household.

$$\underset{\text{(sodium hydrogen carbonate)}}{NaHCO_3} \xrightarrow{\text{Heat}} \underset{\text{(sodium carbonate)}}{Na_2CO_3} + H_2O + CO_2 \uparrow$$

Anhydrous sodium carbonate is generally called soda ash.

Uses:

(i) For making baking powder, which is a mixture of baking soda (sodium hydrogencarbonate) and a mild edible acid such as tartaric acid. When baking powder is heated or mixed in water, the following reaction takes place

$$\underset{\text{(from any acid)}}{NaHCO_3 + H^+} \longrightarrow CO_2 + H_2O + \text{Sodium salt of acid}$$

Carbon dioxide produced during the reaction causes bread or cake to rise making them soft and spongy.

(ii) Sodium hydrogencarbonate is also an ingredient in antacids. Being alkaline, it neutralises excess acid in the stomach and provides relief.

(iii) It is also used in soda-acid fire extinguishers.

(iv) It is used in medicines. It acts as mild antiseptic for infections. It is also present as an ingredient in ant-acids. Being alkaline it neutralises excess acid in the stomach.

➤ **Baking Soda as Antacid**

The acidity in the stomach is caused due to the formation of excess of hydrochloric acid (HCl). Sodium hydrogen carbonate (baking soda) reacts with the acid because of its alkaline nature and neutralises this effect.

$$NaHCO_3 + HCl \longrightarrow NaCl + H_2O + CO_2$$

It therefore, acts as an antacid and is the major constituent of antacid medicines.

➤ **Baking soda in fire extinguishers**

Sodium hydrogen carbonate or baking soda is used in soda acid fire extinguishers. It is in the form of a conical metallic vessel. A strong solution of $NaHCO_3$ is taken in a container. A glass ampoule containing H_2SO_4 and provided with a knob is placed inside the container. When required, the ampoule can be broken by hitting the knob. As a result, the acid will come in contact with sodium hydrogen carbonate. The two will react to evolve CO_2 gas. When enough pressure gets generated inside the container, the gas pushes the water solution which escapes out of the nozzle with force and extinguishes fire.

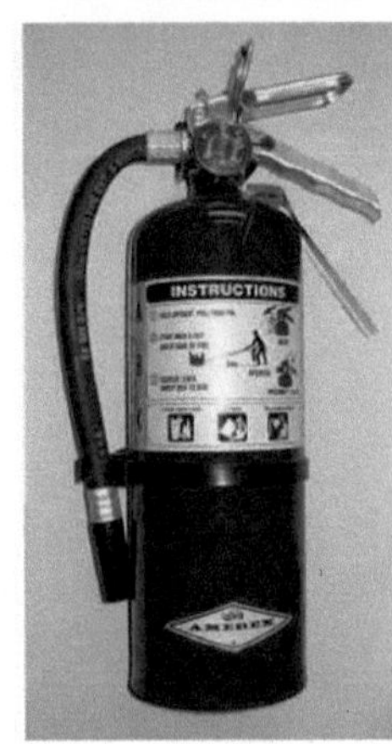

Properties

1. Sodium hydrogen carbonate is a white crystalline solid. It is sparingly soluble in water at room temperature.
2. Aqueous solution of sodium hydrogen carbonate is weakly alkaline in nature due to hydrolysis.
$$NaHCO_3 + H_2O \longrightarrow H_2CO_3 + NaOH$$
3. **Thermal decomposition:** On heating, sodium hydrogen carbonate decomposes to give carbon dioxide.
$$2NaHCO_3 \xrightarrow{\text{Heat}} Na_2CO_3 + CO_2 + H_2O$$
4. **Reaction with acids:** It reacts with acids to liberate carbon dioxide gas with brisk effervescence.
$$2NaHCO_3 + H_2SO_4 \longrightarrow Na_2SO_4 + 2CO_2 + 2H_2O$$
$$NaHCO_3 + HCl \longrightarrow NaCl + CO_2 \uparrow + H_2O$$

Efflorescence

Certain hydrated crystalline salts when exposed to atmosphere lose their water of crystallisation spontaneously and change into amorphous powder.

The spontaneous loss of water of crystallisation, wholly or partly, when crystals with water of crystallisation are exposed to air is called efflorescence and the substances exhibiting efflorescence are called efflorescent substances. For example:

Washing Soda $[Na_2CO_3 \cdot 10H_2O]$; Glauber's salt $[Na_2SO_4 \cdot 10H_2O]$
Blue Vitriol $[CuSO_4 \cdot 5H_2O]$ and Epsom Salt $[MgSO_4 \cdot 7H_2O]$

Deliquescence

Certain crystalline substances when exposed to atmosphere absorb moisture and change into solution. The absorption of moisture from air by crystals to form a solution is called deliquescence. Sodium hydroxide, Potassium hydroxide, Calcium chloride etc. are delinquent substances.

Hygroscopic substances.

Certain substances absorb water from the atmosphere without undergoing change in physical state. Such substances are known as hygroscopic substances.

Anhydrous sodium carbonate, anhydrous copper sulphate, concentrated sulphuric acid are examples of hygroscopic substances.

Illustration 14

A baker found that the cake prepared by him is hard and small in size. Which ingredient has he forgotten to add that would have made the cake fluffy? Give reason.

***Solution*:**

The baker has forgotten to add baking powder. Baking powder is a mixture containing sodium bicarbonate ($NaHCO_3$) and an acidic compound such as potassium hydrogen tartarate or citric acid,

during the preparation of cake/ bread, sodium bicarbonate reacts with the acidic compound to liberate carbon dioxide. The CO_2 so released make the cake/ bread porous and fluffy (light in weight and soft).

Fruit Cake

(v) Washing Soda ($Na_2CO_3.10H_2O$)

The chemical formula of washing soda is $Na_2CO_3.10H_2O$. Anhydrous sodium carbonate is generally called soda ash. (Na_2CO_3). Sodium Carbonate is obtained on commercial scale by **Solvay's process**.

➤ **Raw materials used are**

Sodium chloride (NaCl) in the form of its concentrated solution called brine.

(i) Ammonia (NH_3).

(ii) Lime Stone ($CaCO_3$)

➤ **The reactions taking place in this process are as follow :**

Step I: $NaCl\ (aq) + NH_3\ (g) + H_2O + CO_2\ (g) \longrightarrow NaHCO_3\ (s) + NH_4Cl\ (aq)$

Step II: $2\ NaHCO_3 \xrightarrow{\Delta} Na_2CO_3 + H_2O(l) + CO_2\ (g)$

Step III: $Na_2CO_3\ (s) + H_2O\ (l) \rightarrow Na_2CO_3\ (aq) \xrightarrow{\text{crystallisation}} Na_2CO_3 \cdot H_2O + 9H_2O$

$Na_2CO_3 \cdot 10H_2O$ is obtained by recrystallisation from a saturated solution of soda ash exposed to air. The loss of H_2O by crystalline solid to the atmosphere on exposure to air is called efflorescence.

Uses :

(i) Used for washing clothes.

(ii) Used for softening hard water.

(iii) Sodium carbonate is used for the manufacture of detergents.

(iv) Sodium Carbonate is used in paper and paint industry.

Water of crystallisation – The hydrated salts

Some salts, during crystallisation from their solutions, remain in loose chemical combination with definite molecular proportion of water molecules which also account for their definite crystalline shape. This water is called water of crystallisation.

Water of crystallisation is the definite number of water molecules which are present in loose chemical combination with one formula unit of the ionic solid in crystalline form.

For example, Copper Sulphate crystals are $CuSO_4 \cdot 5H_2O$. Thus, one formula unit of copper sulphate is in combination with five molecules of water. Water of crystallisation can be removed by heating crystals to about 100°C. A salt which contains certain fixed number of water molecules in loose chemical combination with its one formula unit is called **hydrated salt**.

A hydrated salt which completely loses its water of crystallisation is called **anhydrous salt**. For example, $CuSO_4$ is anhydrous copper (II) sulphate. The anhydrous substances left, when hydrated salts are heated, are not crystalline.

- **Manufacturing of Washing Soda**

Washing soda is manufactured by Solvay Process, also called Ammonia-soda process. In addition to this, Le Blanc process and Electrolytic process are also available but are less popular.

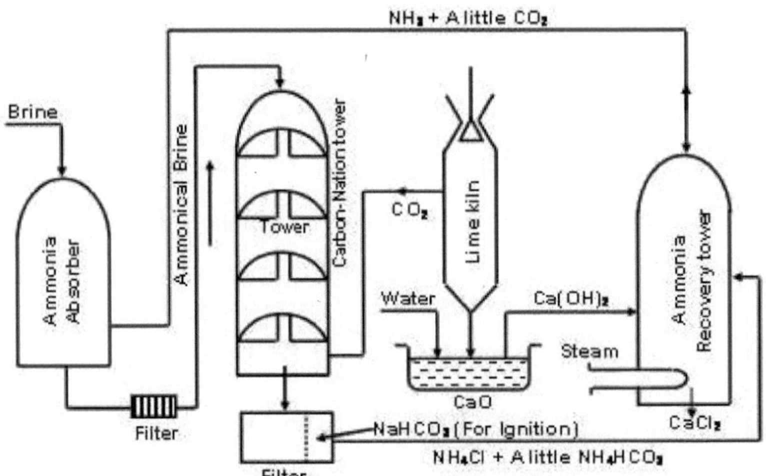

Solvay ammonia process for the manufacture of Na_2CO_3.

Solvay process is being described :

(i) **Saturation tank:** A strong solution of brine (30% of NaCl solution) is introduced from the top of the tank made up of iron. A mixture of ammonia and carbon dioxide which are formed in the ammonia recovery tower is led from a side into the tower. As a result, brine gets saturated with ammonia. Soluble impurities of some calcium and magnesium salts like $CaCl_2$ and $MgCl_2$ associated with sodium chloride are precipitated as carbonates by ammonium carbonate which is formed in the reaction.

$$2NH_3 + CO_2 + H_2O \longrightarrow (NH_4)_2CO_3$$

$$CaCl_2 + (NH_4)_2CO_3 \longrightarrow \underset{(ppt.)}{CaCO_3} + 2NH_4Cl$$

$$MgCl_2 + (NH_4)_2CO_3 \longrightarrow \underset{(ppt.)}{MgCO_3} + 2NH_4Cl$$

The solution is then passed through filters in order to remove these precipitates.

(ii) **Carbonation tower:** It is also made up of iron and is fitted with a number of horizontal plates. Each plate has a hole in the centre covered by a perforated cover. The brine saturated with ammonia (or ammoniated brine) is introduced from the top and the vapours of carbon dioxide from the lime kiln are introduced from the side. As the vapours rise, they come in contact with the ammoniated brine and the following reactions take place:

$$CO_2 + H_2O + NH_3 \longrightarrow NH_4HCO_3$$
$$NaCl + NH_4HCO_3 \longrightarrow NaHCO_3 + NH_4Cl$$

The temperature in the carbonation tower is between 300 – 310 K (very low) and crystals of sodium hydrogen carbonate are formed. Carbon dioxide needed for the reaction is obtained by heating lime stone ($CaCO_3$) in a lime kiln.

$$\underset{\text{(quick lime)}}{CaCO_3} \xrightarrow{\text{heat}} CaO + CO_2$$

Quick lime formed is dissolved in water to form $Ca(OH)_2$ which is led into the ammonia recovery tower as shown in the figure.

(iii) **Filtration:** The solution coming out of the carbonation tower is passed through filters when the precipitated sodium hydrogen carbonate gets separated. The solution containing NH_4Cl and small amount NH_4HCO_3 is taken to the ammonia recovery tower where it meets calcium hydroxide. Sodium hydrogen carbonate formed above is heated strongly in the absence of air (calcined) in a furnace to give sodium carbonate.

$$2NaHCO_3 \xrightarrow{\text{heat}} Na_2CO_3 + H_2O + CO_2$$

(iv) **Ammonia recovery tower:** In this tower, ammonia is formed by the reaction between NH_4Cl and $Ca(OH)_2$ and the reaction mixture is heated with the help of steam coil.

$$2NH_4Cl + Ca(OH)_2 \xrightarrow{\text{heat}} CaCl_2 + 2NH_3 + 2H_2O$$

Ammonium hydrogen carbonate present in the tower also decomposes to evolve NH_3 and CO_2.

$$NH_4HCO_3 \xrightarrow{\text{heat}} NH_3 + CO_2 + H_2O$$

Both these gases are pumped into the saturated tank where they take part in the reaction. Solvay process gives anhydrous sodium carbonate (soda ash) which is completely pure. When crystallised from water, it gives crystals of washing soda.

In laundry, washing soda accomplices several things. The high alkalinity of washing soda helps it act as a solvent to remove a range of stains and unlike bleach, washing soda does not usually stain. It is also used in detergent mixtures to treat hard water; the washing soda binds to the minerals which make water hard, allowing detergent to foam properly so that clothing will come out clean, without any residue. Sodium carbonate is also used by some textile artists, since it helps dyes adhere to fabric, resulting in deeper penetration and a longer lasting color.

Around the house, washing soda can be used to descale things like coffee machines and bathroom tiles which may accumulate mineral deposits as a result of exposure to hard water. It can also be used to strip floors of wax so that they can be refinished, and for other touch cleaning jobs like scrubbing the stove. However, you should wear gloves when cleaning with washing soda because it is very caustic and it can cause severe skin damage. Incidentally, the best way to treat a chemical burn is with **baking soda**, also called **sodium bicarbonate**, as it is a buffer and it will neutralise both acids and alkalis. Apply baking soda to the site of the burn for several minutes, flush the wound with water and seek medical attention.

Illustration 15

What is the difference between baking soda and washing soda?

Solution:

Baking soda and washing soda are two entirely different products. Both baking soda and washing soda are alkaline (bases), but washing soda is stronger base. Although they have some uses in common, they cannot be used in place of each other. For example, washing soda cannot be used for baking purpose in confectionery shop because being stronger base it will results into bitterness in flavour of cake.

(vi) Plaster of Paris $\left(CaSO_4 \cdot \frac{1}{2}H_2O\right)$

Plaster of Paris is hemihydrate (hemi means half and hydrate means water) of calcium sulphate.

Its molecular formula is $CaSO_4 \cdot \frac{1}{2}H_2O$ or $(CaSO_4)_2 \cdot H_2O$.

In Plaster of Paris one molecule of water is shared by two formula units of $CaSO_4$ as,

$$\begin{array}{l} CaSO_4 - H \\ \quad\quad\quad\;\; | \\ CaSO_4 - H - O \end{array} \quad \text{or} \quad \left.\begin{array}{l} CaSO_4 \\ CaSO_4 \end{array}\right\rangle H_2O$$

Preparation of Plaster of Paris

Plaster of Paris is obtained by heating gypsum ($CaSO_4 \cdot 2H_2O$) in a kiln at 373 K (or 100°C).

$$\underset{\text{(gypsum)}}{2\left[CaSO_4 \cdot 2H_2O\right](s)} \xrightarrow[\text{heat}]{373\text{ K }(100°C)} \underset{\text{(Plaster of Paris)}}{\left(CaSO_4\right)_2 \cdot H_2O(s)} + 3H_2O\,(g)$$

$$\underset{\text{(gypsum)}}{CaSO_4 \cdot 2H_2O\,(s)} \xrightarrow[\text{heat}]{373\text{ K }(100°C)} \underset{\text{(Plaster of Paris)}}{CaSO_4 \cdot \frac{1}{2}H_2O\,(s)} + \frac{3}{2}H_2O\,(g)$$

During the preparation of Plaster of Paris, temperature should be controlled carefully. Otherwise, anhydrous calcium sulphate ($CaSO_4$) will be formed. Anhydrous calcium sulphate does not set into hard mass when mixed with water. So, if temperature is not controlled carefully, the Plaster of Paris obtained will have poor setting property.

$$CaSO_4 \cdot 2H_2O \xrightarrow[373\text{ K}]{\text{more than}} \underset{\text{(dead burnt plaster)}}{CaSO_4}$$

Properties of Plaster of Paris

1. Plaster of Paris is a white, odourless powder.
2. At ordinary room temperature, Plaster of Paris absorbs water and a large amount of heat is liberated.
3. When mixed with a limited amount of water (50% by mass), it forms a plastic mass, evolves heat and quickly sets to a hard porous mass within minutes. This is called the **setting process**. During setting, a slight expansion in volume occurs. It is due to this that it fills the mould completely and gives sharp impression. The reaction during process is

$$\underset{\text{(Plaster of paris)}}{CaSO_4 \cdot \frac{1}{2}H_2O\,(s)} + \underset{\text{(water)}}{\frac{3}{2}H_2O\,(l)} \longrightarrow \underset{\text{(gypsum hard mass)}}{CaSO_4 \cdot 2H_2O\,(s)}$$

Uses of Plaster of Paris

1. It is used for producing moulds for industries such as pottery, ceramics. On mixing with water it changes into plastic mass and solidifies due to rehydration. This is called **setting of Plaster of Paris**.

$$\underset{\text{(Plaster of paris)}}{CaSO_4 \cdot \frac{1}{2}H_2O} + \underset{\text{(water)}}{\frac{1}{2}H_2O} \longrightarrow \underset{\text{(gypsum hard mass)}}{CaSO_4 \cdot 2H_2O}$$

   During the process of setting, it undergoes slight expansion (about 1%). Consequently, it produces a very sharp impression of the mould into which it is put.
2. It is used for setting fractured bones in right position in the body. **OR**
   It is used in hospitals for immobilising the affected part in case of bone fracture or strain.
3. It is used for making statues, models and other decorative material.
4. It is used as a fire proofing material and for making chalks.
5. It is used in laboratories for sealing the air gaps in apparatus to make it airtight. It is also used to fill small gaps on walks & roofs.

2.11 ARE THE CRYSTALS OF SALTS REALLY DRY?

Copper sulphate crystals which seem to be dry contain water of crystallisation. When we heat the crystals, this water is removed and the salt turns white.

If we moisten the crystals again with water, we will find that blue colour of the crystals reappears.

Water of crystallisation is the fixed number of water molecules present in one formula unit of a salt. Five water molecules are present in one formula unit of copper sulphate. Chemical formula for hydrated copper sulphate is $Cu\ SO_4.\ 5H_2O$. Now we would be able to answer the question whether the molecule of $Na_2CO_3.10H_2O$ is wet or not.

One other salt, which possesses water of crystallisation is gypsum. It has two water molecules as water of cyrstallisation. It has the formula $CaSO_4.2H_2O$.

POINTS TO REMEMBER

1. An acid may be defined as a substance which releases H^+ ions in a aqueous solution.
2. A base may be defined as a substance which releases OH^- ions in aqueous solution.
3. The nature of a solution whether acidic or basic can be determined with the help of indicators.
4. Indicators are organic dyes which may be natural or synthesised in the laboratory.
5. The common acid-base indicators are phenolphthalein, methyl orange and litmus.
6. The colour of litmus in neutral solution is purple, red in the acidic solution and blue in the basic solution.
7. Phenolphthalein is colourless in neutral and acidic solutions and pink in alkaline solution.
8. Methyl orange is orange is neutral solution, red in acidic solution and yellow in basic solution.
9. Litmus is extracted from 'lichen' a plant belonging to a variety Thallophyta. It is a natural indicator.
10. Methyl orange and phenolphthalein indicators are synthesised in the laboratory.
11. Onion, Vanilla and clove oil are olfactory indicators. They give different smells in acidic and basic solutions.
12. Dilute acids react with active metals to form metal salts and evolve hydrogen gas.
13. Metal oxides react with dilute acids to form salt and water.
14. Both metal carbonates and metal hydrogen carbonates evolve carbon-dioxide gas on reacting with dilute acids.
15. Basicity of an acid is the number of replaceable H atoms present in the acid.
16. Acidity of a base is the number of replaceable OH groups present in the base.
17. Metals like zinc, tin and aluminium react with caustic alkalies like NaOH or KOH to form metal salts and evolve hydrogen gas.
18. Upon passing carbon dioxide gas through lime water solution, it initially becomes milky and milkiness disappears after sometime.
19. Relative strengths of acids and bases can be compared in terms of their degree of dissociation (α).
20. Aqueous solutions of both acid and base conduct electricity due to the presence of ions.
21. Water helps in the dissociation of both acid and base into ions.
22. Acid and base react in aqueous solution to form salt and water. The reaction is known as neutralisation reaction.
23. An indicator helps in checking the completion of the neutralisation reaction.
24. The nature of solutions whether neutral, acidic or basic are expressed in terms of pH values.

25. The pH scale runs from 0 to 14. The pH of neutral solution is 7, that of acidic solution is less than this value and of basic solution is more.

26. Lesser the pH of a solution, more will be its acidic strength. Similarly, higher the pH of a solution, more will be its basic strength.

27. Antacids help in neutralising acidity caused in the stomach due to the formation of excessive hydrochloric acid.

28. Normal salt is formed by the complete neutralisation of an acid by a base.

29. Acidic salts contain some replaceable hydrogen atoms while basic salts contain some replaceable hydroxyl groups.

30. Washing soda is chemically hydrated sodium carbonate ($Na_2CO_3.10H_2O$)

31. Baking powder consists of a mixture of baking soda ($NaHCO_3$) and tartaric acid ($C_4H_6O_6$).

32. Bleaching powder is chemically calcium oxychloride ($CaOCl_2$) and is formed by passing chlorine gas through dry slaked lime.

33. Chlorine released by bleaching powder helps in bleaching clothes.

34. The chemical formula of Plaster of Paris is $CaSO_4.\frac{1}{2}H_2O$.

35. Plaster of Paris is used for setting fractured bones.

36. Upon heating, hydrated salts lose the molecules of water of crystallisation either partially or completely and may also undergo a change in colour.

CONCEPT APPLICATION LEVEL - I [NCERT Questions]

Q.1 You have been provided with three test tubes. One of them contains distilled water and the other two contain an acidic solution and a basic solution, respectively. If you are given only red litmus paper, how will you identify the contents of each test tube?

Ans. If the colour of red litmus paper gets changed to blue, then it is a base and if there is no colour change, then it is either acidic or neutral. Thus, basic solution can be easily identified.

Let us mark the three test tubes as A, B, and C. A drop of the solution in A is put on the red litmus paper. Same is repeated with solution B and C. If either of them changes colour to blue, then it is basic. Therefore, out of three, one is eliminated. Out of the remaining two, any one can be acidic or neutral. Now a drop of basic solution is mixed with a drop of each of the remaining two solutions separately and then the nature of the drops of the mixtures is checked. If the colour of red litmus turns blue, then the second solution is neutral and if there is no change in colour, then the second solution is acidic. This is because acidic and basic solutions neutralize each other. Hence, we can distinguish between the three types of solutions.

Q.2 Why should curd and sour substances not be kept in brass and copper vessels?

Ans. Curd and other sour substances contain acids. Therefore, when they are kept in brass and copper vessels, the metal reacts with the acid to liberate hydrogen gas and harmful products, thereby spoiling the food.

Q.3 Which gas is usually liberated when an acid reacts with a metal? Illustrate with an example. How will you test for the presence of this gas?

Ans. Hydrogen gas is usually liberated when an acid reacts with a metal.

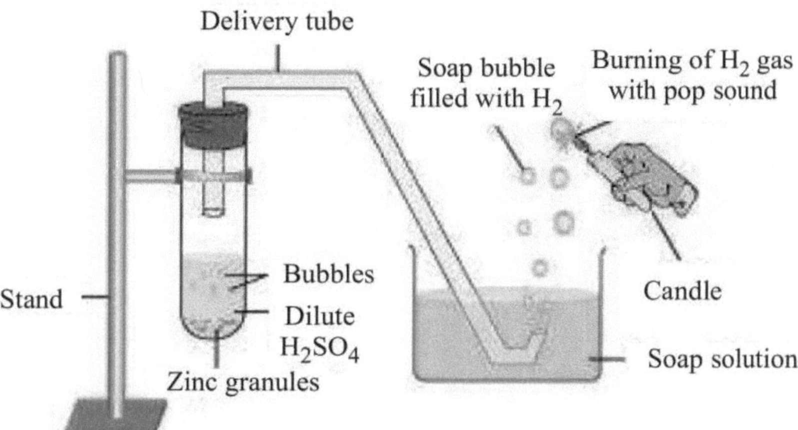

Take few pieces of zinc granules and add 5 ml of diluted acid (dilute H_2SO_4 or HCl). Shake it and pass the gas produced into a soap solution. The bubbles of the soap solution are formed. These soap bubbles contain hydrogen gas.

$$Zn(s) + 2HCl(aq) \longrightarrow ZnCl_2(aq) + H_2(g)$$

We can test the evolved hydrogen gas by its burning with a pop sound when a candle is brought near the soap bubbles.

Q.4 Metal compound A reacts with dilute hydrochloric acid to produce effervescence. The gas evolved extinguishes a burning candle. Write a balanced chemical equation for the reaction if one of the compounds formed is calcium chloride.

Ans.
$$\underset{\text{(calcium carbonate)}}{CaCO_3(s)} + \underset{\text{(hydrochloric acid)}}{2HCl\,(aq)} \longrightarrow \underset{\text{(calcium chloride)}}{CaCl_2\,(aq)} + \underset{\text{(carbon dioxide)}}{CO_2(g)} + \underset{\text{(water)}}{H_2O\,(l)}$$

Q.5 Why do HCl, HNO_3, etc., show acidic characters in aqueous solutions while solutions of compounds like alcohol and glucose do not show acidic character?

Ans. The dissociation of HCl or HNO_3 to form hydrogen ions always occurs in the presence of water. Hydrogen ions (H^+) combine with H_2O to form hydronium ions (H_3O^+). The reaction is as follows:

$$HCl\,(aq) \longrightarrow H^+ + Cl^-$$
$$H^+ + H_2O \longrightarrow H_3O^+$$

Q.6 Why does an aqueous solution of an acid conduct electricity?

Ans. Acids dissociate in aqueous solutions to form ions. These ions are responsible for conduction of electricity.

Q.7 Why does dry HCl gas not change the colour of the dry litmus paper?

Ans. Colour of the litmus paper is changed by the hydrogen ions. Dry HCl gas does not contain H^+ ions. It is only in the aqueous solution that an acid dissociates to give ions. Since in this case, neither HCl is in the aqueous form nor the litmus paper is wet, therefore, the colour of the litmus paper does not change.

Q.8 While diluting an acid, why is it recommended that the acid should be added to water and not water to the acid?

Ans. Since the process of dissolving an acid in water is exothermic, it is always recommended that acid should be added to water. If it is done the other way, then it is possible that because of the large amount of heat generated, the mixture splashes out and causes burns.

Q.9 How is the concentration of hydronium ions (H_3O^+) affected when a solution of an acid is diluted?

Ans. When an acid is diluted, the concentration of hydronium ions (H_3O^+) per unit volume decreases. This means that the strength of the acid decreases.

Q.10 How is the concentration of hydroxide ions (OH^-) affected when excess base is dissolved in a solution of sodium hydroxide?

Ans. The concentration of hydroxide ions (OH^-) would increase when excess base is dissolved in a solution of sodium hydroxide.

Q.11 You have two solutions, A and B. The pH of solution A is 6 and pH of solution B is 8. Which solution has more hydrogen ion concentration? Which of this is acidic and which one is basic?

Ans. A pH value of less than 7 indicates an acidic solution, while greater than 7 indicates a basic solution. Therefore, the solution with pH = 6 is acidic and has more hydrogen ion concentration than the solution of pH = 8 which is basic.

Q.12 What effect does the concentration of $H^+(aq)$ ions have on the nature of the solution?

Ans. Concentration of $H^+(aq)$ can have a varied effect on the nature of the solution. With an increase in H^+ ion concentration, the solution becomes more acidic, while a decrease of H+ ion causes an increase in the basicity of the solution.

Q.13 Do basic solutions also have $H^+(aq)$ions. If yes, then why are these basic?

Ans. Yes, basic solution also has $H^+(aq)$ ions. However, their concentration is less as compared to the concentration of OH ions that makes the solution basic.

Q.14 Under what soil condition do you think a farmer would treat the soil of his fields with quick lime (calcium oxide) or slaked lime (calcium hydroxide) or chalk (calcium carbonate)?

Ans. If the soil is acidic and improper for cultivation, then to increase the basicity of soil, the farmer would treat the soil with quick lime or slaked lime or chalk

$$\underset{\text{(sodium hydrogencarbonate)}}{2NaHCO_3} \xrightarrow{\Delta} \underset{\text{(sodium carbonate)}}{Na_2CO_3} + \underset{\text{(water)}}{H_2O} + \underset{\text{(carbon dioxide)}}{CO_2} \uparrow$$

Q.15 What is the common name of the compound $CaOCl_2$?

Ans. The common name of the compound $CaOCl_2$ is bleaching powder.

Q.16 Name the substance which on treatment with chlorine yields bleaching powder?

Ans. Calcium hydroxide [Ca $(OH)_2$], on treatment with chlorine, yields bleaching powder.

Q.17 Name the sodium compound which is used for softening hard water.

Ans. Washing soda ($Na_2CO_3.10H_2O$) is used for softening hard water.

Q.18 What will happen if a solution of sodium hydrocarbonate is heated? Give the equation of the reaction involved.

Ans. When a solution of sodium hydrocarbonate (sodium hydrogencarbonate) is heated, sodium carbonate and water are formed with the evolution of carbon dioxide gas.

Q.19 Write an equation to show the reaction between Plaster of Paris and water.

Ans. The chemical equation for the reaction of Plaster of Paris and water can be represented as

$$\underset{\text{(Plaster of paris)}}{CaSO_4 \cdot \frac{1}{2}H_2O} + \underset{\text{(water)}}{1\frac{1}{2}H_2O} \longrightarrow \underset{\text{(gypsum hard mass)}}{CaSO_4 \cdot 2H_2O}$$

Q.20 A solution turns red litmus blue, its pH is likely to be

(A) 1 (B) 4 (C) 5 (D) 10

Ans. Bases turn red litmus blue and acids turn blue litmus red. Basic solution has a pH value more than 7. Since the solution turns red litmus blue, its pH is likely to be 10.

Q.21 A solution reacts with crushed egg-shells to give a gas that turns lime-water milky. The solution contains

(A) NaCl (B) HCl (C) LiCl (D) KCl

Ans. B The solution contains HCl.

Q.22 10 mL of a solution of NaOH is found to be completely neutralised by 8 mL of a given solution of HCl. If we take 20 mL of the same solution of NaOH, the amount of HCl solution (the same solution as before) required to neutralise it will be

(A) 4 mL (B) 8mL (C) 12 mL (D) 16 mL

Ans. D 16 mL of HCl solution will be required.

Q.23 Which one of the following types of medicines is used for treating indigestion?

(A) Antibiotic (B) Analgesic (C) Antacid (D) Antiseptic

Ans. C Antacid is used for treating indigestion.

Q.24 Write word equations and then balanced equations for the reaction taking place when

(A) dilute sulphuric acid reacts with zinc granules.

(B) dilute hydrochloric acid reacts with magnesium ribbon.

(C) dilute sulphuric acid reacts with aluminium powder.

(D) dilute hydrochloric acid reacts with iron filings.

Ans. (A) ***Word equation***

$$\text{Zinc} + \text{Sulphuric acid} \longrightarrow \text{Zinc sulphate} + \text{Hydrogen}$$

Balanced equation

$$Zn(s) + H_2SO_4(dil.) \longrightarrow ZnSO_4(aq) + H_2(g)$$

(B) ***Word equation***

$$\text{Magnesium} + \text{Hydrochloric acid} \longrightarrow \text{Magnesium chloride} + \text{Hydrogen}$$

Balanced equation

$$Mg(s) + 2HCl(dil.) \longrightarrow MgCl_2(aq) + H_2(g)$$

(C) ***Word equation***

$$\text{Aluminium} + \text{Sulphuric acid} \longrightarrow \text{Aluminium sulphate} + \text{Hydrogen}$$

Balanced equation

$$2Al(s) + 3H_2SO_4(dil.) \longrightarrow Al_2(SO_4)_3(aq) + 3H_2(g)$$

(D) ***Word equation***

$$\text{Iron} + \text{Hydrochloric acid} \longrightarrow \text{Iron (II) chloride} + \text{Hydrogen}$$

Balanced equation

$$Fe(s) + 2HCl(dil.) \longrightarrow FeCl_2\,(aq) + H_2(s)$$

Q.25 Compounds such as alcohols and glucose also contain hydrogen but are not categorized as acids. Describe an activity to prove it.

Ans. Two nails are fitted on a cork and are kept it in a 100 mL beaker. The nails are then connected to the two terminals of a 6-volt battery through a bulb and a switch. Some dilute HCl is poured in the beaker and the current is switched on. The same experiment is then performed with glucose solution and alcohol solution.

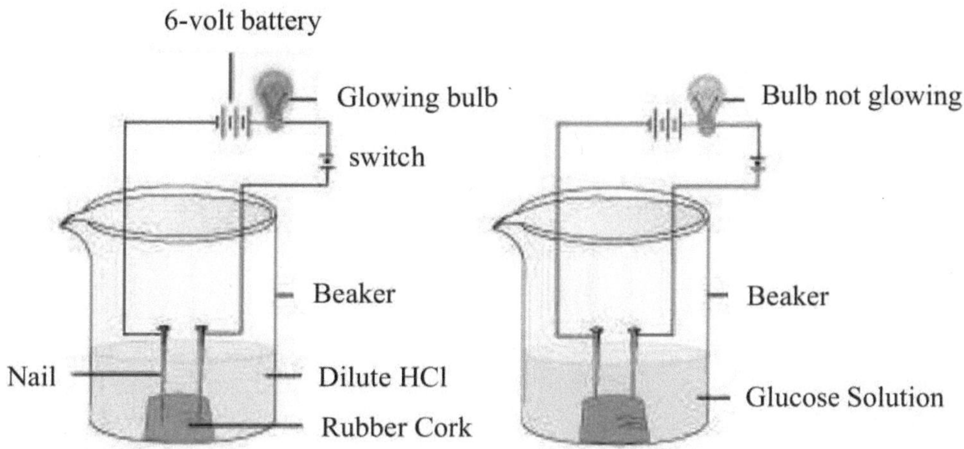

Observations:

It will be observed that the bulb glows in the HCl solution and does not glow in the glucose solution.

Result:

HCl dissociates into H^+ and Cl^- ions. These ions conduct electricity in the solution resulting in the glowing of the bulb. On the other hand, the glucose solution does not dissociate into ions. Therefore, it does not conduct electricity.

Conclusion:

From this activity, it can be concluded that all acids contain hydrogen but not all compounds containing hydrogen are acids. That is why, though alcohols and glucose contain hydrogen, they are not categorised as acids.

Q.26 Why does distilled water not conduct electricity, whereas rain water does?

Ans. Distilled water is a pure form of water and is devoid of any ionic species. Therefore, it does not conduct electricity. Rain water, being an impure form of water, contains many ionic species such as acids and therefore it conducts electricity.

Q.27 Why do acids not show acidic behaviour in the absence of water?

Ans. Acids do not show acidic behaviour in the absence of water because the dissociation of hydrogen ions from an acid occurs in the presence of water only. It is the hydrogen ions that are responsible for the acidic behaviour.

Q.28 Five solutions A, B, C, D and E when tested with universal indicator showed pH as 4, 1, 11, 7 and 9, respectively. Which solution is

(a) neutral?

(b) strongly alkaline?

(c) strongly acidic?

(d) weakly acidic?

(e) weakly alkaline?

Arrange the pH in increasing order of hydrogen-ion concentration.

Ans. (a) Neutral Solution D with pH 7

(b) Strongly alkaline Solution C with pH 11

(c) Strongly acidic Solution B with pH 1

(d) Weakly acidic Solution A with pH 4

(e) Weakly alkaline Solution E with pH 9

The pH can be arranged in the increasing order of the concentration of hydrogen ions as :

$11 < 9 < 7 < 4 < 1$

Q.29 Equal lengths of magnesium ribbons are taken in test tubes A and B. Hydrochloric acid (HCl) is added to test tube A, while acetic acid (CH_3COOH) is added to test tube B. In which test tube will the fizzing occur more vigorously and why?

Ans. The fizzing will occur strongly in test tube A, in which hydrochloric acid (HCl) is added. This is because HCl is a stronger acid than CH_3COOH and therefore produces hydrogen gas at a faster speed due to which fizzing occurs.

Q.30 Fresh milk has a pH of 6. How do you think the pH will change as it turns into curd? Explain your answer.

Ans. The pH of milk is 6. As it changes to curd, the pH will reduce because curd is acidic in nature. The acids present in it decrease the pH.

Q.31 A milkman adds a very small amount of baking soda to fresh milk.

(a) Why does he shift the pH of the fresh milk from 6 to slightly alkaline?

(b) Why does this milk take a long time to set as curd?

Ans. (a) The milkman shifts the pH of the fresh milk from 6 to slightly alkaline because in alkaline condition, milk does not set as curd easily.

(b) Since this milk is slightly basic than usual milk, acids produced to set the curd are neutralized by the base. Therefore, it takes a longer time for the curd to set.

Q.32 Plaster of Paris should be stored in a moisture-proof container. Explain why?

Ans. Plaster of Paris (POP) should be stored in a moisture-proof container because Plaster of Paris, a powdery mass, absorbs water (moisture) to form a hard solid known as gypsum.

$$\underset{\text{(Plaster of paris)}}{CaSO_4 \cdot \frac{1}{2}H_2O} + \underset{\text{(water)}}{1\frac{1}{2}H_2O} \longrightarrow \underset{\text{(gypsum hard mass)}}{CaSO_4 \cdot 2H_2O}$$

Q.33 What is a neutralization reaction? Give two examples.

Ans. A reaction in which an acid and base react with each other to give a salt and water is termed as neutralization reaction. In this reaction, energy is evolved in the form of heat.

For example:

(i) $$\underset{\text{(base)}}{NaOH} + \underset{\text{(acid)}}{HCl} \longrightarrow \underset{\text{(salt)}}{NaCl} + \underset{\text{(water)}}{H_2O}$$

(ii) During indigestion (caused due to the production of excess of hydrochloric acid in the stomach), we administer an antacid (generally milk of magnesia, $Mg(OH)_2$ which is basic in nature). The antacid neutralizes the excess of acids and thus gives relief from indigestion.

$$Mg(OH)_2 + 2HCl \longrightarrow MgCl_2 + 2H_2O$$

Q.34 Give two important uses of washing soda and baking soda.

Ans. Two important used of washing soda and baking soda are as follows:

(1) **Washing soda:**

(a) It is used in glass, soap, and paper industries.

(b) It is used to remove permanent hardness of water.

(2) **Baking soda:**

(a) It is used as baking powder. Baking powder is a mixture of baking soda and a mild acid known as tartaric acid. When it is heated or mixed in water, it releases CO_2 that makes bread or cake fluffy.

(b) It is used in soda-acid fire extinguishers.

CONCEPT APPLICATION LEVEL - II

SECTION-A

Q.1 A drop of liquid is poured on a pH paper such that the colour of pH paper changes to green, the liquid is

(A) Dilute hydrogen chloride solution (B) Dilute sodium hydroxide solution
(C) Sodium chloride solution in distilled water (D) Ammonium chloride solution in water

Q.2 The correct method to find the pH of a solution is

(a) (b) (c) (d)

(A) (a) (B) (b) (C) (c) (D) (d)

Q.3 A student tested the pH of distilled water and found that the colour of pH paper changed to green and when he checked the pH again after dissolving a pinch of common salt in it, the colour of pH paper this time was

(A) yellow (B) red (C) green (D) blue

Q.4 The pH of a sample 'y' at 298K is found to be 10. Which of the following may be the sample 'y' ?

(A) NaOH (B) HCl (C) H_2O (D) CH_3COOH

Q.5 Two solutions X and Y were found to have pH value of 4 and 10 respectively. The inference that can be drawn is

(A) X is base and Y is an acid (B) Both X and Y are acidic solutions
(C) X is an acid and Y is a base (D) Both X and Y are bases

Q.6 A student was given three test tubes I, II and III containing ethanoic acid, sodium bicarbonate solution and water respectively. On dipping a pH paper in them, he observed that the colour turned orange in I, blue in II and green in III. If arranged in increasing order of their pH. the sequence of three test tubes should be

(A) I, II, III (B) II, III, I (C) III, I, II (D) I, III, II

Q.7 pH values of four solutions A, B, C and D are 7, 8, 9, 10 respectively. Put them in a sequence according to their nature :

(A) acidic, acidic, neutral, basic (B) acidic, neutral, basic, basic
(C) acidic, acidic, acidic, neutral (D) neutral, basic, basic, basic

Q.8 A pH paper is first dipped in distilled water and then in dilute solution of lemon juice. The colour of pH paper changes from

(A) colourless to green (B) indigo to orange
(C) green to pink (D) green to orange

Q.9 Four students were given three colourless liquids A, B, C of water, lemon juice and a mixture of water and lemon juice respectively. After testing these liquids with pH paper, following sequences in colour change of pH paper were reported.

i. Blue, Red and Green
ii. Orange, Green and Green
iii. Green, Red and Red
iv. Red, Red and Green

The correct sequence of colours observed is

(A) (i) (B) (ii) (C) (iii) (D) (iv)

Q.10 The pH values of four solutions A, B, C and D as determined by a student are 4, 7,12 and 8 respectively. Arrange the four solutions in the decreasing order of their hydrogen ion concentration.

(A) C,B,D,A (B) C,D,B,A (C) A,C,B,D (D) A,B,D,C

Q.11 Which one of the following will be required to identify the gas evolved when dil HCl is treated with sodium carbonate ?

(A) Red litmus solution (B) Lime water (C) Both (A) and (B) (D) None of these

Q.12 When dilute hydrochloric acid is added to granulated zinc placed in a test tube, the observation made is.

(A) the surface of the metal turns shining
(B) the reaction mixture turns milky
(C) odour of chlorine is observed
(D) a colourless and odourless gas evolves with bubbles

Q.13 A student added dil. HCl to a test tube containing zinc granules and made following observations;

I. The surface of zinc becomes dull and black
II. A gas evolved which burnt with a pop sound
III. The solution remains colourless

The correct observations are :

(A) I and II (B) I and III (C) II and III (D) I, II and III

Q.14 Four experiment set ups are shown below :

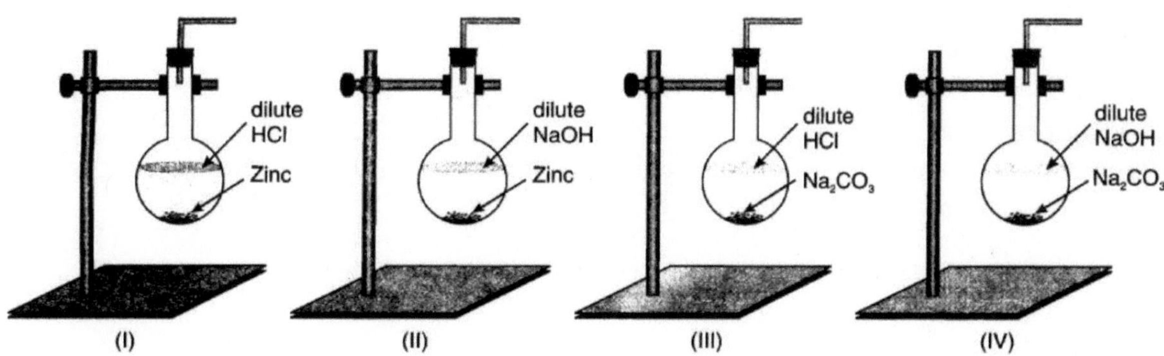

The setups that would result in a rapid evolution of gas would be

(A) I and III (B) II and IV (C) I and II (D) III and IV

Q.15 When hydrochloric acid is added to sodium carbonate we observe :

(A) a colourless gas evolves which turns lime water milky
(B) a brown gas with a pungent smell evolves
(C) a colourless gas evolves which has no effect on lime water
(D) a colourless gas evolves which burns with pop sound

Q.16 On adding a pinch of white powder to some dil HCl to a test tube CO_2 gas is evolved with brisk effervescence.The white powder is
(A) ammonium chloride (B) calcium oxide
(C) sodium carbonate (D) sodium chloride

Q.17 When dilute HCl acid is added to granulated zinc placed in a test tube, the observation made is:
(A) the surface of the metal turns shiny (B) the reaction mixture turns milky
(C) odour of chlorine is observed (D) a colourless and odourless gas evolved

Q.18 On adding a drop of red litmus solution to an aqueous solution of sodium carbonate the colour of red litmus solution changes to blue.On the basis of this observation the nature of the solution should be
(A) alkaline (B) acidic (C) neutral (D) highly acidic

Q.19 Four setups as given below were arranged to identify the gas evolved when dilute hydrochloric acid was added to zinc granules.The most appropriate setup is :

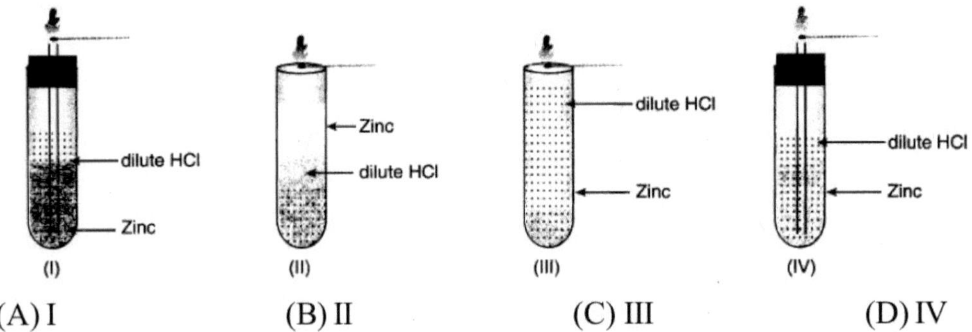

(A) I (B) II (C) III (D) IV

Q.20 What is the effect of HCl on litmus?
(A) red turns into blue (B) blue turns into red
(C) no effect on both colours (D) shows an effect on both blue and red litmus

SECTION - B

(VARY SHORT ANSWER TYPE QUESTION) [1 MARKS]

Q.1 Define pH.
Ans. The pH of a solution is defined as the negative logarithm to the base 10 of the hydrogen ion concentration (H^+) in moles/litre.

Q.2 What would be the pH of an aqueous solution of sodium bicarbonate ?
Ans. Its pH will be greater than 7 as the aqueous solution is alkaline.

Q.3 What is pH of pure water ?
Ans. The pH of pure water is 7.

Q.4 What is meant by pH paper ?
Ans. A pH paper is a strip of paper which is prepared by dipping the strip in the solutions of different indicators and then drying them.

Q.5 What is the pH of rain water? Is it acidic, basic or neutral ?
Ans. It is less than 7. It is acidic in nature.

Q.6 The pH of solutions A, B and C are 3, 7 and 13 respectively. Which solution is (i) acidic (ii) neutral (iii) basic?

Ans. Solution A is acidic, solution B is neutral and solution C is basic.

Q 7 What is the importance of pH in agriculture?

Ans. Plants do not grow well in acidic soils. Thus, if pH of a soil is known, and it is found acidic, the farmer add lime to the soil, so as to remove its acidic nature.

Q.8 On opening the soda water bottle, the dissolved CO_2 comes out. Would the pH of the solution increase or decrease as the gas comes out? Express your answer either way.

Ans Carbondioxide (CO_2) is acidic oxide. As CO_2 comes out of the solution, acidic character of solution decreases and as such pH increases.

Q 9 What happens to pH value, when we add more and more acid to water?

Ans. Its pH value decreases.

Q.10 What are acids?

Ans. Acids are those substances which give H^+ ions in aqueous solutions.

Q.11 What happens when a pinch of washing soda (sodium carbonate) is added to an acid?

Ans. Sodium carbonate reacts with acids to give carbondioxide.

Q.12 How can the deposits of carbonates on metal surface be cleaned?

Ans. Deposits of $CaCO_3$ and $MgCO_3$ on metals can be removed by treating it with dilute acid solution (e.g. dil HCl).

Q.13 What is the utility of the reaction between $NaHCO_3$ and an acid in daily life situation?

Ans. (i) In baking powder (ii) In soda-acid type fire extinguisher and (iii) In ENO fruit salt.

Q.14 How will you test whether the gas evolved in a chemical reaction is carhondioxide ?

Ans. Carbondioxide turns limewater milky.

Q.15 What will be the colour of blue litmus paper on bringing it in contact with a drop of dil. NaOH?

Ans. No change in colour will take place.

Q.16 What happens when zinc is treated with dil. NaOH solution ?

Aus. Hydrogen gas is evolved.

Q.17 Name some other metals which react with alkalis to produce hydrogen?

Ans. Aluminium (Al), Tin (Sn) etc.

Q.18 What happens when dilute solution of sodium hydroxide solution reacts with dilute hydrochloric acid?

Ans. Sodium hydroxide is neutralised by hydrochloric acid and sodium chloride and water are formed.

Q.19 Name the alkali which does not have a metal ion.

Ans. NH_4OH does not have metal ion.

Q.20 Name two soluble bases/alkalis.

Ans. Sodium hydroxide and potassium hydroxide.

Q.21 Write down the reaction taking place when aluminium reacts with sodium hydroxide solution.

Ans. $2Al + 2NaOH + 2H_2O \longrightarrow 2NaAlO_2 + 3H_2\uparrow$

Q.22 If you are provided a blue litmus paper, how can you test an alkali, such as NaOH with it?

Ans. Dip the litmus paper in some acid solution. Its blue colour will change to red. Use this red litmus paper for testing alkali, such as NaOH.

Q.23 Name two natural acid-base indicators. **[SAI-2015]**

Ans. (i) Beetroot extract.

(ii) Extracts of red cabbage leaves.

(iii) Extract of petals of china rose (hibiscus) flower (any two)

Q.24 What are bases?

Ans. Bases are substances that produce hydroxide ions (OH^-) when mixed with water.

Q.25 What is our tooth enamel made-up of ?

Ans. Calcium phosphate, [$Ca_3(PO_4)_2$].

Q.26 At what pH in the mouth is tooth decay faster and why? **[SAI-2014, 2015]**

Ans. At pH of 5.5 or less. Reason: At this pH, the bacteria present in the mouth act on sugars to produce acids which corrode the tooth enamel (calcium phosphate) leading to tooth decay.

Q.27 Why is Plaster of Paris written $CaSO_4.½H_2O$? How is it possible to have half a water molecule attached to $CaSO_4$ **[SAI-2011,15]**

Ans. It is written in this form because two formula units of $CaSO_4$ share one molecule of water.

Q.28 How is the concentration of hydroxide ions (OH^-) affected when excess base is dissolved in a solution of sodium hydroxide? **[SAI-2015]**

Ans. The concentration of hydroxide ions (OH^-) per unit volume increases when excess base is dissolved in a solution of sodium hydroxide.

Q.29 Fresh milk has a pH of 6. When it changes into curd (yogurt) will its pH value increase or decrease? Why? **[SAI-2013, 2015]**

Ans. When milk with pH = 6 changes into curd (yogurt), its pH value will decrease due to the formation of Lactic acid (which is acidic in nature).

Q.30 What is meant by water of crystallisation? **[SAI-2015]**

Ans. Water of crystallisation is the fixed number

Q.31 How chloride of lime chemically differ from calcium chloride? **[SAI-2015]**

Ans. Calcium chloride: $CaCl_2$

Chloride of lime: $CaOCl_2$

(SHORT ANSWER TYPE QUESTION) [2 MARKS]

Q.32 What is chlor-alkali process? Write its chemical equation. Which gas is evolved at cathode and anode? **[SAI-2015]**

Ans. (i) When electricity is passed through an aqueous solution of sodium chloride (called brine), it decomposes to form sodium hydroxide. This process is called chlor-alkali process.

(ii) $2NaCl(aq) + 2H_2O(l) \longrightarrow 2NaOH(aq) + Cl_2(g) + H_2(g)$

(iii) Chlorine gas is evolved at cathode and hydrogen gas at anode.

Q.33 What is universal indicator? State the purpose for which this indicator is used. **[SAI-2015]**

Ans. A universal indicator is a mixture of several synthetic dyes which gives different colours at different concentrations of hydrogen ions $[H^+(aq)]$. It is used for :

(a) Finding whether the given solution is acidic or basic.

(b) Finding the concentration of $H^+(aq)$ ions in the solution.

Q.34 What are antacids? Explain their role in providing relief from stomach ache. Give two examples. **[SAI-2013]**

Ans. (i) Antacids are mild bases.

(ii) Antacids neutralize the effect of extra acid produced in the stomach during indigestion and thus provide relief.

(iii) Example: Magnesium hydroxide, sodium hydrogencarbonate.

Q.35 Give reason why compounds like alcohol and glucose do not show acidic behaviour although they contain hydrogen in them. **[SAI-2010, 2015]**

Ans. Compounds like alcohol and glucose do not dissociate to form hydrogen ions (H^+) when dissolved in water and thus do not show any acidic behaviour.

Q.36 It is seen that basic solutions also contain $H^+(aq)$ ions, then why are they called basic? **[SAI-2011, 2015]**

Ans. The concentration of $H^+(aq)$ ions in basic solution is very less and they are neutralised by hydroxide ions (OH^-) present in the basic solutions.

Q.37 Name the acid present in the following natural sources :

(i) Nettle sting (ii) Vinegar (iii) tomato (iv) Curd **[SAI-2015]**

Ans.

Natural Sources	Acid Present
(i) Nettle sting	Methanoic acid
(ii) Vinegar	Acetic acid
(iii) Tomato	Oxalic acid
(iv) Curd	Lactic acid

Q.38 Although acetic acid is highly soluble in water but still it is a weak acid. Explain, why? **[SAI-2010, 2015]**

Ans. The strength of an acid depends upon the extent of ionisation. Acetic acid is highly soluble in water but it dissociates partially in the aqueous solution to produce a small amount of H^+ ions and, therefore, considered as a weak acid.

Q.39 What happens when nitric acid is added to egg shell? **[SAI-2014]**

Ans. Egg shells contain calcium carbonate . When nitric acid is added then CO_2 gas is evolved with brisk effervescence.

$$CaCO_3 + 2HNO_3 \longrightarrow Ca(NO_3)_2 + H_2O + CO_2\uparrow$$

Q.40 How NaOH is prepared from NaCI ? **[SAI-20I4]**

Ans. NaOH is formed at the (near) cathode when electricity is passed through an aqueous solution of NaCl (Brine solution).

(LONG ANSWER TYPE QUESTION) [3 MARKS]

Q.41 Answer the following questions:

(i) State the colour of phenolphthalein in soap solution.

(ii) Name the by -product of chlor-alkali process which is used for manufacturing of bleaching powder.

(iii) Name one indicator which specifies the various levels of H+ ion concentration. **[SAI-2014, 2015]**

Sol. (i) Pink

(ii) Chlorine gas

(iii) Universal indicator

Q.42 Give three practical applications of neutralisation reaction. **[SAI-2015]**

Ans. (i) Antacids have been developed on the basis of neutralisation reaction.

(ii) Toothpastes are basic in nature which neutralise the excess of acid produced in out mouth.

(iii) Milkman adds a very small amount of baking soda to milk to neutralise the lactic acid produced in the milk.

Q.43 Which of the following substances in water show acidic properties ? State reason.
Sugar, carbon dioxide, acetic acid, alcohol, sulphur dioxide, urea. **[SAI-2015]**

Ans.
- Sugar and alcohol when dissolved in waer do not show acidic nature because they do not ionise in water to produce hydrogen ions or any other ions in solution. They remain as molecules.
- When carbon dioxide is added to water under pressure, it becomes slightly acidic due to formation of carbonic acid, which dissociates to form $H^+(aq)$ ions.
- SO_2 dissolves in water to form sulphurous acid/sulphuric acid which ionises to form H_3O^+ or $H^+(aq)$ ions. This also results in acid rains.
- When urea dissolved in water, the solution of urea is neither acidic nor basic. It is neutral, because urea being an organic compound remains as molecules.

Q.44 The marble statues are often slowly corroded when kept in open for a long time. Give suitable reason. **[SAI-2013,14]**

Ans. Chemically, marbles is calcium carbonate. All metal carbonates and hydrogen carbonates react with acids to give corresponding salt, carbon dioxide and water. Calcium carbonate reacts with acid to form calcium hydrogencarbonate which is soluble in water and thus washed away. So, the marble statues are slowly corroded.

$CaCO_3(s) + H_2O(l) + CO_2 \rightarrow Ca(HCO_3)_2\ (aq)$

Q.45 While eating food, you happen to spill some curry on your white shirt. You immediately scrub it with soap. What happens to its yellow colour on scrubbing with soap ? Why ? What happens to this stain when the shirt is washed with plenty of water ? **[SAI-2015]**

Ans. (i) On scrubbing its colour changes from yellow to reddish brown.

(ii) It happens because soap is basic in nature and the colour of turmeric changes from yellow to reddish brown in basic medium.

(iii) When the shirts is washed with plenty of water, the stain turns yellow again.

Q.46 How would you distinguish between baking powder and washing soda by heating ?

Ans. the chemical formula of baking powder is sodium hydrogencarbonate ($NaHCO_3$) whereas that of washing soda is sodium carbonate ($Na_2CO_3.10H_2O$).

Sodium hydrogencarbonate on heating gives CO_2 gas which will turn lime water milky whereas no such gas is obtained from sodium carbonate.

$$2NaHCO_3 \xrightarrow{Heat} Na_2CO_3 + H_2O + CO_2$$

$$Na_2CO_3 \cdot 10H_2O \xrightarrow{Heat} Na_2CO_3 + 10H_2O$$

Q.47 How the following substances will dissociate to produce ions in their solution **[SAI-2015]**

(a) Hydrochloric acid (b) Nitric acid (c) Sulphuric acid

(d) Sodium hydroxide (e) Potassium hydroxide (f) Magnesium hydroxide

Ans. (a) $HCl + H_2O \rightarrow H_3O^+ + Cl^-$

(b) $HNO_3(l) + H_2O(l) \rightarrow H_3O^+ + NO_3^-$

(c) $H_2SO_4 + H_2O \rightarrow H_3O^+ + HSO_4^-$

(d) $NaOH(s) \xrightarrow{H_2O} Na^+(aq) + OH^-(aq)$

(e) $KOH(s) \xrightarrow{H_2O} K^+(aq) + OH^-(aq)$

(f) $Mg(OH)_2(s) \xrightarrow{H_2O} Mg^{2+}(aq) + 2OH^-(aq)$

Q.48 A white powder is added while baking breads and cakes to make them soft and fluffy. Write the name of the powder. Name its main ingredients. Explian the function of each ingredient. Write the chemical reaction taking place when the powder is heated during baking . **[SAI-2015]**

Ans. Baking powder.

Baking soda and tartaric acid.

On heating or mixing with water, sodium bicarbonate reacts with hydrogen ion from acid and release CO_2 that makes the cake soft and fluffy.

$$NaHCO_3 + H^+ \xrightarrow[\text{(from acid)}]{Heat} Na_2CO_3 + H_2O + CO_2$$

Q.49 Write the balanced equation involved when :

(a) chlorine is passed over dry slaked lime.

(b) sodium bicarbonate reacts with dilute hydrochloric acid

(c) sodium bicarbonate is heated. **[SAI-2015,13]**

Ans. (a) $Ca(OH)_2 + Cl_2 \rightarrow CaOCl_2 + H_2O$

(b) $NaHCO_3 + \text{Dil. } HCl \rightarrow NaCl + CO_2 + H_2O$

(c) $2NaHCO_3 \xrightarrow{\Delta} Na_2CO_3 + H_2O + CO_2$

(VERY LONGANSWER TYPE QUESTION) [5 MARKS]

Q.50 (a) Bee sting leaves a chemical substance that causes pain and irritation. Name the chemical substance. Identify the type of substance which may give relief on the stung area when applied on it.

(b) Mention the pH value below which tooth decay begins. How this fall below this value ? Explain the ill effect of the acidic medium in the mouth. How can this be prevented ?

Ans. (a) Methanoic acid. Using baking soda.

(b) Tooth enamel, made of calcium phosphate does not dissolve in water but is corroded when pH is below 5.5 (acidic).

Bacteria present in the mouth produce acids by degradation of sugar and food particles remaining in the mouth. It can be prevented by using tothpaste, which is generally basic to neutralise excess acid.

(c) **Strong acids :** Those acids that give rise to more H^+ ion concentration. e.g., HCl, H_2SO_4, HNO_3

Weak acids : Those acids that give rise to less H^+ ion concentration. e.g., acetic acid, lactic acid.

Q.51 (i) Explain why is hydrochloric acid a strong acid and acetic acid a weak acid. How can it be verified ? **[SAI-2012,15]**

(ii) You have four solutions A, B, C and D. The pH of solution A is 6, B is 9, C is 12 and D is 7.

(a) Identify the most acidic and most basic solutions.

(b) Arrange the above four solutions in the increasing order of H^+ ion concentration.

(c) State the change in colour of pH paper on dipping in solution C and D.

Ans. (i) HCl will give rise to more H^+ ions and CH_3COOH produces less H^+ ions. The colour of pH paper depends on the concentration of H^+ ion. Colour becomes red for high H^+ ions concentration.

(ii) (a) Most acidic – A ; Most basic – C

(b) C, B, D, A / $C < B < D < A$

(c) In C- blue ; In D -green

Q.52 Identify the compound of calcium which is yellowish white powder and is used for disinfecting drinking water. How is it manufactured ? Write the chemical equation for the reaction involved Mention its two industrial applications. **[SAI-2014]**

Ans. (i) Compound is bleaching powder [Calcium oxychloride ($CaOCl_2$)].

(ii) Bleaching powder is produced by the action of chlorine on dry slaked lime [$Ca(OH)_2$]. In other words, when chlorine is passed over dry slaked lime, bleaching powder is formed

$Ca(OH)_2 + Cl_2 \rightarrow CaOCl_2 + H_2O$

(iii) Bleaching powder is used for :

(a) Bleaching cotton and linen in textile industry.

(b) Bleaching wood pulp in paper factories.

(c) Bleaching washed clothes in laundry.

(d) Disinfecting drinking water to make it germ free.

Q.53 State reasons for the following statements : **[SAI-2015]**

(a) Tape water conducts electricity, whereas distilled water does not.

(b) During summer season, a milkman usually adds a very small amount of baking soda to fresh milk.

(c) Ammonia is a base but does not contain a hydroxyl group.

Ans. (a) Tap water contains salts which dissociate into ions to conduct the charge.

(b) To increase the pH so that milk does not become sour (curdling of milk).

(c) Because ammonia dissolves in water to form OH^- (aq) ions which show the basic property.

Q.54 Fill in the missing data in the following table:

Name of the salt	Formula	Salt obtained from	
		Base	Acid
(i) Ammonium chloride	NH_4Cl	—	—
(ii) Copper sulphate	—	—	H_2SO_4
(iii) Sodium chloride	NaCl	NaOH	—
(iv) Magnesium nitrate	$Mg(NO_3)_2$	—	HNO_3
(v) Potassium sulphate	K_2SO_4	—	—
(vi) Calcium nitrate	$Ca(NO_3)_2$	—	—

Ans.

Name of the salt	Formula	Salt obtained from	
		Base	Acid
(i) Ammonium chloride	NH_4Cl	NH_4OH	HCl
(ii) Copper sulphate	$CuSO_4$	$Cu(OH)_2$	H_2SO_4
(iii) Sodium chloride	NaCl	NaOH	HCl
(iv) Magnesium nitrate	$Mg(NO_3)_2$	$Mg(OH)_2$	HNO_3
(v) Potassium sulphate	K_2SO_4	KOH	H_2SO_4
(vi) Calcium nitrate	$Ca(NO_3)_2$	$Ca(OH)_2$	HNO_3

Q.55 What happens when crystals of washing soda are exposed to air? **[CBSE-2003, 2005]**

Ans. Washing soda undergoes efflorescence and as a result loses nine molecules of water to form white powder,

$$\underset{\substack{\text{(washing soda)} \\ \text{white crystals}}}{Na_2CO_3 \cdot 10H_2O} \xrightarrow{\text{(Air)}} \underset{\substack{\text{(washing soda)} \\ \text{white crystals}}}{Na_2CO_3 \cdot H_2O} + 9H_2O$$

Q.56 Explain giving reasons: **[CBSE-2003]**

(i) Tartaric acid is a component of baking powder used in making cakes.

(ii) Gypsum, $CaSO_4.2H_2O$ is used in the manufacture of cement.

Ans. (i) Role of tartaric acid in baking powder (mixture of tartaric acid and sodium hydrogen carbonate) is to neutralise sodium carbonate formed upon heating sodium hydrogen carbonate.

$$\underset{\text{(sodium hydrogen carbonate)}}{2NaHCO_3} \xrightarrow{\Delta} \underset{\text{(sodium carbonate)}}{Na_2CO_3} + H_2O + CO_2$$

In case it is not done, cake will be bitter and sodium carbonate will also have injurious side effects.

(ii) The role of gypsum, ($CaSO_4.2H_2O$) in the manufacture of cement is to slow down the process of setting of cement.

Q.57 Five solutions A, B, C, D and E when tested with universal indicator show pH as 4, 2, 12, 7 and 9 respectively. Which solution is

(a) neutral (B) strongly alkaline (C) strongly acidic (D) weakly alkaline, (e) weakly acidic, (f) Arrange the pH in increasing order of H^+ ion concentration. **[CBSE-2010]**

Ans. (a) Neutral : D with pH = 7 (b) Strongly alkaline : C with pH = 12 (c) Strongly acidic : B with pH = 2 (d) Weakly alkaline : E with pH = 9 (e) Weakly acidic : A with pH = 4 (f) Increasing order of H^+ ions concentration : C < E < D < A < B

CONCEPT APPLICATION LEVEL - III

Q.1 The pH of the solution of 5×10^{-8} M HCl at 25°C is –
(A) 6.3 (B) 6.9 (C) 7.3 (D) 7.9

Q.2 One of the major enviormental concerns is the phenomenon of acid rain. Rain water is an unpolluted atmosphere will be
(A) Neutral (B) Slightly basic (C) Slightly acidic (D) Strongly acidic

Q.3 In the reaction

$$HC_2O_4^- + PO_4^{3-} \rightleftharpoons HPO_4^{2-} + C_2O_4^{2-}$$

Which are the two bronsted bases
(A) $HC_2O_4^-$, PO_4^{3-} (B) HPO_4^{2-}, $C_2O_4^{2-}$ (C) PO_4^{3-},$C_2O_4^{2-}$ (D) $HC_2O_4^-$, HPO_4^{2-}

Q.4 Ammonium ion (NH_4^+) is
(A) a conjugate acid (B) a conjugate base
(C) Neither an acid nor a base (D) both an acid and a base

Q.5 The pH of a solution containing 0.1N NaOH solution
(A) 1 (B) 10^{-1} (C) 13 (D) 14

Q.6 What is pH of an acidic solution
(A) Greather than 7 (B) Equal to 7 (C) Less than 7 (D) Greater than 10

Q.7 The following acids have been arranged in order decreasing acid strength. Identify the order
ClOH(1), BrOH(2), IOH(3)
(A) $1 > 2 > 3$ (B) $2 > 1 > 3$ (C) $3 > 2 > 1$ (D) $1 > 3 > 2$

Q.8 The set with correct order of acidic is
(A) $HClO > HClO_2 > HClO_3 > HClO_4$ (B) $HClO_4 > HClO_3 > HClO_2 > HClO$
(C) $HClO > HClO_4 > HClO_3 > HClO_2$ (D) $HClO_4 > HClO_2 > HClO_3 > HClO$

Q.9 H_2SO_4 is a
(A) Monoprotic acid (B) Monobasic acid
(C) Polyprotic acid (D) Both (A) and (B) are correct

Q.10 pH of solution is zero. The nature of this solution is
(A) acidic (B) basic (C) Neutral (D) amphoteric

Q.11 Oxygen exhibits (–1) oxidation state
(A) OF_2 (B) H_2O (C) H_2O_2 (D) HClO

Q.12 Nature of methyl orange is –
(A) Acidic (B) Basic (C) Neutral (D) None of these

Q.13 When the pH of the enviornment of protien is changed it is said to be denatured. This is due to
(A) Breakage of peptide bond (B) Breakage of disulfide links
(C) Loss of tertiary structure (D) break down of regroups

Q.14 What is aqua regia ?
(A) 1 : 2 mixture of chromic acid and sulphuric acid
(B) 1 : 3 Mixture of conc. HCl and conc. HNO_3
(C) 1 : 3 mixture of conc. HNO_3 and conc. HCl
(D) 1 : 1 mixture of conc. H_2SO_4 conc. HCl

Q.15 Which gas is evolved when metal carbonates and bicarbonates react with acids ?
(A) O_2 (B) CO_2 (C) H_2 (D) n_2

Q.16 H_3BO_3 is
(A) monobasic and weak lewis acid (B) monobasic and weak bronsted acid
(C) monobasic acid and strong lewis acid (D) Tribasic and weak bronsted acid

Q.17 In I_3^- lewis base is
(A) I_2 (B) I_2^+ (C) I^{2-} (D) I^-

Q.18 Which of the following is not a lewis acid ?
(A) CO (B) $SiCl_4$ (C) SO_3 (D) Zn^{2+}

Q.19 The acid produced in our stomach is
(A) Sulphuric acid (B) Hydrochloric acid (C) Acetic acid (D) Oxalic acid

Q.20 The salt whose aqueous solution turns phenophthalein indicator pink is ?
(A) KCl (B) K_2SO_4 (C) K_2CO_3 (D) KNO_3

Q.21 $Ca(OH)_2(s) + Cl_2(g) \longrightarrow ?$
(A) $Ca(OH)_2 + H_2O$ (B) Slaked lime (C) $CaOCl_2 + H_2O$ (D) Gypsum

Q.22 A Colour less gas B is produced when egg shell is treated with a solution. The gas B turns lime water milky. What are A and B ?
(A) A = NaCl & B = CO_2 (B) A = HCl & B = CO_2
(C) A = NaCl & B = Cl_2 (D) A = H_2SO_4 & B = O_2

Q.23 What is the chemical composition of plaster of pairs
(A) $CaSO_4.2H_2O$ (B) $CaSO_4.H_2O$ (C) $CaSO_4½H_2O$ (D) $CaSO_4.3H_2O$

Q.24 An element X react with dil H_2SO_4 as well as with NaOH to produce salt and $H_2(g)$ Hence it may be concluded that
(I) X is an electropositive element (II) Oxide of X is basic in nature
(III) Oxide of X is acidic in nature (IV) X is an electronegative element
(A) I, II, III (B) IV, I, II (C) III, IV, I (D) I & II only

Q.25 Which of the following is not the raw material for manufacturing of baking soda ?
(A) Common salt (B) Ammonia (C) Lime stone (D) Slaked lime

Q.26 The pH of 0.001 N NaOH solution at 25ºC is
(A) 3 (B) 4 (C) 11 (D) 12

Q.27 pH of Blood is
(A) 6.4 (B) 7.4 (C) 4.7 (D) 6.4

Q.28 What is molecular formula of gypsum ?
(A) $CaCO_3$ (B) $CaSO_4.2H_2O$ (C) CaO (D) $Ca(OH)_2$

Q.29 Strength of caustic soda solution is 2g/litre. pH of this solution will be (log2 = 0.30)
(A) 11.9 (B) 9.7 (C) 10.8 (D) 12.7

Q.30 The bleaching action of chloine is due to its
(A) oxidising nature (B) reducing nature (C) acidic nature (D) All of these

Q.31 One drop of methyl orange solution when added to the solution obtained after electrolysis of a concentrated solution of NaCl with Pt electrodes, the colour of the solution will turn.
(A) Orange (B) Pink (C) Yellow (D) Colourless

Q.32 The tooth paste has ______ medium.
(A) acidic medium (B) basic medium (C) neutral medium (D) may be acidic or basic

Q.33 The pH of solution changes from 4 to 5, the change in H^+ will be
(A) 5 times (B) 10 times (C) 10^{-1} times (D) No change

Q.34 Solvay process is used for the manufacture of
(A) washing soda (B) baking soda (C) bleaching powder (D) none of these

Q.35 Statement–1: pH of 10^{-9} N HCl is 9
Statement–2: pH is defined as the negative logatrithum of $[H^+]$
(A) Both Statement–1 and Statement–2 are correct but Statement–2 is not the correct explanation of Statement–1
(B) Statement–1 is correct and Statement–2 is incorrect
(C) Statement–1 is incorrect but Statement–2 is correct
(D) Both Statement–1 and Statement–2 are correct and Statement–2 is the correct explanation of Statement–1

Q.36 Statement–1 Arrehenius acids will show acidic behaviour both in absence or presence of water
Statement–2 In water acids dissociate and give H^+ ion thux H^+ ions are responsible for the acidic nature of acidx.
(A) Statement–1 is true, Statement–2 is true, Statement–2 is correct explanation for Statement–1
(B) Statement–1 is true, Statement–2 is true, Statement–2 is not correct explanation for Statement–1
(C) Statement–1 is true, Statement–2 is false
(D) Statement–1 is false, Statement–2 is true

Q.37 Statement–1 Curd should not be stored in brass and copper vessels.
Statement–2 Curd contains acid, which reacts with brass and copper.
(A) Statement–1 is true, Statement–2 is true, Statement–2 is correct explanation for Statement–1
(B) Statement–1 is true, Statement–2 is true, Statement–2 is not correct explanation for Statement–1
(C) Statement–1 is true, Statement–2 is false
(D) Statement–1 is false, Statement–2 is true

Q.38

	Column-A		**Column-B**
A	Lactic acid	1.	Food preservative
B.	Benzoic acid	2.	Vinegar
C.	Formic acid	3.	souring of milk in curd
D.	Acetic acid	4.	found in the stings of ants and bees

(A) A-1, B-2, C-3, D-4 (B) A-2, B-4, C-1, D-3
(C) A-3, B-1, C-4, D-2 (D) A-4, B-1, C-2, D-3

Q.39

	Column-A *Parameters*		**Column-B** *Formula*
A	pH	1.	$\frac{[H^+][A^-]}{[HA]}$
B.	K_a	2.	$\frac{[A^+][OH^-]}{[AOH]}$
C.	K_b	3.	$-\log[OH^-]$
D.	pOH	4.	$-\log[H^+]$

(A) A-1, B-2, C-3, D-4 (B) A-2, B-4, C-1, D-3
(C) A-3, B-1, C-4, D-2 (D) A-4, B-1, C-2, D-3

Q.40

	Column-A ***Theory***		**Column-B** ***Acid***
A	Arrhenius	1.	acid is a proton (H^+) donor
B.	Lewis	2.	Acids produce hydrogen ions in an aqueous solution
C.	Bronsted-Lowery	3.	Acid is an e^- acceptor

(A) A-2, B-1, C-3 (B) A-1, B-3, C-2
(C) A-2, B-3, C-1 (D) A-3, B-1, C-2

Q.41 Salt made of non-metallic elements only is :
(A) NaCl (B) NH_4Cl (C) AlN (D) $MgCl_2$

Q.42 Strength of caustic soda solution is 2 g/litre, pH of this solution will be (log 5 = 0.699)
(A) 11.9 (B) 9.7 (C) 10.8 (D) 12.7

Q.43 The pH value of 100 litre aqueous solution containing 4 gram NaOH is:
(A) 3 (B) 9 (C) 11 (D) 14

Q.44 Which of the following solution has the lowest pH value ?
(A) 0.1 Molar NaCl solution (B) 0.01 Molar $NaHCO_3$ solution
(C) 0.001 Molar Na_2CO_3 solution (D) 0.01 Molar NaOH solution

Q.45 Which of the following has the greatest concentration of H^+ – ion ?
(A) 1 mol L^{-1} HCl solution (B) 1 mol L^{-1} H_3PO_2 solution
(C) 1 mol L^{-1} H_2SO_4 solution (D) 1 mol L^{-1} H_2CO_3 solution

ANSWER KEY

CONCEPT APPLICATION LEVEL - II

SECTION-A

Q.1	C	Q.2	C	Q.3	C	Q.4	A	Q.5	C	Q.6	D	Q.7	D
Q.8	C	Q.9	C	Q.10	D	Q.11	B	Q.12	D	Q.13	D	Q.14	A
Q.15	A	Q.16	C	Q.17	D	Q.18	A	Q.19	A	Q.20	B		

CONCEPT APPLICATION LEVEL - III

Q.1	B	Q.2	A	Q.3	C	Q.4	A	Q.5	C	Q.6	C	Q.7	A
Q.8	A	Q.9	C	Q.10	A	Q.11	C	Q.12	B	Q.13	A	Q.14	C
Q.15	B	Q.16	A	Q.17	D	Q.18	A	Q.19	B	Q.20	C	Q.21	C
Q.22	B	Q.23	C	Q.24	A	Q.25	D	Q.26	C	Q.27	B	Q.28	B
Q.29	D	Q.30	A	Q.31	C	Q.32	B	Q.33	C	Q.34	A	Q.35	C
Q.36	D	Q.37	D	Q.38	C	Q.39	D	Q.40	C	Q.41	B	Q.42	D
Q.43	C	Q.44	A	Q.45	C								

3 METALS & NON-METALS

3.1 INTRODUCTION :

Till now, scientists have discovered more than 118 elements. These are classified into metals and Non-metals and metalloids. Metals are electropositive, which are hard, sonorous, malleable, ductile, with tensile strength and good conductor of heat and electricity. Non-metals have just opposite to metals in characteristics. Metalloids are the elements which show the property of both metals and non metals. Metals occur in nature in the free as well as combined state (in minerals). Those minerals from a metal can be extracted profitably and economically are called ores, process is called metallurgy. Metals also from alloys. We will study all these different aspects of elements in this chapter.

3.2 METALS :

(A) PHYSICAL PROPERTIES

(a) Important Characteristics of the Metals :

1. **Physical state :** Solids at room temperature.

   Exception : Mercury (liquid at room temperature).
2. **Shining surfaces** : Property as known as **lustre**.
3. **Conduction :** Good conductors of heat and electricity : eg. Au, Ag

   Exception : Heat (Pb), Electricity (Hg).
4. **Hardness :** Quite hard.

   Exception : Sodium & potassium are soft.
5. **Malleable** : Eg. Fine **Al foils** are used for wrapping different types of food. Thin foils of silver are used for decorating sweets.
6. **Ductile** : All electric wires drawn from different metals are very fine.
7. **Sonorous :** The sound produced on bending a tin foil is known as **'tin cry'**.
8. Generally, have high melting and boiling points.
9. **Density :** Metals have high density and are very heavy.
10. **Valency :** Metals have 1 to 3 electrons in the outermost shell of their atoms.
11. **Electropositive character :** Metals are elements that have a tendency to lose electors and form cations. They normally do not accept electrons.

(b) Important properties of Non-metals

1. **Physical state :** Either gases or solids at room temperature.

   Exception : Bromine (liquid at room temperature).

2. **Surface :** Non-metals vary in colour with generally **dull surfaces**.

   Exception : Diamond, Crystals of iodine have bright lustre.

3. **Conduction :** Mostly Poor conductors of heat and electricity.

   Exception : Graphite

4. **Hardness :** Quite Soft.

   Exception : Diamond

5. **Malleable :** Non-malleable and non-ductile.

6. **Not Sonorous**.

7. **Very low melting and boiling point** as compare to metals.

   Exception : Diamond, Graphite

8. **Reactivity :** They generally form acidic or neutral oxides with oxygen.

Knowledge Enhancer

Noble Metal : Noble metals are metals that are resistant to corrosion or oxidation, unlike most base metals. They tend to be precious metals often due to inertness. Examples include gold, platinum and rhodium.

Precious Metals : A precious metal is a rare metallic chemical element of high economic value. Chemically, the precious metals are less reactive than most elements, have high luster and high electrical conductivity. Historically, precious metals were important as currency, but are now regarded mainly as investment and industrial commodities. The best-known precious metals are gold and silver. While both have industrial uses, they are better known for their uses in art, jewelry and coinage. Other precious metals include the Platinum group metals: ruthenium, rhodium, palladium, osmium, iridium and platinum is the most widely traded.

Based Metal : In chemistry, the term 'base metal' is used informally to refer to a metal that oxidizes or corrodes relatively easily, and reacts variably with dilute hydrochloric acid (HCl) to form hydrogen. Examples include iron, nickel, lead and zinc. Copper is considered as a base metal because it oxidizes relatively easily, although it does not react with HCl. It is commonly used in opposition to noble metal.

Ferrous Metal : The term "ferrous" is derived from the Latin word meaning "containing iron". This can include pure iron, such as wrought iron, or an alloy such as steel. Ferrous metals are often magnetic, but not exclusively.

Alloy : An alloy is a mixture of two or more elements in solid solution in which the major component is a metal. Most pure metals are either too soft, brittle or chemically reactive for practical use. Combining different ratios of metals as alloys modify the properties of pure metals to produce desirable characteristics. The aim of making alloys is generally to make them less brittle, harder, resistant to corrosion, or have a more desirable color and luster. Examples of alloys are steel (iron and carbon), brass (copper and zinc), bronze (copper and tin), and duralumin (aluminium and copper). Alloys specially designed for highly demanding applications, such as jet engines, may contains more than ten elements. Stainless steel (Fe + C + Cr + Ni) are used where resistance to corrosion is important Al and Mg alloys are used for strength and light applications. Nickel-based super alloys are used in high temperature applications such as turbocharger, pressure vessel and heat exchangers. Generally electrical conductivity of an alloy is less than that of pure metal.

(i) There are several metals that are low density, soft and have low melting points, these (the alkali and alkaline earth metals) are extremely reactive, and are rarely encountered in their elemental, metallic form. Some metals like sodium are so soft that they can be even cut with knife. Three metals are magnetic. These are iron, cobalt and nickel. Steel is a mixture of elements but mostly iron, so it is also magnetic. The other metals are not magnetic. Mercury is the only metal which is found in liquid state at room temperature.

(ii) Gold is probably one of the hardest metals. From one gram of the metal, a wire of nearly two kilometres can be drawn. However the metals differ in their ductility capacity.

(iii) Metals such as titanium, chromium, manganese, zirconium, etc. are classified as strategic metals play important role in the country's economy and defence. These metals and their alloys are used in

(a) atomic energy, (b) space science projects (c) jet engines
(d) high grade steels (e) defence equipments

(iv) Iridium is the heaviest metal while lithium is the lighest metal.

Some more properties of Metals :

(i) Ionization energy of an element is the amount of energy required to remove the outermost electron from an isolated atom of the element in gaseous state.

$$A(g) + \text{Ionization energy} \longrightarrow A^{+}(g) + e^{-}$$

Ionization energy of an element is the measure of tendency of an element to lose electrons.

(ii) Thermal and Electrical Conductivity

(A) Study of Thermal Conductivity of Metals

(a) Take an aluminium or copper rod and clamp it on a stand as shown in figure.

(b) Put some wax on one end of the rod.

(c) Start heating the rod, from a place away from the wax, with the help of a burner.

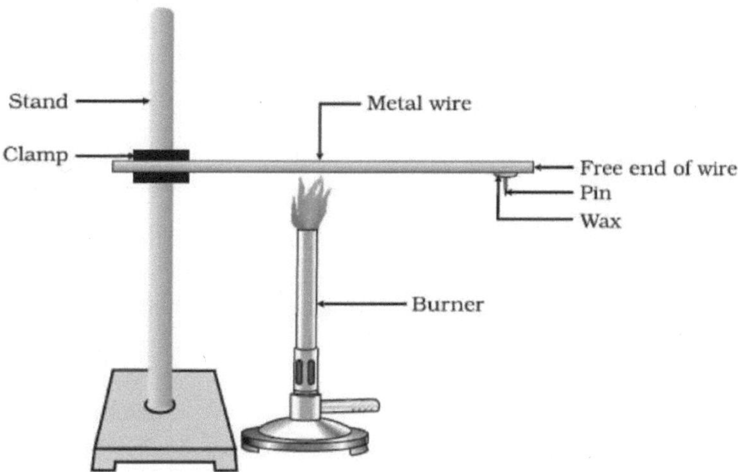

What do you observe?

It is observed that the wax starts melting.

The rod does not melt even after heating for a long time.

This activity demonstrates that the metals are good conductors of heat and have high melting points.

(B) Study of Electrical Conductivity of Metals

(a) Take wires of copper, aluminium, iron etc.

(b) Set up the electric circuit as shown in figure.

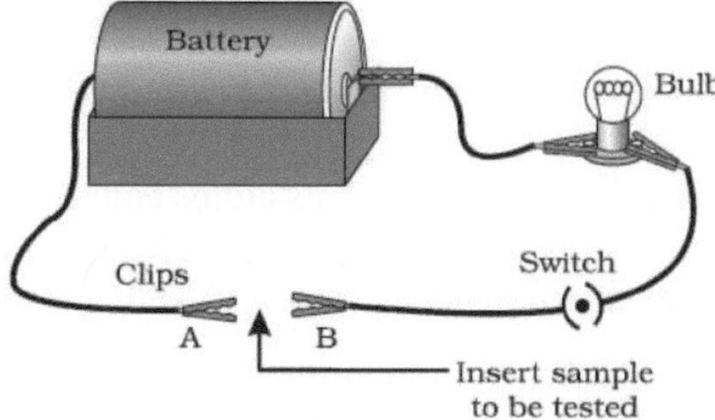

(c) Place the different wires between points A and B one by one and observe whether the bulb glows or not after completing the circuit.

It is observed that bulb glows in case of different metals indicating that metals are good conductor of electricity.

Difference between Metal & Non-metal

Property	Metals	Non – Metals
1. Action with mineral acids	Metals generally react with dilute mineral acids to liberate H_2 gas	Non-metals do not displace hydrogen on reaction with dilute minerals acids
2. Nature of oxides	They form basic oxides. These oxides are ionic in nature. Some oxides like Al_2O_3 are amphoteric also.	Non-metals form acidic or neutral oxides. These oxides are covalent in nature.
3. Combination with hydrogen	Only a few metals combine with hydrogen to form hydrides. These hydrides are ionic in character.	Non-metals combine with hydrogen to form stable hydrides. These hydrides are covalent.
4. Combination with halogens	They combine with halogens to form well defined and stable crystalline solids. For example, NaCl, KBr, etc.	Non-metals form halides which are unstable and undergo hydrolysis readily. For example, PCl_5, PCl_3, etc.
5. Electrochemical behavior	Metals are electropositive in character. They form cations in solutions and are deposited on the cathode when electricity passed through their solutions.	Non-metals are electronegative in character. They form anions in solutions and are liberated at the anode when electricity is passed through their solutions. Hydrogen is an exception. It usually forms positive ions and is liberated at cathode.
6. Oxidising or reducing behaviour	Metals behave as reducing agents. This is because of their tendency to lose electrons.	Non-metals generally behave as oxidizing agents since they have the tendency to gain electrons.

Illustration 1

How does a metal conduct heat?

Solution

When a metal is heated, its atoms gain energy and vibrate more *vigorously*. This energy is transferred to the electrons, which can move through out the metal, they transfer their energy to other electrons and atoms, and thus, heat is conducted.

Illustration 2

How does a metal conduct electricity?

Solution

Metals have low ionisation potential, so they loose electrons, the free e^- (or) mobile electron, move from one kernal (positive charged ion, Ex: Ag^+) to another kernal, so metal conduct electricity.

Try yourself

1. Give one example of a metal which
   (i) is liquid at room temperature
   (ii) can be easily cut out with a knife
   (iii) is the best conductor of heat
   (iv) is the poorest conductor of heat
2. Name two highly malleable metals
3. Name two elements that are alloyed with iron to make stainless steel?

(B) CHEMICAL PROPERTIES OF METALS

Metals are electropositive elements, so they ionise by loss of electrons and form positive ions (cations)

$K \rightarrow K^+ + e^-$, $Mg \rightarrow Mg^{+2} + 2e^-$

The electropositive character of metals gives a certain characteristic chemical properties, these are discussed below.

(I) Reaction of Metals with Oxygen : Almost all metals combine with oxygen to form their respective oxides. Metals oxides are basic in nature.

Metal + Oxygen $\longrightarrow$ Metal oxide

When heated in air sodium burns with golden yellow flame. Potassium burn with pink-violet flame.

All the metals combine with oxygen, and form basic oxides

(a) $4Na + O_2 \longrightarrow 2Na_2O$

$2Cu + O_2 \longrightarrow 2CuO$

(b) Mg does not react with oxygen at room temperature. It combine with oxygen only on heating. Magnesium also combine with nitrogen and forms oxide & nitride.

$2Mg + O_2 \xrightarrow{heat} 2MgO$

$6Mg + 2N_2 \longrightarrow 2Mg_3N_2$ (Magnesium nitride)

(c) $2Zn + 2O_2 \longrightarrow 2ZnO(s)$

(d) Iron does not burn in air even on strong heating but iron filings burn vigorously when sprinkled in the flame of burner. Iron reacts with oxygen or air to form Fe_3O_4.

$3Fe(s) + O_2(g) \longrightarrow Fe_3O_4(s)$

It may be mentioned that oxides of some less electropositive metals are amphoteric in nature. Aluminium & zinc are metals. These metals combine with oxygen and form amphoteric oxide. (Amphoteric oxides reacts with acids and bases)

$2Al + 3O_2 \longrightarrow 2Al_2O_3$

$2Zn + O_2 \longrightarrow 2ZnO$ (Amphoteric oxides)

$Al_2O_3 + 6HCl \longrightarrow 2AlCl_3 + 3H_2O$

$Al_2O_3 + 2NaOH \longrightarrow 2NaAlO_2 + H_2O$ (sodium aluminate)

Alkali (I A group) & Alkaline earth metal (II A group) oxides are soluble in nature and forms metal hydroxides.

$Na_2O\ (s) + H_2O\ (l) \rightarrow 2NaOH\ (Aq)$

$MgO\ (s) + H_2O\ (l) \rightarrow Mg(OH)_2$

But most of the metal oxides are insoluble in nature.

- Different metals show different reactivities towards oxygen.
  Na & K – catches fire when they placed in moist air, So Na & K are kept in kerosene.
- Mg, Al, Zn & Pb reacts with oxygen and forms metal oxide. This oxide layer is called protective oxide layer, it prevent the further oxidation.
- Pb, Ag & Au – do not react with oxygen even at high temperature so they are called noble metals.

$$Na > Mg > Zn > Fe > Cu$$

Anodising: is a process of forming a thick oxide layer of aluminium. During anodising, a clean aluminium article is made the anode and is electrolysed with dilute H_2SO_4. The oxygen gas evolved at the anode reacts with aluminium to make a thicker protective oxide layer. This oxide layer can be dyed easily to give Al – articles to an attractive finish.

(II) Action with water

Metals react with water and produce a metal oxide and hydrogen gas. Metal oxides that are soluble in water dissolve in it to further form metal hydroxide. But all metals do not react with water.

$$\text{Metal} + \text{Water} \longrightarrow \text{Metal oxide} + \text{Hydrogen}$$
$$\text{Metal oxide} + \text{Water} \longrightarrow \text{Metal hydroxide}$$

Metals like potassium and sodium react violently with cold water. In case of sodium and potassium, the reaction is so violent and exothermic that the evolved hydrogen immediately catches fire.

$$2K\,(s) + 2H_2O\,(l) \longrightarrow 2KOH\,(aq) + H_2\,(g) \quad + \text{heat energy}$$
$$2Na\,(s) + 2H_2O\,(l) \longrightarrow 2NaOH\,(aq) + H_2\,(g) \quad + \text{heat energy}$$

The reaction of calcium with water is less violent. The heat evolved is not sufficient for the hydrogen to catch fire.

$$Ca\,(s) + 2H_2O\,(l) \longrightarrow Ca(OH)_2\,(aq) + H_2\,(g)$$

Calcium starts floating because the bubbles of hydrogen gas formed stick to the surface of the metal.

Magnesium does not react with cold water. It reacts with hot water to form magnesium hydroxide and hydrogen. It also starts floating due to the bubbles of hydrogen gas sticking to its surface.

$$Mg(s) + 2H_2O(l) \xrightarrow{\text{heat}} Mg(OH)_2(aq) + H_2(g)$$

Metals like aluminium, iron and zinc do not react either with cold or hot water. But they react with steam to form the metal oxide and hydrogen.

$$2Al\,(s) + 3H_2O\,(g) \longrightarrow Al_2O_3\,(s) + 3H_2\,(g)$$
$$3Fe\,(s) + 4H_2O\,(g) \rightleftharpoons Fe_3O_4\,(s) + 4H_2\,(g)$$

The reaction is reversible in nature.

Metals such as lead, copper, silver and gold do not react with water at all.

Thus, the order of reactivity of some common metals with water.

$$K > Na > Ca >> Mg > Zn > Fe > Cu$$

(III) Reaction With Acids

All metals do not react with dilute hydrochloric acid and sulphuric acids. But when a metal reacts with any of these acids, a salt is formed and hydrogen gas is evolved. The metal replaces the hydrogen atoms in the acid to form a salt.

$$\text{Metal} + \text{dilute acid} \longrightarrow \text{Metal salt} + \text{Hydrogen}$$

(a) Sodium reacts with dilute acid with explosive violence

$$\underset{\text{Sodium metal}}{2Na(s)} + \underset{\text{Hydrochloric acid}}{2HCl(aq)} \longrightarrow \underset{\text{Sodium chloride}}{2NaCl\,(aq)} + H_2(g)$$

This reaction shows that sodium is a very reactive metal.

(b) Magnesium metals reacts rapidly with dilute hydroxhloric acid to form magnesium chloride and hydrogen gas.

$$Mg(s) + 2HCl(aq) \longrightarrow MgCl_2(aq) + H_2(g)$$

(c) Zn reacts with dil. HCl, but less rapidly than Mg. This shows that zinc is less reactive than magnesium

$$Zn(s) + 2HCl(aq) \longrightarrow \underset{\text{Zinc chloride}}{ZnCl_2(aq)} + H_2(g)$$

(d) Iron react very slowly with dil HCl to form ferrous chloride and hydrogen.

$$Fe(s) + 2HCl(aq) \longrightarrow FeCl_2(aq) + H_2(g)$$

(e) $Cu(s) + HCl(aq) \longrightarrow$ No reaction.

Thus, order of reactivity is

$$\boxed{Na > Mg > Zn > Fe > Cu}$$

Hydrogen gas is not evolved when a metal reacts with nitric acid. It is because HNO_3 is a strong oxidising agent. It oxidises the H_2 produced to water and is itself reduced to any of oxides of nitrogen (N_2O, NO, NO_2). But Mg and Mn react with very dilute HNO_3 to evolve H_2 gas.

$$Mn(s) + \underset{\text{(very dilute)}}{2HNO_3(aq)} \longrightarrow Mn\,(NO_3)_2\,(aq) + H_2(g)$$

The rate of formation of bubbles was the fastest in the case of magnesium. The reaction was also the most exothermic in this case. The reactivity decreases in the order Mg > Al > Zn > Fe. In the case of copper, no bubbles were seen and the temperature also remained unchanged. This show that copper does not react with dilute HCl.

Knowledge Enhancer

Aqua regia is a mixture containing 3 parts concentrated hydrochloric acid and 1 part concentrated nitric acid. It was well known to the alchemists for its power to dissolve gold. Aqua regia, which is Latin for 'royal water', is highly corrosive and fuming acid.

It reacts with noble metals such as gold and platinum to form their corresponding chlorides.

$$\underbrace{3HCl + HNO_3}_{\text{Aqua regia}} \longrightarrow \underset{\text{(Nitrosyl chloride)}}{NOCl} + \underbrace{2H_2O + 2Cl}_{\text{(Nascent)}}$$

$$\underset{\text{Gold}}{Au} + 3Cl \longrightarrow \underset{\text{(Auric chloride)}}{AuCl_3} \quad ; \quad \underset{\text{Plantinum}}{Pt} + 4Cl \longrightarrow \underset{\text{(Platinum chloride)}}{PtCl_4}$$

(IV) Reaction with Chlorine

Most of the metals react with chlorine to form chlorides. These chlorides are ionic (or electrovalent) in character. During the formation of these chlorides, metal loses electrons and becomes positively charged whereas chlorine atoms accept electrons and become negatively charged ions (chloride ions). During this reaction metal undergoes oxidation whereas chlorine undergoes reduction. Some examples are given below:

$$\underset{\text{Sodium}}{2Na(s)} + Cl_2(g) \longrightarrow \underset{\text{Sodium chloride}}{2NaCl(s)} \quad ; \quad \underset{\text{Calcium}}{Ca(s)} + Cl_2(g) \longrightarrow \underset{\text{Calcium chloride}}{CaCl_2(s)}$$

$$\underset{\text{Magnesium}}{Mg(s)} + Cl_2(g) \longrightarrow \underset{\text{Magnesium chloride}}{MgCl_2(s)} \quad ; \quad \underset{\text{Zinc}}{Zn(s)} + Cl_2(g) \longrightarrow \underset{\text{Znic chloride}}{ZnCl_2(s)}$$

(V) Reaction with Hydrogen

Most of the metals do not form compounds with hydrogen because metals form compounds by loss of electrons which are accepted by the other element. But hydrogen usually forms compounds with other elements by loss of electrons or by sharing of electrons. It does not accept electrons. However, a few reactive metals such as sodium, potassium and calcium react with hydrogen to form ionic hydrides.

$$\underset{\text{Sodium}}{2Na(s)} + H_2(g) \longrightarrow \underset{\text{Sodium hydride}}{2NaH(s)} \quad ; \quad \underset{\text{Potassium}}{2K(s)} + H_2(g) \longrightarrow \underset{\text{Potassium hydride}}{2KH(s)}$$

$$\underset{\text{Calcium}}{Ca(s)} + H_2(g) \longrightarrow \underset{\text{Calcium hydride}}{CaH_2(s)}$$

These hydrides are highly unstable compounds. They are decomposed with water.

$$NaH(s) + H_2O(l) \longrightarrow NaOH(aq) + H_2(g)$$

(VI) Reaction of Metals with Solutions of Other Metal Salts

Reactive metals can displace less reactive metals from their compounds in solution or molten form. We have seen in the previous sections that all metals are not equally reactive. We checked the reactivity of various metals with oxygen, water and acids. But all metals do not react with these reagents. So we were not able to put all the metal samples we had collected in decreasing order of their reactivity.

It is simple and easy if metal A displaces metal B from its solution, it is more reactive than B.

$$\text{Metal A} + \text{Salt solution of B} \longrightarrow \text{Salt solution of A} + \text{Metal B}$$

Certain metals have the capacity to displace some metals from the aqueous solution of their salts. These reaction are known as metals displacement reactions. It may be noted that *a metal placed higher in the activity series can displace the metal which occupies a lower position form the aqueous solution of its salt or a less reavtive metal can displace more reactive metal from its salt solution.*

For example, if we look at the activity series, we find that zinc occupies a much higher position in the activity series as compared to copper. It is expected to displace copper present in the aqueous solution of its salt (e.g. $CuSO_4$)

$$Zn(s) + CuSO_4(aq) \longrightarrow ZnSO_4(aq) + Cu(s)$$

Activity/Reactivity Series of Metals

The reactivity of metals differs from metal to metal. Some of the metals are reactive, while others are less reactive towards chemical reagents. The elements that can lose electrons easily and form positively charged ions are more reactive. The elements that cannot lose electrons easily are less reactive.

Metals can be arranged in the decreasing order of their reactivity in a series. This series is called the reactivity or activity series of metals. The series has been derived from the reactions discussed above and many other similar reactions.

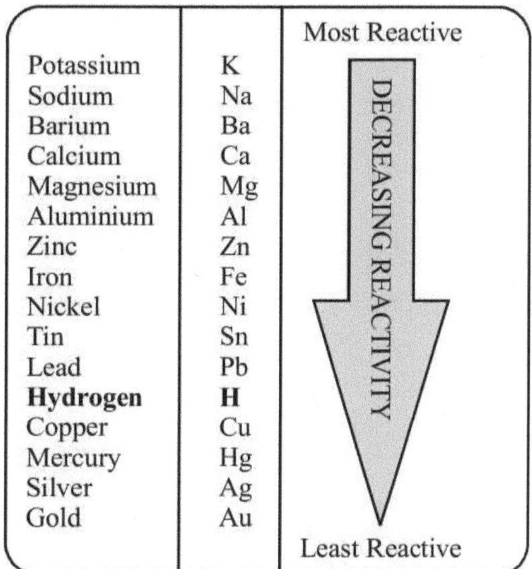

Activity series of some metals

1. The activity series of metals provides a list of metals arranged in order of their decreasing chemical activity. The most active metal, potassium is at the top of the list and the least active metal, gold, is at the bottom.
2. The ease with which a metal loses electrons and forms positive ions in solution, decreases as we go do down the activity series from potassium to gold.
3. Hydrogen is included in the activity series even though it is not a metal. The hydrogen ion (H^+), like other metal ions, has a positive charge in most chemical reactions.

Knowledge Enhancer

During reactions, metals generally undergo oxidation, i.e. they lose electrons to form positive ions. The metals that have low ionization energy, have greater tendency to lose electrons and hence are generally more reactive. Such metals occupy higher positions in the activity series. On the other hand, the metals having high ionization energy do not lose electrons easily and hence are less reactive. Such metals occupy lower positions in the activity series.

Significance of Activity Series

1. The metals above hydrogen in the activity series have greater tendency than hydrogen to give up electrons in their solutions. Such metals are called electropositive metals.
   For example, potassium (K), the first metal in the series is the most electropositive, while gold (Au), the last metal of the series is the least electropositive.
2. The metals above hydrogen in the series can liberate hydrogen when treated with an acid solution. Thus, magnesium and zinc react with dilute solutions of sulphuric acid to produce hydrogen gas.
   $Mg + H_2SO_4 \longrightarrow MgSO_4 + H_2$; $Zn + H_2SO_4 \longrightarrow ZnSO_4 + H_2$
3. A more electropositive metal can replace a less electropositive metal from the solution of a salt of the less electropositive metal. For example, when an iron rod is dipped into a solution of copper sulphate, reddish coloured copper is deposited on the iron rod.
   $Fe + CuSO_4 \longrightarrow FeSO_4 + Cu$
   This is because iron is more electropositive than copper.

Example **:**

Four students A, B, C and D noted that initial colour of the solutions in beakers I, II, III and IV. After inserting zinc rods in each solution and leaving it undisturbed for two hours, noted the colour of each solution again.

$Al_2(SO_4)_3$

$ZnSO_4$

$FeSO_4$

$CuSO_4$

They recorded their observations in the form of table given below:

Student	Colour of the solution	I	II	III	IV
A	Initial Final	Colourless Colourless	Colourless Colourless	Light green Colourless	Blue Colourless
B	Initial Final	Colourless Colourless	Light Yellow Colourless	Light green Light green	Blue Colourless
C	Initial Final	Colourless Light blue	Colourless Colourless	Light green Colourless	Blue Light Blue
D	Initial Final	Light green Colourless	Colourless Colourless	Light green Dark green	Blue Colourless

Which students made the correct observation in all the four beakers?

Solution :

The student A had recorded the correct observations in all the four beakers.

(i) In beaker I, zinc is not in a position to displace aluminium metal, since it is placed below it. Therefore, the solution will remain colourless.

(ii) In beaker II, zinc is in contact with $ZnSO_4$. Therefore, no chemical reaction is possible. The solution will remain colourless.

(iii) In beaker III, zinc will displace iron present in ferrous sulphate solution (light green) to form zinc sulphate which is colourless.

(iv) In beaker IV, zinc will displace copper from copper sulphate solution (blue) to form zinc sulphate which is colourless.

From the above discussion, it is quite clear that the student A has made correct observations initially and also after the experiment.

(VII) Reaction of Metals with Non-Metals

We learnt that noble gases, which have a completely filled valence shell, show little chemical activity. We, therefore, explain the reactivity of elements as a tendency to attain a completely filled valence shell.

We know that a sodium atom has one electron in its outermost shell. If it loses the electron from its M shell then its L shell now becomes the outermost shell and that has a stable octet. The nucleus of this atom still has 11 protons but the number of electrons has become 10, So there is a net positive charge giving us a sodium cation Na^+ .On the other hand chlorine has seven electrons in its ourtermost shell and it requires one more electron to complete its octet. If sodium and chlorine were to react, the electrons lost by sodium could be taken up by chlorine. After gaining an electron, the chlorine atom gets a unit negative charge, because its nucleus has 17 protons and there are 18 electrons in its K, L and M shells. This gives us a chloride anion Cl^-.

So both these elements can have a give and take relation between them as follows.

$$\underset{2,\,8,1}{Na} \longrightarrow \underset{\substack{2,\,8 \\ \text{(Sodium cation)}}}{Na^+} + e^-$$

$$\underset{2,\,8,7}{Cl} + e^- \longrightarrow \underset{\substack{2,8,8 \\ \text{(chloride anion)}}}{Cl^-}$$

$$\dot{Na} + :\overset{\times\times}{\underset{\times\times}{Cl}}\overset{\times}{_\times} \rightarrow (Na^+)\,[:\overset{\times\times}{\underset{\times\times}{Cl}}\overset{\times}{_\times}]^-$$

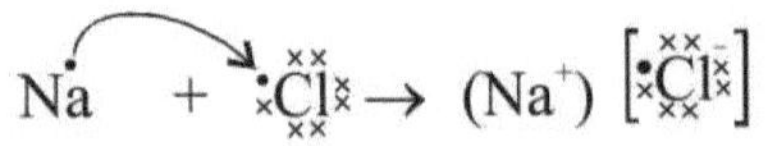

Sodium and chloride ions, being oppositely charged, attract each other and are held by strong electrostatic forces of attraction to exist as sodium chloride (NaCl). It should be noted that sodium chloride does not exist as molecules but aggregates of oppositely charged ions.

Let us see the formation of one more ionic compound, magnesium chloride

$$\underset{2,8,2}{Mg} \longrightarrow \underset{\substack{2,8 \\ \text{(Magnesium cation)}}}{Mg^{2+}} + 2e^-$$

$$\underset{2,8,7}{Cl} + e^- \longrightarrow \underset{\substack{2,8,8 \\ \text{(Chloride anion)}}}{Cl^-}$$

$$Mg: + \begin{matrix} :\overset{\times\times}{\underset{\times\times}{Cl}}\overset{\times}{_\times} \\ :\overset{\times\times}{\underset{\times\times}{Cl}}\overset{\times}{_\times} \end{matrix} \longrightarrow (Mg^{2+})\,[:\overset{\times\times}{\underset{\times\times}{Cl}}\overset{\times}{_\times}]^-_2$$

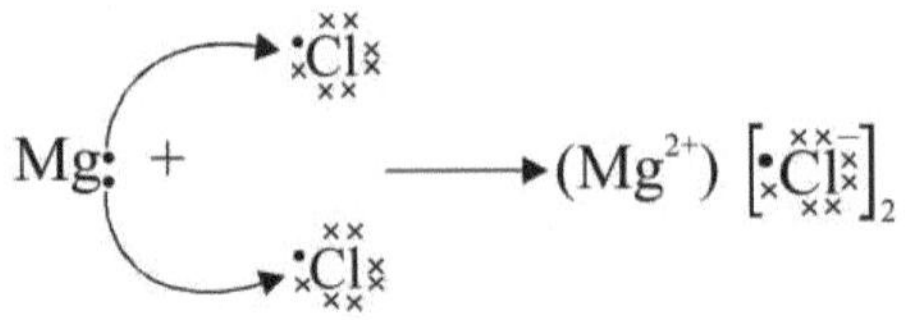

Knowledge Enhancer

(i) The symbols of the elements showing valence electrons with the help of dots (even crosses can be used) in their atoms are known as Lewis symbols which have been used in the formation of ionic bonds are Lewis symbols. For example, Lewis symbols of sodium and magnesium are $\dot{Na}$ and $\dot{\underset{\bullet}{M}}g$ respectively. Similarly Lewis symbols of fluorine and oxygen are $:\dot{\underset{\bullet\bullet}{F}}:$ and $:\dot{\underset{\bullet}{O}}:$ respectively.

(ii) Lewis symbols are normally used only when the atoms are to take part in the bond formation. Ordinary symbols are used when the atoms take part in chemical reactions.

(iii) The number of electrons which an atom either loses or gains in the formation of ionic bond, is known as its valency or electrovalency.

(iv) If an atom loses electrons, its electrovalency is positive. For example, electrovalency of Na is 1+ and that of Ca and Mg are 2+ .

(v) If an atom gains electrons, its electrovalency is negative. For example, electrovalency of Cl is 1– while that of O is 2– .

Illustration 3

The element A and B having electronic configuration 2,8,1 and 2, 8,7 respectively. Which one of them is a metal and which is a non-metal?

Solution

The element A has only one electron in its outermost shell (All inner shells being complete). Therefore, the element A is a metal.

The element B has seven electron in its outermost shell (all inner shells being complete). Therefore, the element B is a non-metal.

Try yourself

4. Which of the following is a metal

(A) ${}^{7}_{3}X$ (B) ${}^{3}_{1}Y$ (C) ${}^{10}_{9}Z$

5. Name any two metal oxide which are amphoteric

3.3 OCCURENCE OF METALS IN NATURE :

A metal is said to occur native or free when it is found in nature in the metallic state. Those metals which remain unaffected by moisture, oxygen and carbon dioxide of the air can occur native or free.

The reactive metals, i.e., the metals which react with moisture, oxygen, carbon dioxide or other chemical reagents, are not found in nature in free state, but in combined state in the form of compounds.

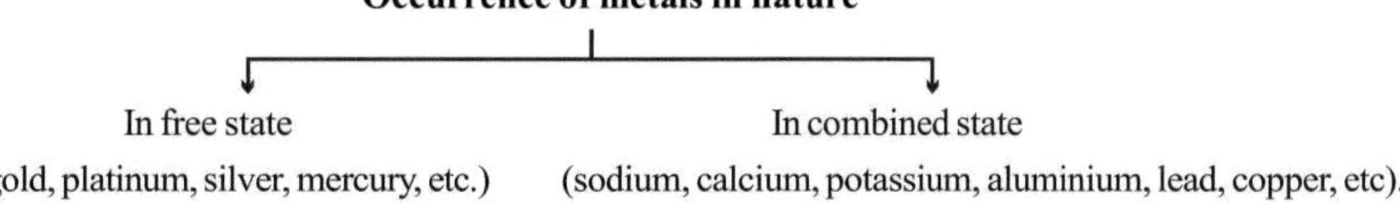

3.3.1 MINERALS AND ORES

Minerals:

Metal-bearing substances, found in the earths crust, are called minerals. In other words, the solid compounds of metals occurring in nature are called minerals.

Metals can also be classified in terms of their nature and behaviour. For example, metals resembling iron in properties like manganese, chromium, nickel are ferrous metals. They have a similar magnetic behaviour like iron and can be used for preparing **magnets**.

Ores:

The minerals from which metals can be obtained on a commercial scale are called ores. In other words, the minerals from which metals can be extracted profitably are called ores.

For example, Earth's crust contains aluminium in the form of two well known minerals bauxite ($Al_2O_3 . 2H_2O$) and china clay (Al_2O_3, $2SiO_2 . 2H_2O$). But the extraction of aluminium is cheaper and easier from bauxite. Hence, ore of aluminium is bauxite.

Thus it can be concluded that –

(i) All ores are minerals, but all minerals are not ores.

(ii) An ore is rich in the amount of the metal. The amount of foreign materials or impurities is low in an ore.

Elements	Ores
Iron	Haematite (Fe_2O_3), Magnetite ($FeO. Fe_2O_3$), Iron pyrites (FeS_2)
Aluminium	Bauxite ($Al_2O_3 . 2H_2O$)
Calcium	Limestone ($CaCO_3$)
Magnesium	Dolomite ($MgCO_3 . CaCO_3$)
Copper	Copper pyrites ($CuFeS_2$)
Mercury	Cinnabar (HgS)
Zinc	Zinc blende (ZnS), Calamine ($ZnCO_3$)
Lead	Lead glance (PbS)
Sodium	Rock salt ($NaCl$)
Silver	Horn silver ($AgCl$)

Flux :

A flux is a substance that is added to the furnace charge (roasted or calcined ore and coke) during the process of smelting to remove the nonfusible impurities present in the ore.

Slag :

Flux combines with the nonfusible impurities to convert them into a fusible substance known as slag. Impurities present in metal oxides may be acidic or basic. For acidic impurities, such as SiO_2 or P_2O_5, a basic flux (e.g., CaO) is added to the mixture during smelting. If basic impurities such as MnO are present, silica is added to the flux.

Impurity		**Flux**	**Slag**
SiO_2	+	CaO	$\longrightarrow CaSiO_3$
P_2O_5	+	$3CaO$	$\longrightarrow Ca_3(PO_4)_2$
MnO	+	SiO_2	$\longrightarrow MnSiO_3$.

Gangue or Matrix :

The ore mined from the earth's crust contains some unwanted substances or impurities, such as sand, rocky or clay materials. These substances are called **gangue or matrix.**

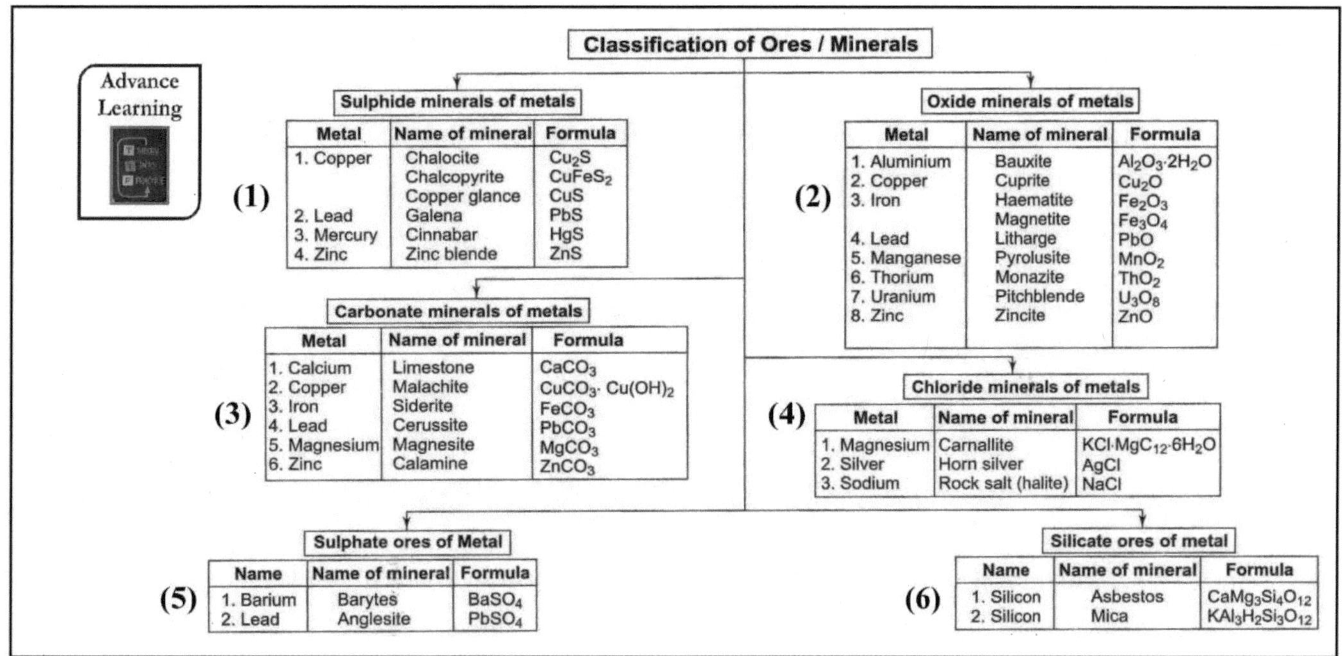
Advance Learning

Classification of Ores / Minerals

(1) Sulphide minerals of metals

Metal	Name of mineral	Formula
1. Copper	Chalocite	Cu_2S
	Chalcopyrite	$CuFeS_2$
	Copper glance	CuS
2. Lead	Galena	PbS
3. Mercury	Cinnabar	HgS
4. Zinc	Zinc blende	ZnS

(2) Oxide minerals of metals

Metal	Name of mineral	Formula
1. Aluminium	Bauxite	$Al_2O_3 \cdot 2H_2O$
2. Copper	Cuprite	Cu_2O
3. Iron	Haematite	Fe_2O_3
	Magnetite	Fe_3O_4
4. Lead	Litharge	PbO
5. Manganese	Pyrolusite	MnO_2
6. Thorium	Monazite	ThO_2
7. Uranium	Pitchblende	U_3O_8
8. Zinc	Zincite	ZnO

(3) Carbonate minerals of metals

Metal	Name of mineral	Formula
1. Calcium	Limestone	$CaCO_3$
2. Copper	Malachite	$CuCO_3 \cdot Cu(OH)_2$
3. Iron	Siderite	$FeCO_3$
4. Lead	Cerussite	$PbCO_3$
5. Magnesium	Magnesite	$MgCO_3$
6. Zinc	Calamine	$ZnCO_3$

(4) Chloride minerals of metals

Metal	Name of mineral	Formula
1. Magnesium	Carnallite	$KCl \cdot MgC_{12} \cdot 6H_2O$
2. Silver	Horn silver	$AgCl$
3. Sodium	Rock salt (halite)	$NaCl$

(5) Sulphate ores of Metal

Name	Name of mineral	Formula
1. Barium	Barytes	$BaSO_4$
2. Lead	Anglesite	$PbSO_4$

(6) Silicate ores of metal

Name	Name of mineral	Formula
1. Silicon	Asbestos	$CaMg_3Si_4O_{12}$
2. Silicon	Mica	$KAl_3H_2Si_3O_{12}$

Remember

(i) Aluminium is the most abundant metal in the earth's crust.

(ii) All minerals of a metal cannot be used for extraction of the metal.

3.4 METALLURGY:

The process of extracting metals from their ores and refining them for use is known as metallurgy. In other words, the process of obtaining a metal from its ores is called metallurgy of the metal.

Metallurgical Operations

The various steps used in metallurgy are :

(1) Enrichment or dressing of the ore.

(2) Conversion of the enriched ore into the oxide of metal.

(3) Extraction of metal from the metal oxide.

(4) Refining or purification of the metal.

(1) Enrichment of Ores :

Ores mined from the earth are usually contaminated with large amounts of impurities such as soil, sand, etc., called **gangue or matrix**. The impurities must be removed from the ore prior to the extraction of the metal. The processes used for removing the gangue from the ore are based on the differences between the physical or chemical properties of the gangue and the ore. Different separation techniques are accordingly employed.

(i) Hydraulic washing ; (ii) Froth floatation;

(iii) Magnetic separation; (iv) Chemical separation/ reaching

(2) Conversion of the enriched ore into the oxide of metal

After concentration the ore is generally subjected to calcination or roasting, depending upon nature of ore.

Calcination : It is the process of heating the ore in a limited supply of air, at a temperature below its melting point.

(i) Volatile impurities are expelled.

(ii) Moisture is expelled.

(iii) Carbonate ores changes into oxide ores.

$$\underset{\text{Bauxite}}{Al_2O_3.2H_2O(s)} \longrightarrow Al_2O_3(s) + 2H_2O(g)$$

$$ZnCO_3(s) \longrightarrow \underset{\text{Calamine}}{ZnO(s)} + CO_2(g)$$

Calcination is carried out in case of carbonate ores or hydrates of oxide ores.

Roasting : It is the process of heating the ore in the excess supply of air, at a temperature below it melting point.

This process results in the following changes.

(i) Volatile impurities are expelled.

(ii) Moisture is expelled

(iii) Sulphide ores change into oxides

$$\underset{\text{Zinc blende}}{2ZnS} + 3O_2 \longrightarrow 2ZnO + 2SO_2$$

Both calcination and roasting are carried out in a special type of furnace called reverberatory furnace.

(3) Extraction of metals from metal oxide :

(A) Extracting Metals Low in the Activity Series

Metals low in the activity series are very unreactive. The oxides of these metals can be reduced to metals by heating alone. For example, cinnabar (HgS) is an ore of mercury. When it is heated in air, it is first converted into mercuric oxide (HgO). Mercuric oxide is then reduced to mercury on further heating.

$$2HgS\ (s) + 3O_2\ (g) \xrightarrow{\text{Heat}} 2HgO\ (s) + 2SO_2\ (g)$$

$$2HgO\ (s) \xrightarrow{\text{Heat}} 2Hg\ (l) + O_2\ (g)$$

Similarly, copper which is found as Cu_2S in nature can be obtained from its ore by just heating in air.

$$2Cu_2S + 2O_2\ (g) \xrightarrow{\text{Heat}} 2Cu_2O\ (s) + 2SO_2\ (g)$$

$$2Cu_2O + Cu_2S \xrightarrow{\text{Heat}} 6Cu\ (s) + SO_2\ (g)$$

(B) Extracting Metals in the Middle of the Activity Series

The metals in the middle of the activity series such as iron, zinc, lead, copper, etc., are moderately reactive. These are usually present as sulphides or carbonates in nature. It is easier to obtain a metal from its oxide, as compared to its sulphides and carbonates. Therefore, prior to reduction, the metal sulphides and carbonates must be converted into metal oxides.

The process of obtaining metals from their compounds is known as reduction. Before reduction the ore is subjected to **roasting and calcination.** The sulphide ores are converted into oxides by heating strongly in presence of excess of air. The process is known as **roasting**. The carbonate ores are changed into oxides by heating strongly in absence of excess of air.

Roasting –

$$2ZnS(s) + 3O_2(g) \longrightarrow 2\,ZnO(s) + 2\,SO_2(g)$$

Calcination –

$$ZnCO_3(s) \longrightarrow ZnO(s) + CO_2(g)$$

(4) Refining or purification of the metal.

(i) Distillation; (ii) Liquation; (iii) Poling Electrolytic Refining

3.5 METALLURGY IN DETAIL:

3.5.1 CONCENTRATION OF ORE

The process of removal of the gangue particle from the ore is called dressing (or) concentration (or) benefaction.

It can be classified into various types, depending upon the nature of impurities

(I) Hand picking;
(II) Hydraulic washing (or) gravity separation (or) levigation
(III) Magnetic separation ;
(IV) Froth floatation;
(V) Leaching (or) chemical separation

(I) Hand picking : If ore particles and impurities (gangue) are different in size & shape, hand picking process can be used to separate it.

For example, Haematite ore is purified by this method

(II) Hydraulic washing (or) gravity separation (or) levigation: This method is based on the difference in specific gravity of the ore & gangue particle. Gangue particles are lighter than the ore particles.

In this method the ore is mixed with water (or) washed with an upward stream of running water, the lighter gangue particles are washed leaving behind the ore particles.

For example, this method is used for concentration of the oxide ores of Iron (Haematite), Tin (Tinstone), Au & Ag etc.

(III) Magnetic separation : If ore or gangue particles are having magnetic nature, then it is concentrated by this method.

This method is based on the difference in the magnetic properties of the ore and the gangue. This method can be applied when either the ore is magnetic or the impurities are magnetic. The other component should be non-magnetic.

Ex. Magnetite, an ore of iron is enriched by applying this method. Here, the ore particle are attracted by the magnetic roller. Similarly, tungstates of iron (impurity) are removed from tin stone (an ore of tin) by this method.

In this method, the powdered, impure ore is dropped over a travelling belt moving around two rollers, one of which has a magnet attached to it. As the impure ore particles roll over the left, the magnetic particles are attracted by the magnetic roller & ore collected just below the magnetic roller, But the non-magnetic particle fall away from the magnetic rollers.

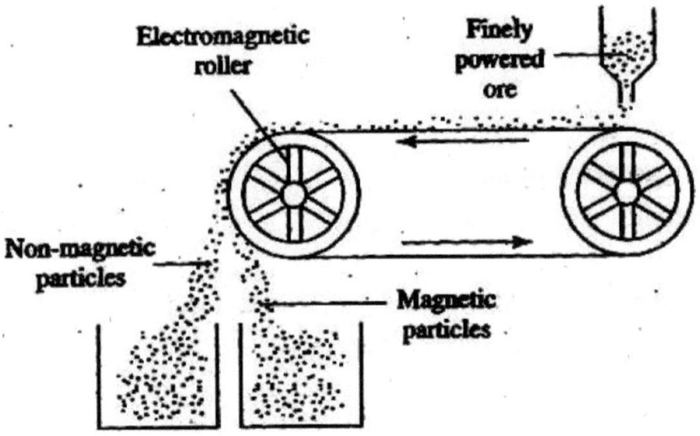

(Fig. Magnetic Separation)

(IV) Froth flotation process : It is used for separating impurities from the sulfide ores. Copper pyrities ($CuFeS_2$), galena (PbS) & zinc blende (ZnS) are concentrated by using this method.

This process based upon the fact that the surface of sulphide ore is wetted by oils, while gange is wetted by water.

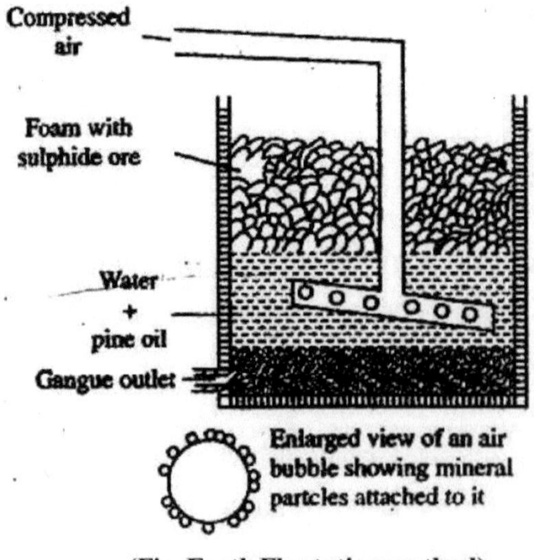

(Fig. Froth Floatation method)

This method is generally applied for the concentration of the sulphide ores. The finely crushed ore is taken in a tank filled with water and a little (about 1%) pine oil or mineral oil is added. A small quantity of a substance such as soap (called collector) is also added. The whole mass is vigorously stirred by passing compressed air (figure) through it when froth is produced. The ore particles get preferentially wetted by the oil while the gangue particles are wetted by the water. The ore thus rises to the top alongwith the froth and can be skimmed off easily. The gangue particles are left behind. The froth containing ore particles is washed with water to recover the concentrated ore. This method is used to concentrate the sulphide ores of copper, lead and zinc.

(V) Leaching (or) chemical separation

This method is based on difference between the chemical properties of the ore and the gangue. The process consists of treatment of the powdered ore with a suitable reagent (such as acids, base (or) other reagents) which can Selectively dissolve, the ore but not the impurities.

Ex: Baeyer's process: pure aluminium oxide is obtained from the Bauxite ore (containing Fe_2O_3 & silicates) by leaching. The powdered ore is treated with concentrated solution of NaOH (base) where Al_2O_3 dissolves in the form of sodium aluminate leaving behind the impurities which can be separated by filtration..

$$Al_2O_3\,(s) + 2NaOH\,(aq) + H_2O\,(l) \longrightarrow \underset{\text{sodium aluminate}}{2NaAlO_2\,(aq)} + H_2O\,(l)$$

Sodium aluminate on dilution (or) by neutralisation with CO_2 gives Aluminium hydroxide (ppt).

$$2NaAlO_2\,(aq) + 2H_2O\,(l) \xrightarrow[\text{(or)}CO_2]{\text{Dilution}} \underset{\text{white ppt}}{Al(OH)_3\,(s)\downarrow} + NaOH\,(aq)$$

$Al(OH)_3$ on heating gives pure alumina.

$$2Al(OH)_3 \xrightarrow{1473\,K} Al_2O_3 + 3H_2O$$

Leaching is also used for extracting metals like Au & Ag by converting these metals (or) their ores into soluble complexes with the help of NaCN (or) KCN (Dilute solution)

$$Ag_2S + NaCN \longrightarrow \underset{\substack{\text{sodium dicyano argentate (I)}\\ \text{(soluble complex)}}}{2Na[Ag(CN)_2]} + Na_2S$$

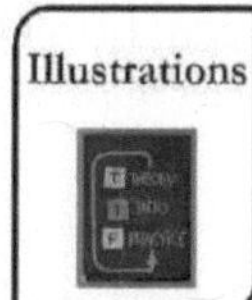

Illustration 4

Define Mineral, Ore and Gangue

Solution

Mineral: The inorganic compounds which occurs naturally in the earth crust are known as minerals for example, $CuFeS_2$, Copper pyrites

Ore: The minerals from which metals can be profitably and conveniently extracted are known as ore, for example, Fe_2O_3 haematite

Gangue: The impurities present in ore is known as gangue for example, SiO_2

3.5.2 CHEMICAL REDUCTION

(I) Before reduction the ore is subjected to roasting and calcination (as discussed earlier)

It is carried by using carbon (or) hydrogen (or) aluminium as reducing agents.

(A) Carbon as a reducing agent (i.e. smelting)

The reduction of metal oxides with carbon is known as smelting. The roasted (or) calcined ore mixed with carbon (in the form of coal, coke (or) charcoal) and heated to a temperature above its melting point in a furnace.

$$MO + C \longrightarrow M + CO$$

Ex: $ZnO\,(s) + C\,(s) \longrightarrow Zn\,(s) + CO\,(g)\uparrow$

$$\underset{\text{Cassiterite}}{SnO_2\,(s)} + 2C\,(s) \xrightarrow[1573\,K]{1437\text{ to}} Sn + 2CO\,(g)\uparrow$$

The carbon monoxide produced can also bring about the reduction of metal oxide to free metal.

Ex: $ZnO + CO \longrightarrow Zn + CO_2\uparrow$

$Fe_2O_3 + CO \longrightarrow 2FeO + CO_2\uparrow$

$FeO + CO \longrightarrow Fe + CO_2\uparrow$

Important application for carbon reduction is to extract the Iron which is carried out in a blast furnace.

(B) Hydrogen as a reducing agent

Metals like W, Mo $\longrightarrow$ Cannot be reduced by carbon

They can be reduced by passing a current of hydrogen

$$WO_3 + 3H_2 \longrightarrow W + 3H_2O$$

Hydrogen is rarely used as reducing agent, because it is highly expensive & also inflammable.

(II) Reduction with aluminium:

Certain metal oxides such as Cr_2O_3 and MnO_2 are not easily reduced with carbon. In such cases, aluminium is used as reducing agent because it is more electropositive than chrominum or manganese. The process of reducing of oxides with aluminium is called Aluminothermy. Some examples are :

$$Cr_2O_3(s) + 2Al(s) \longrightarrow Al_2O_3(s) + 2Cr(l)$$

$$3MnO_2(s) + 4Al(s) \longrightarrow 2Al_2O_3(s) + 3Mn(l)$$

The reduction of oxides of metals using aluminium as reducing agent is a highly exothermic reaction. The heat produced during the reaction is sufficient to melt the metal. Hence, the metal is produced in the molten state.

Aluminothermic process is sometimes used for welding metals. For example, the reaction Fe_2O_3 with aluminium is used to join railway tracks or cracked machine parts.

$$Fe_2O_3 + 2Al(s) \longrightarrow \underset{\text{Molten iron}}{2Fe(l)} + Al_2O_3(s)$$

This reaction known as thermite or thermite reaction.

(III) Reduction with Magnesium

In some cases, the reduction is carried out by alkaline earth elements like magnesium.

$$\underset{\text{Titanium tetrachloride}}{TiCl_4} + 2Mg \longrightarrow 2MgCl_2 + Ti$$

(IV) Electrolytic Reduction

The highly electropositive metals (that is the metals occupying higher positions in the reactivity series) such as sodium, calcium, magnesium, etc. cannot be obtained by chemical reduction methods. Such metals are extracted by the electrolytic reduction. In order to obtain these metals their salts are electrolysed in fused state. The commonly used salts are halides. For example, sodium metal is extracted by electrolysis of molten sodium chloride. The chlorine gas is liberated at anode (the positively charged electrode) whereas sodium metal is liberated at cathode (the negatively charged electrode).

$$NaCl \longrightarrow Na^+ + Cl^-$$

At anode : $2Cl^- \longrightarrow Cl_2 + 2e^-$

At cathode : $2Na^+ + 2e^- \longrightarrow 2Na$

The overall reaction may be represented as :

$$2NaCl \xrightarrow{\text{Electrolysis}} 2Na + Cl_2$$

Similarly, aluminium is obtained by electrolytic reduction of aluminium oxide (Al_2O_3) dissolved in molten cryolite (Na_3AlF_6) using graphite electrodes. The reactions taking place are:

At cathode : $Al^{3+} + 3e^- \longrightarrow Al(l)$

At anode: $2O^{2-} \longrightarrow O_2(g) + 4e^-$

$$2C(s) + O_2(s) \longrightarrow 2CO(g)$$

$$2CO(s) + O_2(s) \longrightarrow 2CO_2(g)$$

Thus, on the basis of reactivity we can group the metals into the following three categories:

(i) Metals of low reactivity; (ii) Metals of medium reactivity; (iii) Metals of high reactivity

Different reduction processes are to be used for obtaining the metals falling in each category.

The relation between the reduction process employed and the position of the metals in the activity series is depicted in table.

Table : Position of the metal in the Activity Series and the Related Reduction Process

Position in the Activity Series	Element	Reduction Process
Metals found near the top of the activity series	K, Na, Ca, Mg, Al	Electrolysis
Metals found in the middle of the activity series	Zn, Fe, Pb	Reduction using carbon or some other reducing agent
Metals found in the lower regions of the activity series	Cu, Hg, Ag	Reduction by heat alone
Metals found at the bottom of the activity series	Pt, Au	Found in native state

3.5.3 REFINING (OR) PURIFICATION OF METALS

The process of purifying the crude metal is called refining depends upon nature of the metal & nature of impurities following methods are used

(a) Distillation (b) Liquation (c) Oxidation (d) Electro-refining
(e) Zone refining (f) Fractional crystallisation (g) Vapour phase refining

(a) Distillation: Based upon boiling point difference

Distillation is a method of heating impure liquid to its boiling point & cooling the vapours to get the pure liquid.

Low boiling metal like, Zn, Hg, Cd etc can be refined by this method. The impure metal is heated so it is converted into liquid & the pure metal is converted into vapors, leaving the non-volatile impurities in the container, the pure metal vapours on cooling condensed into pure metal.

(b) Liquation process: Based upon melting point difference

When the M.P. of the metal is lower than the impurities, this technique is used.

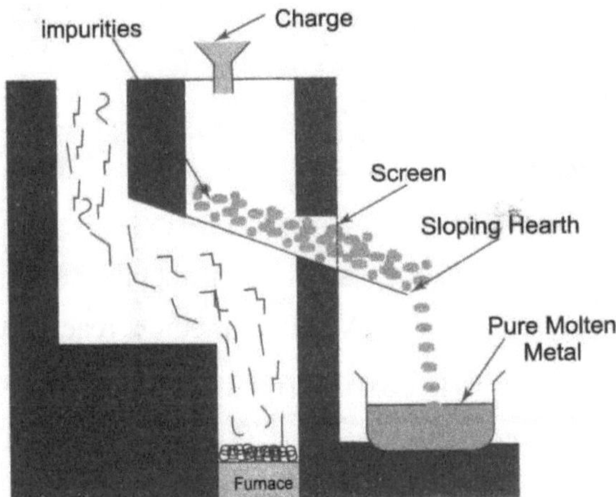

Low melting point metals such as Bi, Hg, Sn, Pb etc are refined by the process.

The crude metal is heated in an inert atmosphere of carbon monoxide on slopping hearth. The metal, melts & flows down the hearth, leaving behind the high melting impuries.

(c) Oxidation process: If impurities have greater affinity for oxygen (or) impurities are oxidised more readily than the metal.

Ex: Cu, Ag, Sn, etc.

(i) Bassemerisation: This is carried out in a specially designed furnace called Bessemer converter. The impure metal is melted & a hot blast of air is passed through it. Impurities are removed as volatile oxides which escapes out.

(ii) Cupellation: This method is used, when the impure metal contain the impurities of other metals, which form volatile oxides. The crude metal is taken in a boat shaped pan and a blast of air is blown into it. The impurities are converted into volatile oxides which escapes.

This process is used for removing the impurities of lead from silver.

(iii) **Poling**: If crude metal contains impurties of the oxide of the metal itself. The crude metal is melted in a big container and is stirred with green poles of wood. Gaseous hydrocarbons (CH_4, C_2H_6 etc.) released from the green poles reduce the oxides of the metal to the pure state by taking up oxygen.

Crude copper (i.e. blister copper) having the impurities

$$3Cu_2O + CH_4 \longrightarrow 6Cu + 2H_2O + CO$$

Stannic oxide is also purified by this method.

(d) **Electro-refining**: Used for Cu, Au, Ag, Pb, Zn & Al. In this method

The impure metal act as Anode & pure metal strip is taken as Cathode (both are same metals), these electrodes are suspended in an electrolyte, (soluble salt of the same metals).

On passing electric current, metal ions from the electrolyte are reduced to metal, which is deposited on the cathode in the form of pure metal & an equivalent. Amount of metal from the anode goes into the electrolyte solution.

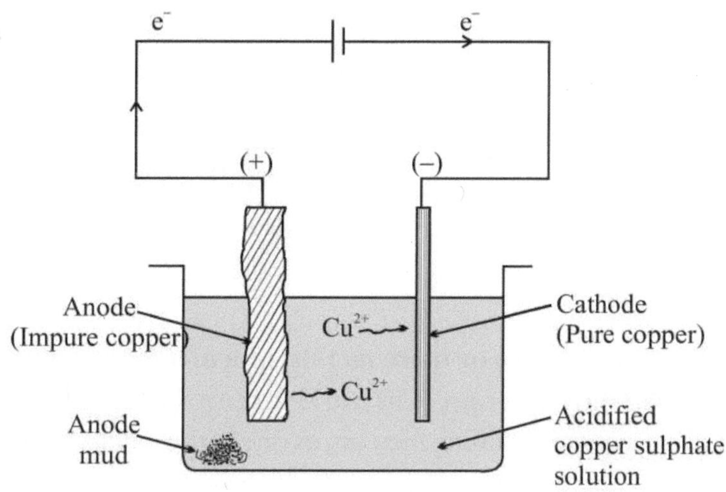

At Anode: M(Impure) $\rightarrow M^{n+} + ne^-$

At Cathode: $M^{n+} + ne^- \rightarrow$ M (pure)

Ex: In the electrolysis of copper, metals like Zn remains in the solution as cations.

Where as metals such as Au, Ag etc form the Anode mud because its lie lower in activity series with respect to Zn.

(e) **Zone refining (or) Fractional distillation**: The method is based on the principle that when an impure metal in the molten state is allowed to cool, only the metal crystallises, while the impurities remain in the molten mass (or) melt (Impurities are more soluble).

This method gives high purity, metals like Ga, In, Si which are used in semi conductors are purified by this method.

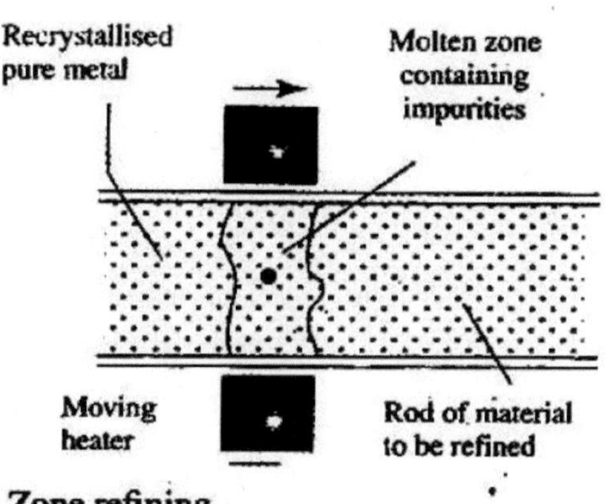

Zone refining.

The impure metal is converted into a rod which is heated at one end with a moving circular heater. As the heater is slowly moved along the length of the rod, the pure metal crystallises out of the melt, where as the impurites pass into the adjacent molten zone. This process is repeated number of times till the impurities are driven completely towards one end and the pure metal towards the other end. The entire process is carried out in an inert atmosphere to prevent the oxidation of the metal.

(f) **Vapour phase refining**: The crude metal is heated with specific reagent at low temperature, so that it is converted into unstable volatile compound, leaving behind the impurities. The unstable voltatile compound is decomposed at a high temperature to give the pure metal.
It is two types:

(i) **Mond process**: Mond process is used for refining of Nickle. Impure Nickle is heated with carbon monoxide to form volatile Nickle carbonyl, leaving behind the impurities.

$$\underset{}{\text{Ni (Impure)}} + 4CO \xrightarrow{330\text{-}350\text{ K}} \underset{\text{vapor}}{[Ni(CO)_4]} \xrightarrow{\Delta} \underset{\text{pure}}{Ni} + 4CO$$

(ii) **Van-Arkel method**: The impure metal heated with Iodine-vapors at high temperature to give vapors of metallic tetra iodide, (unstable). At high temperature these are decomposed to give pure metal. Zirconium (Zr) & Titanium (Ti) are purified by this method

$$\underset{\text{Im pure}}{Ti} + \underset{\text{Vapours}}{2I_2} \xrightarrow[50-250°C]{500\text{ k}} \underset{\text{Vapours}}{TiI_4} \xrightarrow[1400°C]{1700\text{ k}} \underset{\text{pure metal}}{Ti} + 2I_2$$

3.6 ALLOYS :

The homogeneous mixture of two or more metals, or a metal and a nonmetal is called an alloy. For examples, brass is an alloy of copper (Cu) and zinc (Zn). Similarly, steel is mainly an alloy of iron (Fe) and carbon (C). An alloys containing mercury as one of the metals is called an amalgum.

➢ **Preparation**

(i) Alloys are commonly prepared by melting the desired metals in proper proportions. The melt is allowed to cool and solidify. The solid substance formed is called an alloy.

(ii) By compressing together the various constituents of the alloys under high pressure.

(iii) By simultaneous electro deposition of metals.

➢ **Properties of Alloys**

Alloys have certain characteristic properties :

(i) They are harder than their constituents but less ductile and malleable.

(ii) They are resistant to corrosion.

(iii) The melting point of an alloy may be higher or lower than any of its constituents.

(iv) The properties of an alloy are much more improved and pronounced than those of its constituents. For example, aluminium is a light metal and it is not very strong. But Duralumin, an alloy of Aluminium, is light and very strong.

(v) The colour of an alloy is different from the metals from which it is formed. For example, both Silver and zinc are almost white but the alloy formed from them are pink in colour.

- **Types of alloys :** There are two types of alloys :
  - (i) **Ferrous Alloys :** These are the alloys which contain iron as one of the constituents, such as nickel steel, stainless steel etc.
  - (ii) **Non-ferrous Alloys :** These are the alloys which do not contain iron as one of the constituents such as bronze, brass etc.

Few Examples of Alloys

- **Alloys of Gold :** The purity of gold is expressed in carats. 24 carat gold is pure gold. But pure gold is very soft and, therefore, cannot be used in making ornaments or coins. It is generally alloyed with copper or silver to make it hard and useful. 22 carat gold means that the alloy contains 22 parts of gold in 24 parts of the alloy.
- **Amalgam :** An amalgam is an alloy of mercury and one or more metals. Most of the metals form amalgam with mercury. But iron and Platinum are noticable exceptions. Therefore, amalgams can be stored in iron bottles.

  Some of the amalgams are definite intermetallic compounds, such as sodium amalgam (NaHg), magnesium amalgam (MgHg), silver amalgam (Ag_5Hg_8), etc. Amalgams of sodium and aluminium are good reducing agents. Amalgam of silver, tin, Cadmium and copper have been utilized as dental fillings. Amalgams may be solid or liquid.
- **Alloy Steels**

  Steel : Steel is an alloy of iron and carbon, the carbon content being 0.15–1.7%. Small quantities of other elements such as manganese, silicon, chromium, Molybdenum, cobalt and nickel are added to impart desirable mechanical and chemical properties that cannot be obtained by using carbon alone. Such steels are known as **alloy steels.**

  Stainless Steel : Steel that contains over 11–12% of chromium is known as **stainless steel.** Stainless steel does not rust or stain. It is, therefore, used to serve a variety of purposes in industrial, chemical and domestic fields.

  A particularly useful alloy is the steel known as 18–8 which contains Cr (18%), Ni (8%) and C (0.08%). It is now apparent that the ingredient which is instrumental in influencing the properties of steel is carbon.

Alloys of Aluminium

Alloy	Percentage Composition	Uses
Magnallium	Al = 95%, Mg = 5%	Pressure cookers, balance beams some light instruments.
Duralumin	Al = 95%, Cu = 4%, Mg = 0.5%, Mn = 0.5%	Making parts of aeroplanes and automobiles, pressure cookers etc.

Alloys of Copper

Alloy	Percentage Composition	Uses
Bronze	Cu = 90, Sn = 10	For making statues, coins, utensils etc.
Brass	Cu = 80, Zn = 20	For making utensils, parts of machinery, condenser tubes, wires etc.
Gun metal	Cu = 90, Sn = 10	For making gun barrels.
Bell metal	Cu = 80, Sn = 20	For making bells and gongs.
German silver	Cu = 60, Zn = 20, Ni = 20	For making silver wares, resistance wires.
Phosphor bronze	Cu = 95, Sn = 4.8, P = 0.2	For making springs, electric switches.
Monel metal	Cu = 30, Ni = 67	For making corrosion resistant pumps and Fe and Mn = 3 containers for storing acids.

Alloys of Silver

Alloy	Percentage Composition	Uses
Coinage silver	Ag = 90, Cu = 10	For making silver coins.
Silver solder	Ag = 63, Cu = 30, Zn = 7	For soldering.
Dental alloy	Ag = 33, Hg = 52, Sn = 12.5 Cu = 2, Zn = 0.5	For filling teeth.

Alloys of Tin and Lead

Alloy	Percentage Composition	Uses
Solder	Pb = 50, Sn = 50	For soldering broken pieces.
Type metal	Pb = 70, Sb = 20, Sn = 10	For making printing type.

Alloys of Iron or Alloy Steels

Alloy	Percentage Composition	Uses
Stainless steel	Fe = 73, Cr = 18, Ni = 8 and C = 1	Utensile, cycle and automobile parts shaving blades, watch cases.
Nickel steel	Fe = 96 – 98, Ni = 2 – 4	Cables, automobile and aeroplane parts, armour plates, gears and drilling machines.
Alnico	Fe = 60, Ni = 20, Al = 12, Co = 8	Permanent magnets.
Chrome steel	Fe = 98, Cr = 2	Axels, ball bearings, files and cutting tools.

3.7 CORROSION OF METALS :

Slow destruction of metals due to chemical reactions on their surface by oxygen, carbon dioxide, moisture, sulphur dioxide, hydrogen sulphide, etc., of the atmosphere, is known as **corrosion of metals**.

Due to corrosion, small holes appear on the surface of the metal and the strength of the metal goes on decreasing. The process of corrosion is caused by the reaction of the metal with oxygen of air or with oxygen dissolved in water.

In corrosion, the metal atoms give up electrons (i.e. they are oxidized) and are converted into ions.

$$M \rightarrow M^{+} + e$$

The ions move from one part of the metal to another more easily in the presence of moisture. This is because moisture provides the medium through which ions can flow.

Factor Determining the Rate of Corrosion

The process of corrosion is speed up in the following circumstances.

1. **The metals are in contact with each other**

   The corrosion of a more electropositive metal is speed up when it is in contact with a less electropositive metal. Two metals form an electrochemical (galvanic) cell in the presence of moisture. Electrons begin to flow from the more electropositive (or more reactive) to the less electropositive (or less reactive) metal. Thus, the more electropositive metal is lost as ions. For example, when iron and copper are in contact, electrons flow from iron to copper because iron is more electropositive than copper. Thus, the more reactive metal iron forms ions. The process of iron going away as ions is slower in the absence of copper.

2. **Polluting materials in air**

   The air near industrial units is generally polluted with CO_2, SO_2, H_2S etc. Gases coming out of chimneys contain these gases in abundance. We know that these gases are also responsible for the corrosion of metals. Therefore, the process of corrosion is speed up in presence of these pollutants.

   (a) Silver articles become black after some time when exposed to air. This is because it reacts with sulphur in the air to form a coating of silver sulphide.

   (b) Copper reacts with moist carbon dioxide in the air and slowly loses its shiny brown surface and gains a green coat. This green substance is basic copper carbonate.

   (c) Iron when exposed to moist air for a long time acquires a coating of a brown flaky substance called rust.

(d) **Activity**

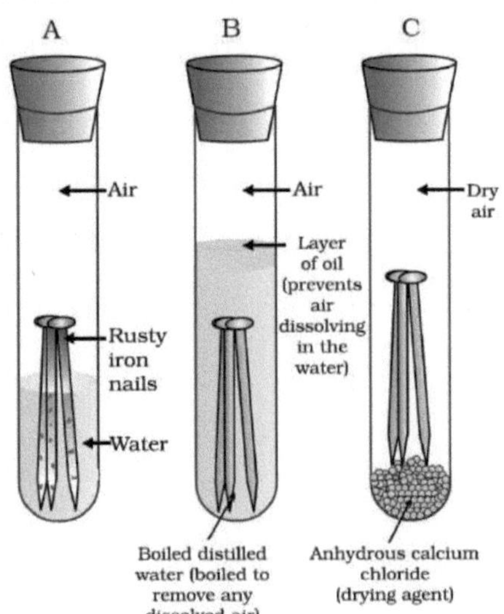

- Take three test tubes and place clean iron nails in each of them.
- Label these test tubes A, B and C. Pour some water in test tube A and cork it.
- Pour boiled distilled water in test tube B, add about 1 mL of oil and cork it. The oil will float on water and prevent the air from dissolving in the water.
- Put some anhydrous calcium chloride in test tube C and cork it. Anhydrous calcium chloride will absorb the moisture, if any, from the air.
- Leave these test tubes for a few days and then observe (figure). You will observe that iron nails rust in test tube A, but they do not rust in test tubes B and C. In the test tube A, the nails are exposed to both air and water. In the test tube B, the nails are exposed to only water, and the nails in test tube C are exposed to dry.

Preventive measures

The metallic surface can be coated with appropriate chemicals (ex: bisphenol, oxides etc.)

- Paints are very good corrosion-inhibitors. If they contain red lead zinc chromate or lead chromate. Since these forms the protective coatings.
- Concrete coating & phosphate coating (Fe & Mn-phophates) are very effective against atmospheric corrosion.
- Steel plants & nuclear plants etc are protected by the method of Anodic potential.
- Anodised 'Al' is resistant to corrosion. It is the reason that the bodies of the buses & cars have 'Al' strips around it.
- Glycol in coolant for automobiles is good corrosion inhibitor addition of small quantity of cyanovanador to the thermostats (or) radiators of cars can protect them from corrosion.
- Copper & Brass items can be protected by covering them with p-chlorobenzohydroxamic Acid.

Illustrations

Illustration 5

What is 24 carat gold? How will you convert it into 18 carat gold?

Solution

24 carat gold is pure gold. It is very soft for which reason it can not be used for making jewellery. To make it 18 carat, 18 parts of pure gold in alloyed with 6 parts of either silver or copper.

Illustration 6

What is rust ? Write its chemical formula?

Solution

The deposition of brown, flasy substance on the surface of iron is known as rust. Rust is mainly hydrated iron(III) oxide $Fe_2O_3.xH_2O$, $Fe(OH)_3$

$$Fe + H_2O + O_2 \rightarrow Fe_2O_3.xH_2O + Fe(OH)_3$$

Comparison of Pig Iron, Wrought Iron and Steel

Pig Iron	Wrought Iron	Steel
Composition		
1. Iron : upto 94 % 2. Carbon : 2.5–4.0% 3. Impurities : Less Than 2% (Si, P, S, Mg)	Almost pure iron Carbon : 0.1 – .25% Impurities : negligible	Less pure than wrought iron Carbon : 0.1–1.7% Impurities : negligible
Properties		
1. Hard, brittle, non-malleable, non-ductile.	Soft, tough, malleable, ductile, does not crack under strain.	Hardness depends on the carbon content, malleable and ductile.
2. Lacks tensile strength Cannot be welded, forged, tempered or shaped by hammering even while hot.	Can be welded, forged, tempered and by hammering while hot but has less strength than steel.	Can be welded, forged, tempered and shaped by hammering while hot. Has maximum tensile strength.
3. Does not rust easily.	Resists corrosion better than pig iron.	Ordinary steel rusts. Hence alloyed.
4. Has a low melting point (1200°C)	Melting point around 1500°C.	Melting point ranges between 1200 – 1500°C.

3.7.1 RUSTING

When iron is exposed to moist air, a reddish-brown coating of a mixture of ferric oxide (Fe_2O_3) and ferric hydroxide ($Fe(OH)_3$) is deposited on the surface of the metal. The slow conversion of iron into a mixture of Fe_2O_3 and $Fe(OH)_3$ by water and atmospheric oxygen is known as **rusting.**

Rusting of iron is an oxidation reaction that occurs due to the attack of water and oxygen. It has been found that rusting does not take place in air-free water. It also does not occur in presence of oxygen alone. Both water and oxygen are essential for rusting. Thus, the following conditions are necessary for rusting :

(i) Presence of oxygen or air (ii) Presence of water or moisture

The process of rusting is continuous. The strength of iron decreases gradually and finally the metal is destroyed completely.

(A) Prevention of Rusting

Iron can be prevented from rusting by the following ways :

1. Rusting of iron can be prevented by covering its surface with paint, grease, enamel, that does not allow air and moisture to come in contact with it and no rusting occurs. This is known as **barrier protection**.
2. Rusting of iron can be prevented by **galvanization**. Zinc metal does not corrode on exposure to air. So zinc coating protect iron from rusting. Zinc itself forms a protective coating of basic zinc carbonate [$Zn(OH)_2.ZnCO_3$].

3. Rusting can be prevented by coating the surface of iron object with chromium, tin, nickel or aluminium. These metals resist corrosion. Hence, they protect iron from rusting. They may be coated by **electroplating**.
4. Rusting can also be prevented by converting it into an alloy with chromium and nickel. This alloy is called **stainless steel**.
5. Rusting of iron can be prevented by coating it surface with iron (II, III) oxide, Fe_3O_4.
6. Rusting is prevented by **sacrificial protection** in which a more reactive metal is connected to iron objects so that the more reactive metal gets oxidized in preference to the iron object. For example, Mg or Zn being more reactive than Fe are connected to Fe, which are oxidized and said to be scarified. Iron pipes beneath the soil are protected by connecting them to rolls of magnesium (Mg) or Zinc sheets by Sacrificial Protection.

(B) Uses of Iron

1. Iron find wide application in house construction, eg. in the **reinforcement** of roofs and other parts of buildings.
2. Wrought iron and cast iron are largely used in the manufacture of locomotives, railway lines, springs, cubes, etc.
3. Iron has its important therapeutic uses in the treatment of **hypochromic anemias.** The iron deficiency condition impair the formation of haemoglobin and many other functions of red blood cells. Any of iron compounds may be used in therapy and inorganic salts are equally effective for the purpose.
4. All plants, animals and human beings require iron to live. The largest percentage of iron in human beings is present in red blood cells, which are main part of **haemoglobin**. Small quantities of iron are also found in muscles and tissues.
5. Iron is the basic material for thousands of manufactured goods from small pins to mammoth buildings. Iron combines readily with various non-metals such as sulphur and oxygen. Enormous quantities of iron metal is used producing **alloys**, eg. steel (one of the most useful and cheapest metals) is produced by adding a small amount of carbon to iron. Several precious stones, including topaz, turquoise and spinel also contain iron.

3.8 USES OF METALS

Metals are used in the form of pure metals, alloys and in the form of metal compounds.

3.8.1 USE OF PURE METALS

➢ **Zinc**:

(i) It is used to galvanise iron to prevent it from rusting.
(ii) It is used in making alloys such as brass and bronze.

➢ **Iron:** It is used as a catalyst in the manufacture of ammonia by the Haber's Process.

➢ **Mercury:** It is used in preparing amalgams.

➢ **Silver and Gold:**

(i) Both are used in making ornaments and jewellary.

(ii) Both are used in making coins.

➢ **Chromium and Nickel:**

(i) Both these metals are used in electroplating, cycle, motorcycle and other automobile parts.

(ii) They are mixed with other metals to prepare useful alloys.

➢ **Titanium**: Titanium is a light metal. It has a high melting point and boiling point. It is highly resistant to corrosion and has a high tensile strength, even higher than that of steel. Due to these properties, it has the following uses :

(i) Preparing steel for defence installations (military hardware) marine instruments, aircraft frames. Hence referred to as a **'strategic element'**.

(ii) Titanium is used in nuclear reaction.

(iii) Titanium is used for making strong structures for construction of buildings.

3.8.2 SOME IMPORTANT METALS COMPOUNDS USED IN DAILY LIFE :

➢ **Silver Nitrate ($AgNO_3$)** : It is also known as lunar caustic It is colourless, transparent, crystalline solid and soluble in water.

Uses :

(i) As laboratory reagent, (ii) In preparation of marking inks,

(iii) In photography (iv) In silvering of mirror,

(v) In manufacturing of other salts of silver.

➢ **Silver Bromide (AgBr)**: It is pale yellow coloured crystalline compound, insoluble in water.

Uses : In photography

➢ **Potash Alum** : ($K_2SO_4 . Al_2(SO_4)_3 24H_2O$)

Potash alum is a double salt of aluminum sulphate and potassium sulphate. It is soluble in water. In potash alum crystalline water is found in large amount, so on heating it expands in volume.

Uses: In softening of water.

➢ **Blue Vitrol or copper sulphate ($CuSO_4.5H_2O$)** :

Copper sulphate is also known as blue vitrol. It is blue coloured, crystalline substance. On heating it gradually releases the crystalline water

$$CuSO_4.5H_2O \xrightarrow{373\,K} CuSO_4.H_2O \xrightarrow{413K} CuSO_4 \xrightarrow{443K} CuO + SO_2$$

Uses :

(i) In electroplating (ii) In electric batteries.

(iii) The mixture of $CuSO_4$ and lime is known as bordeaux mixture, it is used as fungicide,

(iv) In dyeing of clothes , (v) In preservation of wood

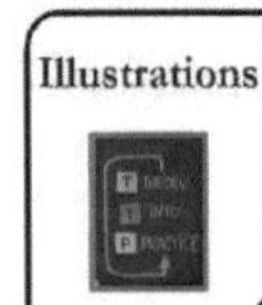

Illustration 7

In the manufacture of iron lime stone added to the blast furnace why?

Solution

Limestone mixed with charge get decomposed in to CaO and CO_2. Calcium oxide reacts with silica present in the ore to produce fusible slag.

$$\underset{\text{Lime}}{CaO} + \underset{\text{Silica}}{SiO_2} \rightarrow \underset{\text{Slag (Calcium silicate)}}{CaSiO_3}$$

Illustration 8

Give the formation of slag in the metallurgy of copper

Solution

$$\underset{\text{Impurity}}{FeO} + \underset{\text{flux}}{SiO_2} \rightarrow \underset{\text{Slag}}{FeSiO_3}$$

Try yourself

6. Which of the following is not an ore
   (A) Bauxite (B) Malachite (C) Zinc blende (D) Pig iron
7. Carbonates and sulphide ores are usually converted into oxide ores why?
8. Write down the chemical formula of compound
   (i) Potash alum (ii) Blue vitrol (iii) Lunar caustic

3.9 NON-METALS :

Important properties of Non-metals

1. **Physical state :** Either gases or solids at room temperature.
   Exception : Bromine (liquid at room temperature).
2. **Surface :** Non-metals vary in colour with generally **dull surfaces**.
   Exception : Diamond, Crystals of iodine have bright lustre.
3. **Conduction :** Mostly Poor conductors of heat and electricity.
   Exception : Graphite
4. **Hardness :** Quite Soft.
   Exception : Diamond
5. **Malleable :** Non-malleable and non-ductile.
6. **Not Sonorous.**
7. **Very low melting and boiling point** as compare to metals.
   Exception : Diamond.
8. **Reactivity :** They generally form acidic or neutral oxides with oxygen.

Non-Metals : Only 22 nonmetallic elements, of which 11 are gases, one is a liquid and the rest 10 are solids. Non-mentals are placed on the right-hand side of the periodic table.

At room temperature, non-metals are either solids or gases, except bromine, which is a liquid. Hydrogen (H_2), nitrogen (N_2), oxygen (O_2), chlorine (Cl_2) etc., are example of some gaseous non-metals. Carbon, sulphur (S_8), phosphorus (P_4), etc., are solids. **They play an important role in our daily life.**

(A) PHYSICAL PROPERTIES

1. Non-metallic solids are **brittle**. If they are hammered or stretched, they break into pieces. Carbon in the form of graphite is very soft.
2. Non-metals **do not have any lustre**, i.e., they do not have a shining surface. But **iodine**, which has a lustrous appearance, is an exception.
3. Non-metals are generally soft elements, except diamond (an allotropic form of carbon), which is the hardest known substance.
4. Non-metals do not conduct heat and electricity because unlike metals, they have no free electrons. But there is an exception. Graphite, an allotropic form of carbon, is a good conductor of electricity.

(B) CHEMICAL PROPERTIES

Due to energy considerations, non-metals cannot form positively charged ions by the loss of electrons. In fact, they form negatively charged ions (anions) by the gain of electrons. Hence, they are known as electronegative elements.

$Cl + e^- \longrightarrow Cl^-$; $O + 2e^- \longrightarrow O^{2-}$; $S + 2e^- \longrightarrow S^{2-}$.

(I) Reaction with Oxygen

Non-metals combine with oxygen to form oxides. These oxides are either acidic or neutral. They never form basic oxides. The non-metallic oxides are formed by sharing of electron pairs between the atoms of non-metal and oxygen. Hence, these are convalent compounds.

$$C(s) + O_2(g) \longrightarrow CO_2(g)$$

$$S(s) + O_2(g) \longrightarrow SO_2(g)$$

Both carbon dioxide (CO_2) and sulphur dioxide are acidic oxides. They dissolve in water to form acids.

$$P_2O_5(s) + 3H_2O(l) \longrightarrow 2H_3PO_4(aq)$$
(Phosphoric acid)

$$CO_2(g) + H_2O(l) \longrightarrow H_2CO_3(aq)$$
(Carbonic acid)

$$SO_2(g) + H_2O(l) \longrightarrow H_2SO_3(aq)$$
(Sulphurous acid)

Note : Certain oxides of non-metals are neutral. These oxides are neither acidic nor basic. These oxides donot have any effect on litmus paper.

Examples of neutral oxides are carbon monoxide (CO), nitrous oxide (N_2O), etc.

(II) Reaction with Acids

Non-metals do not displace hydrogen from dilute acids. For example, carbon or sulphur does not react with dilute acids. Hydrogen can only be displaced from dilute acids if electrons are supplied to the H^+ ions of the acid.

$$H_2SO_4\,(aq) \longrightarrow 2H^+\,(aq) + SO_4^{2-}\,(aq)$$

$$2H^+\,(aq) + 2e^- \longrightarrow H_2(g)$$

A non-metal is an electron acceptor. It cannot supply electrons to H^+ ions. Therefore, it does not displace hydrogen from dilute acids.

(III) Reaction with Chlorine

With chlorine, non-metals form covalent chlorides. The covalent chloride is generally a volatile liquid or a gas.

$$H_2(g) + Cl_2(g) \longrightarrow 2HCl\,(g)$$

(Hydrogen chloride)

$$P_4(s) + 6Cl_2(g) \longrightarrow 4PCl_3\,(g)$$

(Phosphorus trichloride)

$$P_4(s) + 10Cl_2(g) \longrightarrow 4PCl_5\,(l)$$

(Phosphorus pentachloride)

(IV) Reaction with Hydrogen

Non-metals combine with hydrogen to form hydrides. For example, ammonia (NH_3), methane (CH_4), hydrogen sulphide (H_2S), water (H_2O), etc. These hydrides are stable compounds and are formed by sharing of electron pairs between the non-metal and hydrogen.

$$N_2(g) + 3H_2(g) \longrightarrow 2NH_3(g)$$

$$H_2(g) + S(l) \longrightarrow H_2S(g)$$

$$2H_2(g) + O_2(s) \longrightarrow 2H_2O(l)$$

(water)

3.9.1 SULPHUR

Atomic number	:	16
Atomic mass	:	32
Electronic configuration	:	$1s^2\,2s^2\,2p^6\,3s^2\,3p^4$
Symbol	:	S
Valencies	:	$+2, +4$ and $+6$, while in some compounds -2.

Sulphur is known to man since ancient time. In Sanskrit, sulphur is known as 'sulvari' which means 'destroyer of copper'. This is because it destroys the metallic properties of copper. Lavoisier studied its properties and identified it as an clement Sulphur is found in nature in free state and combine state.

➢ **Combine State**

(a) **Sulphates :** Gypsum ($CaSO_4.2H_2O$), Epsom salt ($MgSO_4.7H_2O$), Glauber's salt ($Na_2SO_4.10H_2O$)

(b) **Sulphides :** Cinnabar (HgS), Galena (PbS), Iron pyrites (FeS_2), Copper pyrites ($CuFeS_2$), Zinc blend (ZnS).

(c) **Organic matter :** In insulin, glucosionates of plants and animals, nature, gas petroleum, crude oil, coal gas, water springs.

➢ **Allotropes of sulphur**

Allotropes and allotropy : Two or more forms of an element which have different structure and other physical properties but have same chemical properties are known as allotropes of the element This property of elements is known as allotropy .

Sulphur has two allotropes the crystalline and non crystalline.

(A) **Crystalline allotropes:** Crystalline sulphur is found in two allotropic forms.

(i) **Rhombic sulphur** : This allotrope of sulphur is also known as α (alfa) sulphur At normal temperature this allotrope of sulphur is highly stable. It is insoluble in water but soluble in carbon disulphide When it is heated at 368.6 K (95.6° C), it is converted into other allotrope, monoclinic sulphur

(ii) **Monoclinic sulphur** : It is also known as β (beta) sulphur. It is found in the form of needle shaped crystals. Thus it is also known as prismatic sulphur. It is insoluble in water and soluble in carbon disulphide. This allotrope of sulphur is stable above 368.6 K temperature Below this temperature it is converted to α sulphur Both allotropcs of sulphur coexist at 368.6 K This temperature is known as transition temperature.

$$\text{Rhombic sulphur} \underset{}{\overset{368.6K}{\rightleftharpoons}} \text{monoclinic sulphur}$$

Both these allotropes of sulphur have 58 structure that forms a distorted ring.

(B) **Non crystalline sulphur** : This sulphur is found in three allotropic forms

(i) **Plastic sulphur** : When boiling sulphur is poured in cold water a soft rubber like substance is obtained which is known as plastic sulphur. This is an unstable allotrope of sulphur which gets converted slowly, into rhombic sulphur, It is also known as γ (gamma) sulphur. Plastic sulphur is unsynchronized chain structure.

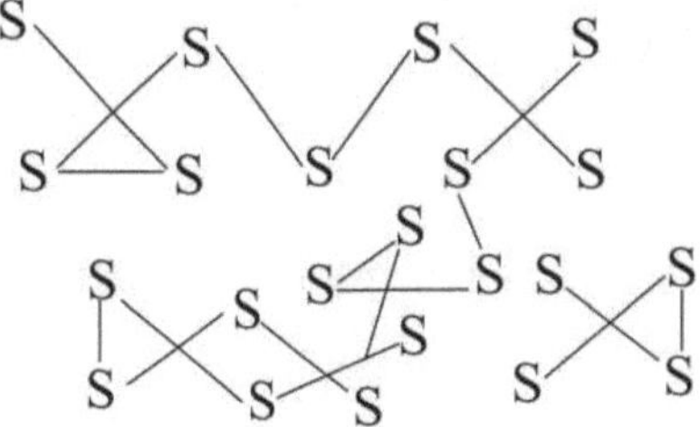

Distorted ring of S_8 molecle in rhombic and monoclinic sulphur

Chain of S. molecules in plastic sulphur.

(ii) **δ (delta) sulphur or milk of sulphur**: It is white coloured non crystalline sulphur It is used for preparing medicines.

(iii) **Colloidal sulphur** : This allotrope of sulphur is obtained by passing H_2S gas in dilute nitric acid solution.

$H_2S + 2HNO_3$ (dilute) $\rightarrow$ $2NO_2 + 2H_2O + S$

This sulphur is soluble in Carbon disulphide but insoluble in water. On heating or after some times, this sulphur gets transformed into rhombic sulphur. It is also used in preparation of medicines.

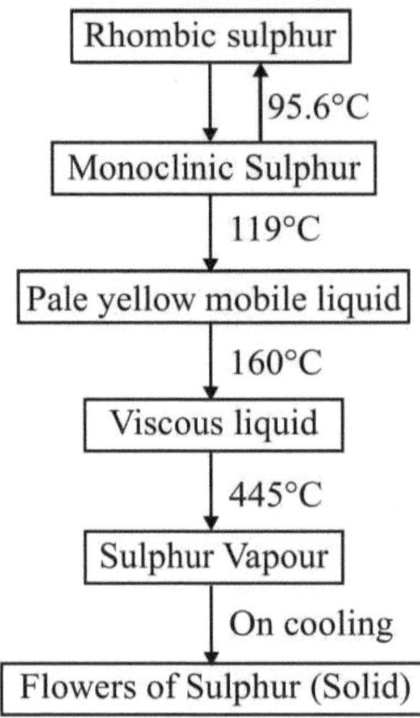

➢ **Use of sulphur:**

(i) sulphur is extensively used for industrial production of sulphuric acid.

(ii) It is used in gun powder and in manufacturing of match sticks.

(iii) It is used as powerful insecticide.

(iv) Sulphur is used in preparation of medicines, sulphur containing medicines are useful for skin diseases and blood purification,

(v) It is used in vulcanization of rubber.

3.9.2 PHOSPHORUS

Atomic number	:	15
Atomic mass	:	31
Electronic configuration	:	$1s^2\ 2s^2\ 2p^6\ 3s^2\ 3p^3$
Symbol	:	P
Valencies	:	+ 3,+ 5

Phosphrous is a Greek work meaning phos = light and phero = carry. This implies that phosphorus is an element that glows in darkness. Phosphrous was discovered by Brand a German scientist in 1669. He obtained this element for first time by distillation of a mixture of urine, sand and coal.

It is not found in free state in nature because it is highly reactive. In combined state, it is found in the form of phosphate compounds.

The principal minerals of phosphrous are

(i) Phosphorite $Ca_3(PO_4)_2$

(ii) Flourapatite $3Ca_3(PO_4)_2.CaF_2$

(iii) Chlorapatite $3Ca_3(PO_4)_2.CaCl_2$

➢ **Allotropes of phosphorus** : There are many allotropes of phosphorus, they are as follows.

(i) White or yellow phosphorus,

(ii) Red phosphorus,

(iii) Black phosphorus,

(iv) Violet / purple phosphorus,

(v) Dark red phosphorus.

Out of these white, red and black phosphorus are more common.

- **White phosphorus** is of white colour when it is pure but gradually it turns yellow. It has garlic like smell and is poisonous. It is a molecular solid having tetrahedral P_4 units. In this arrangement P-P-P bond angle is 60° and the structure is more strained. Due to this white phosphorus is more reactive. It catches fires in presence of air thus it is kept in cold water. It is soft and can be easily cut with knife.

- **Red phosphorus**: It has a complex chain structure. It is odourless and its ignition point is high. In red phosphorus, P-P-P bond angle is 100°.

- **Black phosphorus**: Due to its layered structure it is more stable. In this allotrope many layer of phosphorus atoms are interconnected. Similar to red phosphorus, it is also odourless.

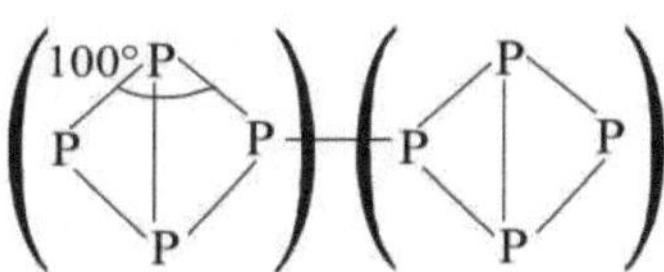

Red phosphorus

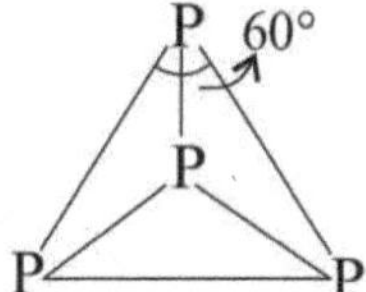

White phosphorus

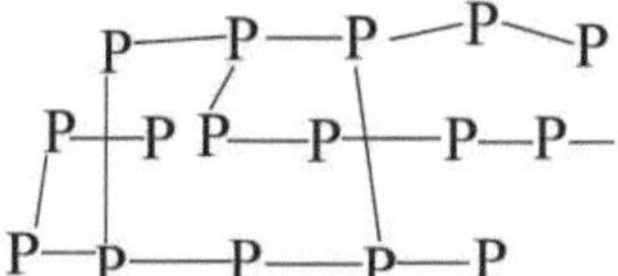

Black Phosphorus

➢ **Uses of phosphorus :**

(i) White phosphorus is used to prepare smoke clouds, fire balls, presentation of fire game and to manufacture coloured match sticks.

(ii) Red phosphorus is used to prepare match sticks,

(iii) Red Phosphorus is used to prepare phosphorus bronze alloy. This alloy contains copper, tin and phosphorus.

(iv) Compounds of phosphorus like zinc phosphide and calcium phosphide are used to kill rats.

3.9.3 SOME IMPORTANT COMPOUNDS OF NON-METALS

1. **Ozone(O_3)**: Ozone is an allotrope of oxygen. Nascent oxygen is obtained from this compound, so it is a strong oxidizing agent. A layer of ozone is also found in the atmosphere. This layer prevents the harmful U.V. radiations coming from sun. Thus act as a protective layer. Following are important industrial uses of ozone gas.

   (i) In production of artificial silk, (ii) As bleaching agent.
   (iii) As disinfectant. (iv) For purifying drinking water.
   (v) Ozone used as disinfectant and also for purifying air.
   (vi) Used for preparation of potassium permangnate.

2. **Hydrogen peroxide (H_2O_2)**

   It's chemical structure

   H–O–O–H.

   It exhibit both oxidizing and reducing properties. Usually its oxidizing properties are more Its important uses are as follows :

   (i) The oxidizing property is employed in rejuveniling (re-brightening) of old paintings whose original lead coating has turned dirty due to its reaction with H_2S present in atmosphere, resulting in formation of PbS Hydrogen peroxide oxidises this yellow lead sulphide to white lead sulphate

   $$\underset{\text{yellow}}{PbS} + 4H_2O_2 \longrightarrow \underset{\text{white}}{PbSO_4} + 4H_2O$$

   (ii) Dilute solution of hydrogen peroxide is used as a disinfectant for wounds.
   (iii) Concentrated H_2O_2 is used as rocket fuel oxidant.
   (iv) The main industrial application of it is the bleaching of silk, hair, ivory, wool, wood etc
   (v) It is used in medicine, cosmetics etc.

3. **Ammonia (NH_3)** :

   Structure of ammonia

   $$H - \ddot{N} - H$$
   $$\quad |$$
   $$\quad H$$

   (i) Ammonia is used for manufacturing of nitrogen containing fertilizers (like ammonium nitrate, urea, ammonium phosphate and ammonium sulphate)
   (ii) Ammonia is used for manufacturing of nitric acid.
   (iii) It is used as freezing agent thus it is also used in ice factories
   (iv) Used in synthesis of artificial silk.
   (v) Used for producing explosives.
   (vi) It is useful in removing stains of fats, oils, grease etc. from clothes.
   (vii) Dilute ammonia is used in medicines and cosmetics.

4. **Nitric acid (HNO_3) :**

Structure of nitric acid

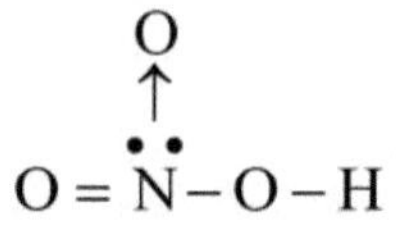

$$O = \overset{\overset{O}{\uparrow}}{\ddot{N}} - O - H$$

Nitric acid is a strong oxidizing agent Its main industrial applications are as follows.

(i) Nitric acid is used for preparation of ammonium nitrate which is used as fertilizer,

(ii) It is also useful for preparation of other nitrates which are used in explosives and fire crackers. For example - potassium nitrate (KNO_3), nitroglycerine, trinitrotoluene etc are explosive.

(iii) Used for oxidation of rocket fuels.

(iv) Used for manufacturing of dyes, medicines, artificial silk etc.

(v) In purification of gold and silver.

(vi) Used for manufacturing of sulphuric acid.

5. **Sulphuric acid (H_2SO_4) :**

Structure of sulphuric acid

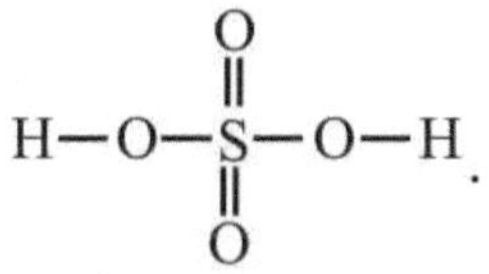

$$H-O-\underset{\underset{O}{\|}}{\overset{\overset{O}{\|}}{S}}-O-H$$

Main industrial uses are -

(i) manufacturing of hydrochloric acid, nitric acid and fertilizers,

(ii) purification of petrol,

(iii) In dye industry

(iv) In metallurgy for the extraction of metals,

(v) In batteries.

(vi) In electroplating

(vii) In detergent industry

Infact sulphuric acid is used in the synthesis of hundreads of industrial products, thus it is also known as king of acids.

6. **Hydrochloric acid (HCl):**

Also known as acid of common salt. Its important uses are as follows-

(i) As an important reagent in laboratory

(ii) A Mixture of three part of HCI and one part of HNO_3 is called aquaregia in which metals are soluble,

(iii) In iron and steel industry.

(iv) In textile industry,

(v) In manufacture of gum and dyes,

(vi) Manufacturing of chlorine gas which in turn used to prepare bleaching powder. It is used for the purification of drinking water.

(vii) For synthesis of metal and non metal chlorides.

7. **Ammonium chloride (NH_4Cl) :** $[NH_4]^+ Cl^-$

It is commonly known as 'Nausadar' Its main uses are as follows-

(i) Soldering material is prepared by ammonium chloride, it is used for polishing utensils,

(ii) It is used in electric battery,

(iii) Used in colouring clothes,

(iv) Also used as medicine

(v) As reagent in laboratory.

8. **Silica (SiO_2) :** [O = Si = O]

In nature, silica is found in different forms Sand is present in nature in abundance which is a form of silica. It is more useful because of its hardness. Its main uses are as follows-

(i) Silica is used in the manufacturing of glass,

(ii) Jasper a semi precious stone, a form of silica

(iii) Silica form other silicates which arc used in electrical appliances, chemical laboratory equipment, optical lenses, prism etc.

(iv) Silicon is prepared from silica, which is used in semi conductor, transistor and alloys,

(v) Kieselguir is an allotrope of silica, is used for manufacturing dynamite.

POINTS TO REMEMBER

1. The elements which have intermediate properties between those of metals and non-metals are called metalloids.

2. Allotropes are two or more different forms of the same element.

3. Reaction of metals with oxygen: Almost all metals combine with oxygen to form metal oxides. But all metals do not react with oxygen at the same rate. Different metals show different reactivities towards oxygen. Metal oxides are basic in nature. But some metal oxides are amphoteric oxides.

4. Amphoteric oxides: Metal oxides which show both acidic as well as basic behaviour are known as amphoteric oxides. Such metal oxides which react with both acids as well as bases to produce salts and water. For example: aluminium oxide, zinc oxide, etc.

5. **Aqua regia:** Aqua regia is a freshly prepared mixture of concentrated hydrochloric acid and concentrated nitric acid in the ratio of 3:1.

6. **Anodising:** It is a process of forming a thick oxide layer of aluminium. During anodising, a clean aluminium article is made the anode and is electrolysed with dilute sulphuric acid. The oxygen gas evolved at the anode reacts with aluminium to make a thicker protective oxide layer. This aluminium oxide coat makes it resistant to further corrosion.

7. **Reaction of metals with solution of other metal salts:**

   Metal A + Salt solution of B $\rightarrow$ Salt solution of A + Metal B (Metal A is more reactive than metal B)

8. **Reactivity series:** The reactivity series is a list of metals arranged in the order of their decreasing activities.

9. **Reaction of metals with non-metals:** When a metal and a non-metal react with each other, transfer of electrons take place from metal to non-metal.

10. **Ionic compounds:** The compounds that formed by complete transference of electrons from a metal to non- metal are known as ionic compounds. Ionic compounds have strong electrostatic force of attraction between the positive and negative ions.

11. **Properties of ionic compounds:**

    (a) **Physical nature:** Ionic compounds are solids and are somewhat hard.

    (b) **Melting and Boiling points:** Ionic compounds have high melting and boiling points.

    (c) **Solubility:** Electrovalent compounds are generally soluble in water and insoluble in solvents such as kerosene, petrol, etc.

    (d) **Conduction of Electricity:** Ionic compounds do not conduct electricity in the solid state but conduct electricity in the molten state or when dissolved in water.

12. **Corrosion:** The process of slowly eating away of the metal due to attack of air, water, etc. on the surface of the metal is called corrosion.

13. The rusting of iron can be prevented by painting, oiling, greasing, galvanising, chrome plating, anodising or making alloys.

14. Galvanisation is a method of protecting steel and iron from rusting by coating them with a thin layer of zinc. The galvanised article is protected against rusting even if the zinc coating is broken.

15. **Alloys:** An alloy is a homogeneous mixture of two or more metals, or a metal and a non-metal.

16. **Alloys and their constituents:**

Alloy Constituents Brass :Copper, zinc

Bronze :Copper, tin

Steel: Iron, carbon

Stainless steel :Iron, nickel, chromium

Solder :Lead, tin

17. **Mineral:** The elements or compounds, which occur naturally in the earth's crust, are known as minerals.

18. **Ore:** The minerals contain a very high percentage of a particular metal and from which the metal can be profitably extracted is called ore.

19. **Gangue:** The unwanted materials or impurities present in the ores are called gangue.

20. **Enrichment of ore:** Ores mined from the earth are usually contaminated with gangue. The removal of gangue from the ore is called enrichment of ore. The process used for enrichment of ores is based on the differences between the physical or chemical properties of the gangue and the ore.

21. **Metals low in the activity series:** Metals low in the activity series are very non-reactive. The oxides of these metals can be reduced to metals by heating alone.

22. **Metals in the middle of the activity series:** The metals in the middle of the activity series are moderately reactive. These are usually present as sulphides or carbonates in nature. They are first converted to metal oxides and then in the next step the metal oxides are reduced to metal.

23. **Conversion of ore into oxide form:** It can be done in two ways:

Roasting : The process of heating the sulphide ore in the presence of sufficient supply of air to convert it into oxide is called roasting.

Calcination : The process of heating the carbonate ore in the presence of limited supply of air to convert it into oxide is called calcination.

24. **Metals towards the top of the reactivity series:** These are highly reactive metals. Example: Sodium, calcium, magnesium, aluminium are obtained by electrol ysis of molten chlorides. These metals are obtained by electrolytic reduction.

CONCEPT APPLICATION LEVEL - I [NCERT Questions]

Q.1 (i) Metal that exists in liquid state at room temperature ?

Ans. Mercury

(ii) Metal that can be easily cut with a knife ?

Ans. Sodium

(iii) Metal that is the best conductor of heat ?

Ans. Silver

(iv) Metals that are poor conductor of heat ?

Ans. Lead

Q.2 Explain the meanings of malleable and ductile.

Ans. **Malleable:** Substances that can be beaten into thin sheets are called malleable. For example, most of the metals are malleable.

Ductile: Substances that can be drawn into thin wires are called ductile. For example, most of the metals are ductile.

Q.3 Define the following terms.

(i) Mineral (ii) Ore (iii) Gangue

Ans. (i) **Mineral:** Most of the elements occur in nature as in combined state as minerals. The inorganic element or compounds which occur naturally in earth's crust are known as minerals. The chemical composition of minerals is fixed.

(ii) **Ore:** Minerals from which metals can be extracted profitably are known as ores.

(iii) **Gangue:** The impurities such as sand, silt, soil, gravel, etc. associated with the minerals are called gangue.

Q.4 Write equations for the reactions of

(i) iron with steam

(ii) calcium and potassium with water

Ans. (i)

$$\underset{\text{Iron}}{3Fe(s)} + \underset{\text{water}}{4H_2O} \longrightarrow \underset{\text{Iron (II, III) oxide}}{Fe_3O_4(aq)} + \underset{\text{Hydrogen}}{4H_2(g)}$$

(ii)

$$\underset{\text{Calcium}}{Ca(s)} + \underset{\text{water}}{2H_2O(l)} \longrightarrow \underset{\text{Calcium hydroxide}}{Ca(OH)_2\ (aq)} + \underset{\text{Hydrogen}}{H_2(g)} + \text{Heat}$$

$$\underset{\text{Potassium}}{2K(s)} + \underset{\text{water}}{2H_2O} \longrightarrow \underset{\text{Potassium hydroxide}}{2KOH(aq)} + \underset{\text{Hydrogen}}{H_2(s)} + \text{Heat}$$

Q.5 Samples of four metals A, B, C and D were taken and added to the following solution one by one. The results obtained have been tabulated as follows.

Metal	Iron (II) Sulphate	Copper (II) sulphate	Zinc sulphate	Silver nitrate
A	No reaction	Displacement		
B	Displacement		No reaction	
C	No reaction	No reaction	No reaction	Displacement
D	No reaction	No reaction	No reaction	No reaction

Use the Table above to answer the following questions about metals A, B, C and D.

(i) Which is the most reactive metal?

(ii) What would you observe if B is added to a solution of copper (II) sulphate?

(iii) Arrange the metals A, B, C and D in the order of decreasing reactivity.

Ans. Explanation

$A + FeSO_4 \longrightarrow$ No reaction, i.e., A is less reactive than iron.

$A + CuSO_4 \longrightarrow$ Displacement, i.e., A is more reactive than copper.

$B + FeSO_4 \longrightarrow$ Displacement, i.e., B is more reactive than iron.

$B + ZnSO_4 \longrightarrow$ No reaction, i.e., B is less reactive than zinc.

$C + FeSO_4 \longrightarrow$ No reaction, i.e., C is less reactive than iron.

$C + CuSO_4 \longrightarrow$ No reaction, i.e., C is less reactive than copper.

$C + ZnSO_4 \longrightarrow$ No reaction, i.e., C is less reactive than zinc.

$C + AgNO_3 \longrightarrow$ Displacement, i.e., C is more reactive than silver.

$D + FeSO_4/CuSO_4/ZnSO_4/AgNO_3 \longrightarrow$ No reaction,

i.e., D is less reactive than iron, copper, zinc, and silver. From the above equations, we obtain:

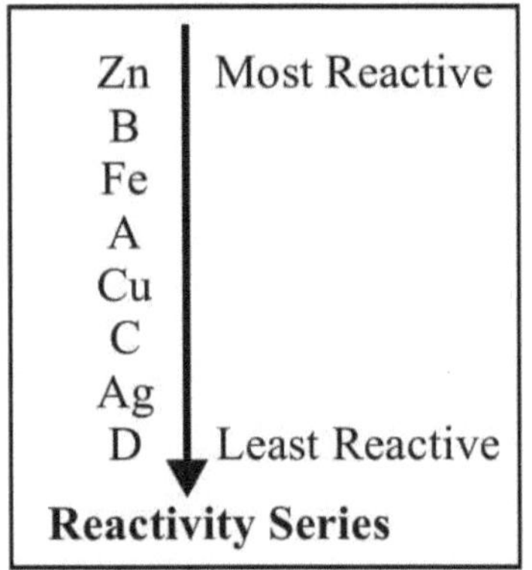

(i) B is the most reactive metal.

(ii) If B is added to a solution of copper (II) sulphate, then it would displace copper.

$B + CuSO_4 \longrightarrow$ Displacement

(iii) The arrangement of the metals in the order of decreasing reactivity is:

$B > A > C > D$

Q.6 Which gas is produced when dilute hydrochloric acid is added to a reactive metal? Write the chemical reaction when iron reacts with dilute H_2SO_4.

Ans. Hydrogen gas is evolved when dilute hydrochloric acid is added to a reactive metal. When iron reacts with dilute H_2SO_4, iron (II) sulphate with the evolution of hydrogen gas is formed.

$$Fe(s) + H_2SO_4(aq) \longrightarrow FeSO_4(aq) + H_2(g)$$

(Ferrous sulphate)

Q.7 What would you observe when zinc is added to a solution of iron (II) sulphate? Write the chemical reaction that takes place.

Ans. Zinc is more reactive than iron. Therefore, if zinc is added to a solution of iron (II) sulphate, then it would displace iron from the solution.

$$Zn(s) + FeSO_4(aq) \longrightarrow ZnSO_4(aq) + Fe(s)$$

Q.8 (i) Write the electron-dot structures for sodium, oxygen and magnesium.

(ii) Show the formation of Na_2O and MgO by the transfer of electrons.

(iii) What are the ions present in these compounds?

Ans. (i) The representation of elements with valence electrons as dots around the elements is referred to as electron-dot structure for elements.

(a) Sodium (2, 8, 1) = $\dot{\text{N}}\text{a}$

(b) Oxygen (2, 6) = $:\ddot{\text{O}}:$

(c) Magnesium (2, 8, 2) = $\ddot{\text{M}}\text{g}$

(ii) $2\,\dot{\text{N}}\text{a} + \text{O} \longrightarrow (Na^+)_2\,[:\text{O}:]^{2-}$

$\text{Mg}: + \text{O} \longrightarrow (Mg^{2+})\,[:\text{O}:]^{2-}$

(iii) The ions present in Na_2O are Na^+ and O^{2-} ions and in MgO are Mg^{2+} and O^{2-} ions.

Q.9 Name two metals which are found in nature in the free state.

Ans. The metals at the bottom of the reactivity series are mostly found in free state. For example: gold, silver, and platinum.

Q.10 What chemical process is used for obtaining a metal from its oxide?

Ans. The chemical process used for obtaining a metal from its oxide is reduction. In this process, metal oxides are reduced by using suitable reducing agents such as carbon or by highly reactive metals to displace the metals from their oxides. For example, zinc oxide is reduced to metallic zinc by heating with carbon.

$$ZnO(s) + C(s) \xrightarrow{\Delta} Zn(s) + CO(g)$$

Manganese dioxide is reduced to manganese by treating it with aluminium powder. In this case, aluminium displaces manganese from its oxide.

$$3MnO_2(s) + 4Al(s) \longrightarrow 3Mn(s) + 2Al_2O_3(s) + Heat$$

Oxides of more reactive metals are reduced by electrolysis.

Q.11 Metallic oxides of zinc, magnesium and copper were heated with the following metals.

Metal	Zinc	Magnesium	Copper
Zinc oxide	—	—	—
Magnesium oxide	—	—	—
Copper oxide	—	—	—

In which cases will you find displacement reactions taking place?

Ans.

Metal	Zinc	Magnesium	Copper
Zinc oxide	No reaction	Displacement	No reaction
Magnesium oxide	No reaction	No reaction	No reaction
Copper oxide	Displacement	Displacement	No reaction

Q.12 Which metals do not corrode easily?

Ans. More reactive a metal is, more likely it is to be corroded. Therefore, less reactive metals are less likely to get corroded. This is why gold plating provides high resistance to corrosion.

Q.13 What are alloys?

Ans. Alloys are homogeneous mixtures of two or more elements. The elements could be two metals, or a metal and a non-metal. An alloy is formed by first melting the metal and then dissolving the other elements in it. For example, steel is an alloy of iron and carbon.

Q.14 Which of the following pairs will give displacement reactions?

(A) NaCl solution and copper metal
(B) $MgCl_2$ solution and aluminium metal
(C) $FeSO_4$ solution and silver metal
(D) $AgNO_3$ solution and copper metal.

Ans. (D), $AgNO_3$ solution and copper metal

Q.15 Which of the following methods is suitable for preventing an iron frying pan from rusting?

(A) Applying grease
(B) Applying paint
(C) Applying a coating of zinc
(D) all of the above.

Ans. (C), Applying a coating of zinc (We can also apply grease and paint to prevent iron from rusting. However, in case of iron frying pan, grease and paint cannot be applied because when the pan will be heated and washed again and again, the coating of grease and paint would get destroyed.)

Q.16 An element reacts with oxygen to give a compound with a high melting point. This compound is also soluble in water. The element is likely to be

(A) calcium (B) carbon (C) silicon (D) iron

Ans. (A) The element is likely to be calcium.

Q.17 Food cans are coated with tin and not with zinc because

(A) zinc is costlier than tin. (B) zinc has a higher melting point than tin.

(C) zinc is more reactive than tin. (D) zinc is less reactive than tin.

Ans. (C) Food cans are coated with tin and not with zinc because zinc is more reactive than tin.

Q.18 You are given a hammer, a battery, a bulb, wires and a switch.

(a) How could you use them to distinguish between samples of metals and non-metals?

(b) Assess the usefulness of these tests in distinguishing between metals and nonmetals.

Ans. (a) With the hammer, we can beat the sample and if it can be beaten into thin sheets (that is, it is malleable), then it is a metal otherwise a non-metal. Similarly, we can use the battery, bulb, wires, and a switch to set up a circuit with the sample. If the sample conducts electricity, then it is a metal otherwise a non-metal.

(b) The above tests are useful in distinguishing between metals and non-metals as these are based on the physical properties. No chemical reactions are involved in these tests.

Q.19 What are amphoteric oxides? Give two examples of amphoteric oxides.

Ans. Those oxides that behave as both acidic and basic oxides are called amphoteric oxides. Examples: aluminium oxide (Al_2O_3), zinc oxide (ZnO).

Q.20 Name two metals which will displace hydrogen from dilute acids, and two metals which will not.

Ans. Metals that are more reactive than hydrogen displace it from dilute acids. For example: sodium and potassium. Metals that are less reactive than hydrogen do not displace it. For example: copper and silver.

Q.21 In the electrolytic refining of a metal M, what would you take as the anode, the cathode and the electrolyte?

Ans. In the electrolytic refining of a metal M:

Anode $\longrightarrow$ Impure metal M

Cathode $\longrightarrow$ Thin strip of pure metal M

Electrolyte $\longrightarrow$ Solution of salt of the metal M

Q.22 Pratyush took sulphur powder on a spatula and heated it. He collected the gas evolved by inverting a test tube over it, as shown in figure below.

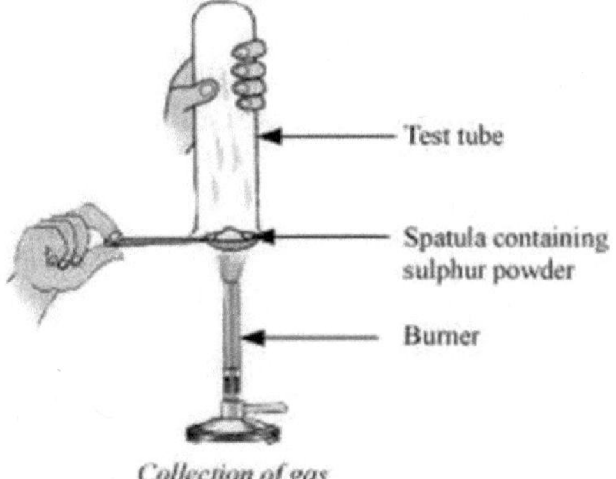

Collection of gas

(a) What will be the action of gas on

(i) dry litmus paper? (ii) moist litmus paper?

(b) Write a balanced chemical equation for the reaction taking place.

Ans. (a) (i) There will be no action on dry litmus paper.

(ii) Since the gas is sulphur dioxide (SO_2), it turns moist blue litmus paper to red because sulphur dioxide reacts with moisture to form sulphurous acid.

(b) $S(s) + O_2(g) \longrightarrow SO_2(g)$ (Sulphur dioxide)

$SO_2(g) + H_2O(l) \longrightarrow H_2SO_3(aq)$ (Sulphurous acid)

Q.23 State two ways to prevent the rusting of iron.

Ans. Two ways to prevent the rusting of iron are:

(i) Oiling, greasing, or painting: By applying oil, grease, or paint, the surface becomes water proof and the moisture and oxygen present in the air cannot come into direct contact with iron. Hence, rusting is prevented.

(ii) Galvanisation: An iron article is coated with a layer of zinc metal, which prevents the iron to come in contact with oxygen and moisture. Hence, rusting is prevented.

Q.24 What type of oxides is formed when non-metals combine with oxygen?

Ans. Non-metals combine with oxygen to form acidic oxides.

For example: $S(s) + O_2(g) \longrightarrow SO_2(g)$

Acid in nature

Q.25 Give reasons

(a) Platinum, gold and silver are used to make jewellery.

(b) Sodium, potassium and lithium are stored under oil.

(c) Aluminium is a highly reactive metal, yet it is used to make utensils for cooking.

(d) Carbonate and sulphide ores are usually converted into oxides during the process of extraction.

Ans. (a) Platinum, gold, and silver are used to make jewellery because they are very lustrous. Also, they are very less reactive and do not corrode easily.

(b) Sodium, potassium, and lithium are very reactive metals and react very vigorously with air as well as water. Therefore, they are kept immersed in kerosene oil in order to prevent their contact with air and moisture.

(c) Though aluminium is a highly reactive metal, it is resistant to corrosion. This is because aluminium reacts with oxygen present in air to form a thin layer of aluminium oxide. This oxide layer is very stable and prevents further reaction of aluminium with oxygen. Also, it is light in weight and a good conductor of heat. Hence, it is used to make cooking utensils.

(d) Carbonate and sulphide ores are usually converted into oxides during the process of extraction because metals can be easily extracted from their oxides rather than from their carbonates and sulphides.

Q.26 You must have seen tarnished copper vessels being cleaned with lemon or tamarind juice. Explain why these sour substances are effective in cleaning the vessels.

Ans. Copper reacts with moist carbon dioxide in air to form copper carbonate and as a result, copper vessel loses its shiny brown surface forming a green layer of copper carbonate. The citric acid present in the lemon or tamarind neutralises the basis copper carbonate and dissolves the layer. That is why, tarnished copper vessels are cleaned with lemon or tamarind juice to give the surface of the copper vessel its characteristic lustre.

Q.27 Differentiate between metal and non-metal on the basis of their chemical properties.

Ans.

	Metal	Non-metal
1.	Metals are electropositive.	Non-metals are electronegative.
2.	They react with oxygen to form basic oxides. $4Na + O_2 \longrightarrow 2Na_2O$ These have ionic bonds	They react with oxygen to form acidic or neutral oxides. $C + O_2 \longrightarrow CO_2$ These have covalent bonds.
3.	They react with water to form oxides and hydroxide. Some metals react with cold water, some with hot water and some with steam. $2Na + 2H_2O \longrightarrow 2NaOH + H_2 \uparrow$	They do not react with water.
4.	They react with dilute acids to form a salt and evolve hydrogen gas. However, Cu, Ag, Au, Pt, Hg do not react. $2Na + 2HCl \longrightarrow 2NaCl + H_2 \uparrow$	They do not react with dilute acids. These are not capable of replacing hydrogen.
5.	They react with the salt solution of metals. Depending on their reactivity, displacement reaction can occur. $CuSO_4 + Zn \longrightarrow ZnSO_4 + Cu$	They do not react with the salt solution of non-metals.
6.	They act as reducing agents (as they can easily lose electrons). $Na \longrightarrow Na^+ + e^-$	These act as oxidizing agents (as they can gain electrons). $Cl_2 + 2e^- \longrightarrow 2Cl^-$

Q.28 A man went door to door posing as a goldsmith. He promised to bring back the glitter of old and dull gold ornaments. An unsuspecting lady gave a set of gold bangles to him which he dipped in a particular solution. The bangles sparkled like new but their weight was reduced drastically. The lady was upset but after a futile argument the man beat a hasty retreat. Can you play the detective to find out the nature of the solution he had used?

Ans. He must have dipped the gold metal in the solution of aqua regia 3 : 1 mixture of conc. HCl and conc. HNO_3. Aqua regia is a fuming, highly corrosive liquid. It dissolves gold in it. After dipping the gold ornaments in aqua regia, the outer layer of gold gets dissolved and the inner shiny layer appears. That is why the weight of gold ornament reduced.

Q.29 Give reasons why copper is used to make hot water tanks and not steel (an alloy of iron).

Ans. Copper does not react with cold water, hot water, or steam. However, iron reacts with steam. If the hot water tanks are made of steel (an alloy of iron), then iron would react vigorously with the steam formed from hot water.

$$\underset{\text{Iron}}{3Fe} + \underset{\text{Steam}}{4H_2O} \longrightarrow \underset{\text{Iron (II, III) oxide}}{Fe_3O_4} + \underset{\text{Hydrogen}}{4H_2}$$

That is why copper is used to make hot water tanks, and not steel.

Q.30 Why is sodium kept immersed in kerosene oil?

Ans. Sodium and potassium are very reactive metals and combine explosively with air as well as water. Hence, they catch fire if kept in open. Therefore, to prevent accidental fires and accidents, sodium is stored immersed in kerosene oil.

Q.31 Why do ionic compounds have high melting points?

Ans. Ionic compounds have strong electrostatic forces of attraction between the ions. Therefore, it requires a lot of energy to overcome these forces. That is why ionic compounds have high melting points.

CONCEPT APPLICATION LEVEL - II

SECTION-A

MULTIPLE CHOICE QUESTIONS

Q.1 When a non-metal reacts with chlorine, it forms
(A) an ionic chloride (B) a covalent chloride (C) a tetrachloride (D) a dichloride

Q.2 Which of the following metals will displace hydrogen from steam, dilute acids and alkalies?
(A) Iron (B) Mercury (C) Zinc (D) Calcium

Q.3 The final acid obtained during the manufacture of H_2SO_4 by contact process is:
(A) H_2SO_4 (conc.) (B) H_2SO_4 (dil.) (C) H_2SO_4 (aq) (D) $H_2S_2O_7$

Q.4 $Cu_2S + 2\,Cu_2O \rightarrow 6\,Cu + SO_2$ reaction occurs in -
(1) calcination of copper (2) roasting of copper
(3) smelting of copper (4) bessemerisation of copper

Q.5 A process employed for the concentration of sulphide ore is :
(A) Froth floatation (B) Roasting (C) Electrolysis (D) Bessemerisation

Q.6 Zone refining is used for the :
(A) Concentration of an ore (B) Reduction of metal oxide
(C) Purification of metal (D) Purification of an ore.

Q.7 Which of the following processes is used for the concentration of Bauxite ($Al_2O_3 . 2H_2O$)?
(A) Froth floatation (B) Leaching (C) Liquation (D) Magnetic separation

Q.8 In the thermite process, the reducing agent is :
(A) Nickel (B) Zinc (C) Sodium (D) Aluminium

Q.9 Metal always found in free state is
(A) Gold (B) Silver (C) Copper (D) Sodium

Q.10 Chemically rust is :
(A) hydrated ferrous oxide (B) hydrated ferric oxide
(C) only ferric oxide (D) none of these

Q.11 Which is used as catalyst in Haber's process?
(A) Cr (B) Al (C) Ni (D) Fe

Q.12 SO_2 reacts with Cl_2 in the presence of sun light to form
(A) Sulphuryl chloride (B) Sulphonyl chloride (C) Sulphur dioxide (D) None of these

Q.13 Sulphur readily dissolves in
(A) Water (B) sodium hydroxide (C) hydrochloric acid (D) carbon disulphide

Q.14 In the preparation of vanaspati ghee from an cdible oil, the chemical reaction taking place in the presence of Ni catalyst is called.
(A) oxidation (B) dehydration (C) hydrogenation (D) dehydrogenation

Q.15 Sugar reacts with concentrated sulphuric acid to give the smell of burning sugar. It is due to the formation of
(A) CO_2 (B) SO_2 (C) C (D) both CO_2 and SO_2

Q.16 When concentrated H_2SO_4 comes in contact with sugar, it becomes black due to:
(A) Hydrolysis (B) Hydration (C) Decolourisation (D) Dehydration

Q.17 The important ore of iron is
(A) Siderite (B) Haematite (C) Pyrites (D) Bauxite

Q.18 Which of the following processes is used in the extractive metallurgy of magnesium?
(A) Fused salt electrolysis (B) Self reduction
(C) Aqueous solution electrolysis (D) Thermite reduction

Q.19 The process of electrolysis is used for obtaining such metals which are
(A) highly reactive (B) moderately reactive
(C) highly unreactive (D) all types of metals

Q.20 Which of the following reactions canot occure ?
(A) $2AgNO_3(aq) + Fe(s) \rightarrow Fe(NO_3)_2(aq) + 2Ag(s)$
(B) $CuSO_4(aq) + Zn(s) \rightarrow ZnSO_4(aq) + Cu(s)$
(C) $CuSO_4(aq) + 2Ag(s) \rightarrow Cu(s) + Ag_2SO_4(aq)$
(D) $2AgNO_3(aq) + Zn(s) \rightarrow Zn(NO_3)_2(aq) + 2Ag(s)$

Q.21 An alloy of zinc and copper is dissolved in dilute hydrochloric acid. Hydrogen as is evolved. In this evolution of gas
(A) only zinc reacts with dilute hydrochloric acid
(B) only copper reacts with dilute hydrochloric acid
(C) both zinc and copper react with dilute
(D) only copper reacts with water

Q.22 An element reacts with oxygen to give a compound with a high melting point. this compound is also soluble in water. The element is likely to be
(A) Calcium (B) Carbon (C) Silicon (D) Iron

Q.23 'Duralumin' is an alloy of aluminium with
(A) iron, manganese and magnesium (B) copper, manganese and magnesium
(C) copper, chromium and magnesium (D) iron, nickel and magnesium

Q.24 The reactivities of iron, magnesium, sodium and zinc towards water are in the following order
(A) $Fe > Mg > Na > Zn$ (B) $Zn > Na > Mg > Fe$
(C) $Na > Mg > Zn > Fe$ (D) $Mg > Na > Fe > Zn$

Q.25 In the laboratory process of hydrogen production we use impure zinc because :
(A) pure zinc is very costly (B) there is risk of explosion with pure
(C) impurity in zinc act as catalyst (D) pure zinc is not easily available

Q.26 Copper is extracted from the ore copper pyrite by smelting in a blast furnace. The flux used and the slag formed are as given below :
(A) Flux CaO, Slag $CaSiO_3$ (B) Flux SiO_2, Slag $CaSiO_3$
(C) Flux FeO, Slag $FeSiO_3$ (D) Flux SiO_2, Slag $FeSiO_3$

SECTION-B

(VERY SHORT ANSWER TYPE QUESTION) [1 MARKS]

Q.1 Name two metals which can occure in free state as well as in the combined state. **[SAI-2014,15]**

Ans. Copper (Cu) and Silver (Ag).

Q.2 (i) Name a metal which does not stick to glass.
(ii) Name the metal which is commonly used in thermite welding. **[SAI-2012]**

Ans. (i) mercury (Hg).
(ii) Aluminium (Al)

Q.3 Blue colour of copper sulphate solution disappears when some aluminium powder is added in it. **[SAI-2015,14]**

Ans. Aluminium is more reactive than copper.

Q.4 Why is sodium kept immersed in kerosene oil ? **[SAI-2010,15]**

Ans. Sodium reacts with air and water vigorously at room temperature. So it is kept in kerosene.

Q.5 Give a reason why platinum, gold and silver are used to make jewellery ? **[SAI-2013]**

Ans. These are most ductile, malleable and shining property

Q.6 Give reasons why silver metal does not easily combine with oxygen but silver jewellery tarnishes after sometime ? **[SAI-2014, 15]**

Ans. It is due to the formation of the layer of silver disulphide which is black in colour. So it appears tarnished.

Q.7 Why should the metal sulphides and carbonates be converted to metal oxides in the process of extraction of metal from them ? **[SAI-2014, 15]**

Ans. It is easier to obtain metal from its oxide as compared from its sulphides and carbonates.

Q.8 Why magnesium ribbon starts floating when it is placed in hot water ? **[SAI-2015]**

Ans. It starts floating due to the bubbles of hydrogen gas sticking to its surface.

Q.9 Why are ionic compounds usually hard ? **[SAI-2015]**

Ans. Due to strong forc of attraction between cation and anion these are firmly bonded in a definite crystallie pattern. As a result, ionic compounds are generally hard.

Q.10 Explain why a salt which does not conduct electricity in the solid state but becomes a good conductor in molten state ? **[SAI-2015]**

Ans. In molten (fused) state or in aqueous state, ions are in free form and they can move towards opposite electrodes under the influence of electricity. So they are good conductor of electricity

(SHORT ANSWER TYPE QUESTION) [2 MARKS]

Q.11 Write one example each of a : **[SAI-2014,15]**
(i) metal which is so soft that can be cut with a knife and a non-metal which is the hardest natural substance.
(ii) metal and a non-metal which exist as liquid at room temperature.

Ans. (i) Sodium, Diamond.
(ii) Metal–Mercury, Non–metal–Bromine.

Q.12 Explain, how mercury is extracted from its sulphide ore cinnabar. Give equations of the reactions involved. **[SAI-2014, 15]**

Ans. Roasting.

$$2HgS(s) + 3O_2(g) \xrightarrow{\text{Heat}} 2HgO(s) + 2SO_2(g)$$
$$2HgO(s) \xrightarrow{\text{Heat}} 2Hg(l) + O_2(g)$$

Q.13 Can we place silver nitrate in an iron vessel ? Give reason for your answer with a balanced chemical equation. **[SAI-2013]**

Ans. Instrous metals. These metals have little affinity for oxygen and thus,are not attacked easily by air or moisture.

Q.14 (a) Name two metals which evolve hydrogen gas with nitric acid.
(b) Write product of any one of the metals. **[SAI-2011, 15]**

Ans. (a) (i) Magnesium (Mg), (ii) Manganese (Mn).
(b) Magnesium nitrate [$Mg(NO_3)_2$].

Q.15 Give reason, why copper is used to make hot water tanks and not steel (an alloy or iron). **[SAI-2014]**

Ans. Because copper is good conductor of heat and non-corrosive (does not react with steam unlike steel which reacts).

Q.16 Write one example each of :
(a) A metal having low melting point and a non-metal having high melting point.
(b) A metal which is poor conductor or electricity and a non-metal which is good conductor of electricity. **[SAI-2015]**

Ans. (a) Low melting point metal–Gallium, High melting point non-metal–Diamond
(b) Metal, which is poor conductor of electricity– Lead
Non-metal, which is good conductor of electricity–Graphite.

Q.17 (i) Why metals like Cu, Al etc. becomme dull in appearance after sometime ?
(ii) Name the compound formed on the surface of copper which makes it dull. **[SAI-2013, 15]**

Ans. (i) Metals like Cu and Al become dull in appearance because of the formation of their oxides on them.
(ii) Green coating of basic copper carbonate [$CuCO_3.Cu(OH)_2$] and black coating copper (II) oxide [CuO].

Q.18 The following reaction takes place when aluminium powder is heated with MnO_2.
$3MnO_2(s) + 4Al(s) \rightarrow 3Mn(l) + 2Al_2O_3(l) + \text{Heat}$ **[SAI-2015]**
(a) Is aluminium getting reduced ?
(b) Is MnO_2 getting oxidised ?

Ans. (a) No, because oxygen is added to aluminium, therfore, it is getting oxidised.
(b) No, since manganese has lost oxygen, therefore, it is getting reduced.

Q.19 A non- metal A is an important constituent of our food and forms two oxides B and C. Oxide B is toxic whereas C causes global warming. **[SAI-2014]**
(a) Identify A, B and C.
(b) To which group of Periodic Table does A belong ?

Ans. (a) A is carbon, B is carbon monoxide and C is carbon dioxide.
(b) Its belong to IV A

Q.20 Non-metals form two types of oxides. Choose these two types from the following oxides :
SO_2, NO_2, CO, H_2O, N_2O **[SAI-2015]**

Ans. Acidic oxides : SO_2 and NO_2
neutral oxides : CO, H_2O and N_2O.

Q.21 What will happen when : **[SAI-2015]**
(i) Magnesium is treated with very dilute nitric acid ?
(ii) Steam is passed over red hot iron ?

Ans. (i) Magnesium reacts with very dilute nitric acid giving out hydrogen gas.
$$Mg + 2HNO_3 \rightarrow Mg(NO_3)_2 + H_2$$
(ii) It forms iron (II, III) oxide giving out hydrogen gas.
$$3Fe(s) + 4H_2O(g) \rightarrow Fe_3O_4(s) + 4H_2(g)$$

Q.22 Explain why: **[SAI-2014]**
(i) Aluminium metal connot be obtained by reduction of Al_2O_3 with coke.
(ii) Alloys have usually less electrical conductivity.

Ans. (i) Aluminium is a very reactive metal. it cannot be obtained from its compounds by heating with carbon because carbon cannot reduce aluminium oxide.
(ii) Alloy being a homogeneous mixture of two or more metals or metal with a non-metal has less electrical conductivity. When a metal is doped (mixed) with any other metal or non-metal, its conductivity decreases.

Q.23 Give reason why : **[SAI-2012,11,14]**
(a) Aluminium is a good cnductor of electricity. Moreover, when exposed to air, its surface gets covered with exposed to air, its surface gets covered with thin layer of oxides which prevents metal underneath from further corrosion.
(b) Carbonate and sulphide ores are usually converted into oxides during the process of extraction ?

Ans. (a) Aluminium is a good conductor of electricity. Moreover, when exposed to air, its surface gets covered with thin layer of oxides which prevents metal underneath from further corrosion.
(b) It is easier to obtain a metal from its oxide as compared to its sulphides and carbonates.

Q.24 (a) 'Sodium is a highly reactive metal and it cannot be obtained from its oxide by heating with carbon.' Give reason.
(b) How can sodium be obtained from sodium chloride ? **[SAI-2013, 15]**

Ans. (a) Sodium cannot be obtained from its oxide by heating with carbon because carbon cannot reduce the oxides of sodium.
(b) Soium can be obtained from sodium chloride by the process of electrolytic reduction.

Q.25 A metal 'X' combines with a non-metal 'Y' by the transfer of electrons to form a compound Z.
(i) State the type of bond in Z. **[SAI-2015]**
(ii) What can you say about its melting point and boiling point ?
(iii) Will it dissolve in kerosene or petrol ?
(iv) Will it be a good conductor of electricity or not ?

Ans. (i) Ionic/electrovalent.
(ii) High melting and boiling point
(iii) It will not dissolve in kerosene or petrol but in the inorganic solvent such as water.
(iv) It will conduct electricity in the aqueous or molten state.

Q.26 Out of the two metals P and Q, P is less reactive than Q. Suggest an activity to arrange these metals in the order of their decreasing reactivity. Support your answer with a suitable chemical equation. **[SAI-2012,13]**

Ans. Activity : In a test tube, a small amount of salt solution of P is taken and metal Q is added into it. Q being more reactive, displaces metal P from its salt solution.
Chemical equation : Metal Q + Salt solution of P $\longrightarrow$ Salt solution of Q + Metal P.

(LONG ANSWER TYPE QUESTION) [3 MARKS]

Q.27 Compound X and aluminium are used to join railway tracks. (a) Identify the compound X. (b) Name the reaction. (c) Write down its reaction.

Ans. (a) $X - Fe_2O_3$
(b) Thermite reaction
(c) $Fe_2O_3(s) + 2Al(s) \rightarrow 2Fe(l) + Al_2O_3(s) + \text{Heat}$

Q.28 When a metal X is treated with cold water, it gives a basic salt Y with molecular formula XOH (Molecular mass = 40) and liberates a gas Z which easily catches fire. Identify X, Y and Z and also write the reaction involved. **[SAI-2015]**

Ans. $X - Na$, $Y - NaOH$, $Z - H_2$
$2Na + 2H_2O \rightarrow 2NaOH + H_2 + \text{Heat energy}$

Q.29 A metal A, which is used in thermite process, when heated with oxygen gives an oxide B, which is amphoteric in nature. Identify A and B. Write down the reactions of oxide B with HCl and NaOH. **[SAI-2015]**

Ans. $A–Al$, $B–Al_2O_3$
$Al_2O_3 + 6HCl \rightarrow 2AlCl_3 + 3H_2O$
$Al_2O_3 + 2NaOH \rightarrow 2NaAlO_2 + H_2O$

Q.30 Give reasons for the following : **[SAI-2015]**
(i) Most metals conduct electricity well.
(ii) The reaction of iron (III) oxide, Fe_2O_3 with heated aluminium is used to join cracked machine parts.
(iii) Sodium, potassium and lithium are stored under oil.

Ans. (i) Metal conduct electricity because they have electrons which are free to move. Thus, they offer little resistance to the flow of current
(ii) The reaction of iron(III) oxide, (Fe_2O_3) with heated aluminium oxide is highly reactive. The amount of heat evolved is so large that the iron metal is produced in the molten state. For this reason, this reaction is used to join cracked machine parts.

$$\underset{\text{Iron (III) oxide}}{Fe_2O_{3(s)}} + \underset{\text{Aluminium}}{2Al_{(s)}} \xrightarrow{\text{Heat}} \underset{\text{Molten iron}}{2Fe_{(l)}} + \underset{\text{Aluminium oxide}}{Al_2O_{3(s)}}$$

(iii) There are two reasons for this :

(a) These metals are very reactive and may even catch fire when they come in contact with oxygen of the air.

(b) These metals can also combine with moist air containing carbon dioxide and further forming a carbonate layer on metal surface.

Q.31 (i) Define the term 'anode mud'. Name the electrode made of pure metal.

(ii) Give the reactions taking place at cathode and at anode during the electrolytic refining of copper.

Ans. (i) • The insoluble impurities which settle down at the bottom of the anode are known as anode mud.

• Cathode.

(ii) At anode : $Cu(s) \rightarrow Cu^{2+} (aq) + 2e^-$

At cathode : $Cu^{2+}(aq) + 2e^- \rightarrow Cu(s)$

Q.32 Write balanced equation in each case :

(a) Magnesium is treated with very dilute HNO_3.

(b) Aluminium powder is added to Fe_2O_3.

(c) Zinc sulphide is roasted. **[SAI-2013, 2014]**

Ans. (a) $Mg + 2HNO_3 \rightarrow Mg(NO_3)_2 + H_2$

(b) $Fe_2O_3 + 2Al \rightarrow Al_2O_3 + 2Fe$

(c) $2ZnS + 3O_2 \rightarrow 2ZnO + 2SO_2\uparrow$

Q.33 An element 'P' reacts vigorously with water. The product so formed, turns red litmus to blue. Write the equation of reactions of the element 'P' with water and oxygen both. Write two uses of any one salt of element 'P' **[SAI-2012, 2015]**

Ans. • Element P is calcium (Ca).

(i) $Ca(s) + 2H_2O(l) \longrightarrow Ca(OH)_2(aq) + H_2(g)$

(ii) $Ca(s) + O_2(g) \longrightarrow CaO(s)$

Uses of Ca:

(i) As disinfectant for dringking water.

(ii) For bleaching clothes and textile fabrics.

Q.34 A, B and C are three elements which undergo chemical reactions according to the following equations :

$A_2O_3 + 2B \longrightarrow B_2O_3 + 2A$

$3CSO_4 + 2B \longrightarrow B_2(SO_4)_3 + 3C$

$3CO + 2A \longrightarrow A_2O_3 + 3C$ **[SAI-2012, 2014]**

(a) Which element is the most reactive ?

(b) Which element is the least reactive ?

(c) What is the type of reactions lised above ?

Ans. (a) Most reactive element is 'B' as it has replaced both 'A' and 'C' from their compounds.

(b) Element 'C' is least reactive as it has been replaced by both 'A' and 'B'.

(c) Displacement reaction.

Q.35 (i) State the type of chemical reaction used to extract metals at the top of reactivity series from their naturally occurring compounds like oxides or chlorides ? Why carbon cannot be used to reduce their oxides ?

(ii) Write a complete balacned chemical equation to show extraction of Al through molten aluminium oxide. Identify the electrode where aluminium is liberated. **[SAI-2013, 2014]**

Ans. (i) Decomposition reaction → electrolytic decomposition because these metals have more affinity for oxygen than carbon.

(iii) $2Al_2O_3 \xrightarrow{\text{Electrolytic decomposition}} 4Al(l) + 3O_2(g)$

(VERY LONGANSWER TYPE QUESTION) [5 MARKS]

Q.36 Pure iron is soft and stretches easily when hot :

(a) How do these properties of iron change when: **[SAI-2015]**

(i) small amount of carbon is mixed with it ?

(ii) nickel and chromium are mixed with it ?

(b) Define an alloy. How is an alloy prepared ?

(c) An alloy has low melting point and is therefore, used for electrical fuse. Name the alloy and write its constituents.

Ans. (a) (i) When a small amount of carbon is mixed, the iron becomes hard and strong.

(ii) When iron is mixed with nickel and chromium, we get stainless steel

(b) Homogeneous mixture of two or more metals or a metal and a non-metal is known as an alloy.it is prepared by first melting the priary metal and then, dissolving the other elements in it in definite proportions.

(c) Solder, Pb and Sn.

Q.37 (a) Write chemical equation for the reactions taking place when :

(i) manganese dioxide is heated with aluminium powder. **[SAI-2014, 15]**

(ii) Steam is passed over red hot iron.

(iii) Magnesium reacts with hot water.

(b) The oxide X_2O_3 is unaffected by water. Name a method by which metal X can be obtained from its ore. Give one reason as to why have you chosen this method ?

Ans. (a) (i) $3MnO_2(s) + 4Al(s) \longrightarrow 2Al_2O_3(s) + 3Mn(l) + \text{Heat}$

(ii) $3Fe(s) + 4H_2O(g) \longrightarrow Fe_3O_4(s) + 4H_2(g)$

(iii) $Mg(s) + 2H_2O(s) \longrightarrow Mg(OH)_2(aq) + H_2(g)$

(b) It must be Al_2O_3. Aluminium metal can be obtained by electrolysis of molten Al_2O_3. This is because Al_2O_3 cannot be reduced by carobn.

Q.38 Metal 'M' reacts vigorously with water to form a compound S and a gas G. The solution of S turns red litmus blue whereasgas G turns red litmus blue whereas gas G which is lighter than air, burns with a popping sound. Metal M has low melting point and kept in kerosene.

(a) Identify the metal M and compound S. Write their chemical name and chemical formula.

(b) What is the nature of compound ?

(c) Identify the gas G and mention its one use.

(d) Write balanced equation for the reaction which takes place when metal M reacts with water.

(e) Why this metal M cannot be kept in water ? **[SAI-2013, 14]**

Ans. (a) Metal M is sodium (Na) and compound S is sodium hydroxide (NaOH).

(b) The nature of the compound is basic.

(c) The gas G is hydrogen (H_2). It is used as a fuel.

(d) $2Na(s) + 2H_2O(l) \longrightarrow 2NaOH(aq) + H_2(g) + \text{Heat energy}$

(e) Because it reacts violently with water and catches fire.

CONCEPT APPLICATION LEVEL - III

Q.1 A metal occurs in nature as in are X which on heating in air converts to Y. Y reacts with urreacted X to give the metal. The metal is
(A) Hg (B) Cu (C) Zn (D) Fe

Q.2 Metals like Na, K, Ca and Mg are extracted by electrolysis of their chlorides in molten salte. These metals are not extracted by reduction of their oxides with carbon because
(a) Reduction with carbon is very expensive
(b) Carbon readily makes alloys with these metals
(c) Carbon has less affinity for oxgen
(d) Carbon is a waker reducing agent than these metals.
(A) a and b (B) b and c (C) c and d (D) d and a

Q.3 The metal that can be obtained by electrolysis of an aqueous solution of its salts is :
(A) Zn (B) Cr (C) Mg (D) Ca

Q.4 Which of the following cannot be used to extract a metal from its ore ?
(A) Electrolytic reduction (B) Carbon reduction
(C) Reaction with oxygen (D) Reaction with more electropositive metal

Q.5 Choose the correct sets which represent the oxides as $\rightarrow$ Acidic : basic : neutral : amphoteric respectively
(i) $CO_2 : MgO : N_2O : H_2O$ (ii) $SO_2 : NO : CO : Al_2O_3$
(iii) $P_2O_5 : ZnO : NO : Al_2O_3$ (iv) $SO_3 : CaO : N_2O : PbO$
(A) i & ii (B) ii & iii (C) iii & iv (D) i & iv

Q.6 Highly pure dilute solution of Na in liquid NH_3 :
(A) will be colourless (B) Exhibits electrical conductivity
(C) Produces sodium amide (D) Produces hydrogen gas

Q.7 Arrange the following compounds, the one that gats hydrolysed to form metallic hydroxide, hydrogen peroxide and oxygen is :
(A) Na_2O (B) Na_2O_2 (C) KO_2 (D) Li_2O

Q.8 The characteristic not related to alkali metal is :
(A) Their ions are isoelectronic with noble gases
(B) Low melting points
(C) Low electronegativity
(D) High ionisation energy

Q.9 When sodium is treated with sufficient oxygen/air, the product obtained is :
(A) Na_2O (B) Na_2O_2 (C) NaO_2 (D) NaO

Q.10 The reaction of sodium is highly exothermic with water. The rate of reaction is lowered by :
(A) Lowering the temperature (B) Mixing with alcohol
(C) Mixing with acetic acid (D) Making an amalgam

Q.11 Tin dissolves in excess of sodium hydroxide solution to form :
(A) $Sn(OH)_2$ (B) Na_2SnO_3 (C) Na_2SnO_2 (D) SnO_2

Q.12 Which of the following metal is used for drying organic solvents
(A) magnesium (B) sodium (C) platinum (D) Nickel

Q.13 A metal M readily forms water soluble sulphate MSO_4, water insoluble hydroxide $M(OH)_2$ and oxide MO which becomes inert on heating. The hydroxide is soluble in NaOH. Then M is :
(A) Mg (B) Ca (C) Be (D) Sr

Q.14 Be and Al exhibit many properties which are similar. But the two elements differ in :
(A) forming covalent bonds
(B) forming polymeric hydrides
(C) Exhibiting maximum covalency in compounds
(D) Exhibiting amphoteric nature in their oxides

Q.15 Which of the following metals does not form ionic hydride ?
(A) Ba (B) Mg (C) Ca (D) Sr

Q.16 The salts of which of the following give green colour in fire works ?
(A) Na (B) K (C) Ba (D) Ca

Q.17 Which of the following metal dissolves in KOH with the evolution of hydrogen ?
(A) Ca (B) Mg (C) Sr (D) Be

Q.18 A metal X on heating in nitrogen gas gives Y. Y on treatment with H_2O gives a colourless gas which when passed thrangh $CuSO_4$ solution gives a blue colour. Y is
(A) $Mg(NO_3)_2$ (B) Mg_3N_2 (C) NH_3 (D) MgO

Q.19 In electrochemical corrosion of metals the metal undergoing corrosion becomes :
(A) Anode (B) Cathode (C) inert (D) None of thes above

Q.20 'X' is a substance which chemically combines with impurities associated with the ore to form easily fusile mass 'Y'. Here X and Y are :
(A) Flux, Slag (B) Slag, Flux (C) Gangue, Slag (D) Reductant, Flux

Q.21 'X' is the product formed when sulphure reacts with oxygen, it dissolves in water is produce 'Y' choose the correct option for x and y.
(A) SO_2 acid (B) SO_3, neutral (C) SO_2 base (D) SO_3 acid

Q.22 The property of a material to resist shock and impact is called
(A) Retraction (B) Resilience (C) Tension (D) All of the aobve

Q.23 $Cu_2S + 2\,Cu_2O \rightarrow 6\,Cu + SO_2$ reaction occurs in -
(A) calcination of copper (B) roasting of copper
(C) smelting of copper (D) bessemerisation of copper

Q.24 Which one of the following metal oxides shows both acidic and basic characters ?
(A) SO_2 (B) K_2O (C) Cu_2O (D) Al_2O_3

Q.25 In iron metallurgy, lime stone is used -
(A) to obtain heat energy
(B) to reduce iron oxide into iron
(C) as an iron ore
(D) to remove sand (SiO_2)

Q.26 Which alloy of aluminium is used for making aircrafts
(A) Alnico
(B) Y-Alloy
(C) Duralumin
(D) Aluminium Bronze

Q.27 The substance which are put into the blast furnace in the manufacture of iron :
(A) Iron ore, CaO, $Ca(OH)_2$ and $CaSiO_3$
(B) Iron ore, Coke, Like stone and $CaSiO_3$
(C) Iron ore, coke, Lime stone and Hot air
(D) Iron ore, CaO, Lime stone and hot air

Q.28 When a metal is alloyed with mercury the resulting alloy [Amalgum] will have
(A) Less electrical conductivity than pure mtal
(B) Lower melting point than pure
(C) Both A and B are correct
(D) Both A and B are wrong

Q.29 A compound 'X' green coloured solid, gets oxidised to reddish brown solid in presence of air. 'X' on heating gives brown coloured solid 'Y' and two pungent gases 'A' and 'B' 'A' turns acidified potassium dichromate solution green, X, Y, A, B and type of reaction is :
(A) $CuSO_4$, CuO, SO_2, SO_3 decomposition
(B) $FeSO_4$, Fe, SO_2, SO_3 Oxidation
(C) $FeSO_4$, Fe_2O_3, SO_2, SO_3 decomposition
(D) $FeSO_4$, Fe_2O_3, SO_3, SO_2 decomposition

Q.30 A metal carbonate X on treatment with a mineral acid liberates a gas which when passed through aqueous solution of a substance Y gives back X. The substance Y on reaction with the gas obtained at anode during electrolysis of brine gives a compound Z which can decolorise coloured fabrics. The compounds X,Y and Z respectively are
(A) $CaCO_3$, $Ca(OH)_2$, $CaOCl_2$
(B) $Ca(OH)_2$, CaO, $CaOCl_2$
(C) $CaCO_3$, $CaOCl_2$, $Ca(OH)_2$
(D) $Ca(OH)_2$, $CaCO_3$, $CaOCl_2$

Q.31 Metals like sodium, potassium calcium and magnesium are extracted by electrolysis of their chlorides in molten state. These metals are not extracted by reduction of their oxides with carbon because
a) reduction with carbon is very expensive
b) carbon readily makes alloys with these metals.
c) carbon has less affinity for oxygen
d) carbon is a weaker reducing agent than these metals.
(A) (a) and (b)
(B) (b) and (c)
(C) (c) and (d)
(D) (d) and (a)

Q.32 A metal occurs in nature as its ore X which on heating in air converts to Y.Y reacts with unreacted X to give the metal. The metal is :
(A) Hg
(B) Cu
(C) Zn
(D) Fe

Q.33 An element X has electronic configuration 2, 8, 1and another element Y has electronic configuration 2, 8, 7. They form a compound Z. The property that is not exhibited by Z is :
(A) it has high melting point
(B) It is a good conductor of electricity in its pure solid state
(C) It breaks into pieces when beaten with hammer.
(D) It is soluble in water.

Q.34 The metals which liberate hydrogen gas with dilute hydrochloric acid as well as caustic soda solution are:
(A) Na and K (B) Zn and Al (C) Fe and Mn (D) Cu and Ag

Q.35 The metal that can be obtained by electrolysis of an aqueous solution of its salts is :
(A) Zn (B) Cr (C) Mg (D) Ca

Q.36 Arrange the following metals in the order of their decreasing reactivity ?
Fe, Cu, Mg, Ca, Zn, Ag
(A) Ca > Zn > Mg > Cu > Ag > Fe (B) Ca > Zn > Cu > Mg > Ag > Fe
(C) Ca > Mg > Zn > Fe > Cu > Ag (D) Ca > Mg > Fe > Zn > Cu > Ag

Q.37 Which element forms maximum multiple bonds ?
(A) N (B) P (C) As (D) Bi

Q.38 On additon of which metal the blue coloured copper sulphate solution turns into colourless solution ?
(A) Ag (B) Hg (C) Zn (D) Au

Passage Based Questions(Q.39 to Q.40)

Generally, the metals form basic order whereas non-metals form acidic oxides. Only a few metals forms hydrides with hydrogen and these hydrides are unstable while the non-metals form stuble hydrides. Metal atoms can donate electrons easily hence they act as redusing agents and the non-metals can accept electrons readily therefore they act as oxidizing agents. Metals having highee reactivity with have higher tendency to displace less reactive metal ions from its salt solution

Q.39 Which among the following can form only basic oxide ?
(A) Sodium (B) Zinc (C)Aluminium (D) Silicon

Q.40 Which of the following will form a stable hydride ?
(A) Born (B) Silicon (C) Sodium (D) Both (A) and (B)

Q.41 **Match the following**

	Column I	**Column II**
(i)	strongest reducing agent in aqueous solution	(a) Thalium
(ii)	Shows inert pair effect	(b) Cesium
(iii)	Forms peroxide on heating with excess of oxygen	(c) Lithium
(iv)	Used in photo cells	(d) Sodium

(A) (i)-d, (ii)-b, (iii)-a, (iv)-c (B) (i)-c, (ii)-a, (iii)-d, (iv)-b
(C) (i)-c, (ii)-b, (iii)-a, (iv)-d (D) (i)-b, (ii)-d, (iii)-a, (iv)-c

Q.42

Column I	**Column II**
(i) Zn	(a) Cuprite
(ii) Hg	(b) Carnalite
(iii) Cu	(c) Calamine
(iv) Mg	(d) Cinnabar

(A) (i)-(c), (ii)-(d), (iii)-(a), (iv)-(b) (B) (i)-(d), (ii)-(c), (iii)-(a), (iv)-(b)
(C) (i)-(b), (ii)-(d), (iii)-(a), (iv)-(c) (D) (i)-(a), (ii)-(d), (iii)-(d), (iv)-(b)

Q.43

Column I	Column II
(i) Self reduction	(a) Pb
(ii) Carbon reduction	(b) Ag
(iii) Complex formation & displacement by metal	(c) Cu
(iv) Electrolytic reduction	(d) Na

(A) (i)-(a,b), (ii)-(b,c), (iii)-(b), (iv)-(d)
(B) (i)-(a,c), (ii)-(a,c), (iii)-(b), (iv)-(d)
(C) (i)-(a,c), (ii)-(b), (iii)-(a,c), (iv)-(d)
(D) (i)-(a,b), (ii)-(b,c), (iii)-(d), (iv)-(b)

Q.44

Column I	Column II
(i) Steel	(a) Cu and Sn
(ii) Brass	(b) Cu and Zn
(iii) Bronze	(c) Fe,C and Cr
(iv) Magnalium	(d) Al and Mg

(A) (i)-(c), (ii)-(b), (iii)-(d), (iv)-(a)
(B) (i)-(c), (ii)-(b), (iii)-(a), (iv)-(d)
(C) (i)-(b), (ii)-(c), (iii)-(a), (iv)-(d)
(D) (i)-(b), (ii)-(c), (iii)-(d), (iv)-(a)

Q.45

Column I	Column II
(i) Aircrafts	(a) Stainless steel
(ii) Utensils	(b) Bronze
(iii) Medals	(c) Magnalium
(iv) Balance been	(d) Duralumin

(A) (i)-(a), (ii)-(b), (iii)-(d), (iv)-(c)
(B) (i)-(a), (ii)-(b), (iii)-(c), (iv)-(d)
(C) (i)-(d), (ii)-(a), (iii)-(b), (iv)-(c)
(D) (i)-(d), (ii)-(a), (iii)-(c), (iv)-(b)

Q.46 **Statement-1 :** Alkali metals dissolve in liquid NH_3 to give blue solutions
Statement-2 : Alkali metals in liquid NH_3 give solvated specie of the type $[M(NH_3)_n]^+$ (M = alkali metals)
(A) Statement-1 and Statement-2 are correct but Statement-2 is the correct explanation of Statement-1.
(B) Statement-1 and Statement-2 are correct but Statement-2 is **NOT** the correct explanation of Statement-1.
(C) Statement-1 is correct and Statement-2 is not correct.
(D) Statement-1 is not correct and Statement-2 is correct.

Q.47 Statement-1 : Metal and non-metals react by mutual transfer of electrons.
Statement-2 : Non- metals form bonds with other non-metals by sharing of electrons.
(A) Statement-1 and Statement-2 are correct but Statement-2 is the correct explanation of Statement-1.
(B) Statement-1 and Statement-2 are correct but Statement-2 is **NOT** the correct explanation of Statement-1.
(C) Statement-1 is correct and Statement-2 is not correct.
(D) Statement-1 is not correct and Statement-2 is correct.

Q.48 **Statement-1 :** In the extraction of magnesium from fesed anhydrous magnesium chloride, air gap of the electrolytic cell is replaced by inert gas.

Statement-2 : Oxidation of magnesium metal can easily be prevented during its extration by electrolytic reduction of anlydrous magnesium chloride.

(A) Statement-1 and Statement-2 are correct but Statement-2 is the correct explanation of Statement-1.

(B) Statement-1 and Statement-2 are correct but Statement-2 is **NOT** the correct explanation of Statement-1.

(C) Statement-1 is correct and Statement-2 is not correct.

(D) Statement-1 is not correct and Statement-2 is correct.

Q.49 Which of the following is true about the two statements?

Statement I : Reactivity of aluminium decreases when it is dipped in nitric acid

Statement II : A protective layer of aluminium nitrate is formed when aluminium is dipped in nitric acid.

(A) Statement-1 and Statement-2 are correct but Statement-2 is the correct explanation of Statement-1.

(B) Statement-1 and Statement-2 are correct but Statement-2 is **NOT** the correct explanation of Statement-1.

(C) Statement-1 is correct and Statement-2 is not correct.

(D) Statement-1 is not correct and Statement-2 is correct.

ANSWER KEY

CONCEPT APPLICATION LEVEL - II

SECTION-A

Q.1	B	Q.2	C	Q.3	D	Q.4	B	Q.5	A	Q.6	C	Q.7	B
Q.8	D	Q.9	A	Q.10	B	Q.11	D	Q.12	A	Q.13	D	Q.14	C
Q.15	C	Q.16	D	Q.17	B	Q.18	A	Q.19	A	Q.20	C	Q.21	A
Q.22	A	Q.23	B	Q.24	C	Q.25	C	Q.26	D				

CONCEPT APPLICATION LEVEL - III

Q.1	B	Q.2	C	Q.3	C	Q.4	C	Q.5	D	Q.6	B	Q.7	C
Q.8	D	Q.9	B	Q.10	D	Q.11	B	Q.12	B	Q.13	A	Q.14	C
Q.15	B	Q.16	C	Q.17	D	Q.18	B	Q.19	A	Q.20	B	Q.21	A
Q.22	B	Q.23	D	Q.24	D	Q.25	D	Q.26	C	Q.27	C	Q.28	C
Q.29	C	Q.30	A	Q.31	C	Q.32	B	Q.33	B	Q.34	B	Q.35	B
Q.36	C	Q.37	A	Q.38	C	Q.39	A	Q.40	D	Q.41	B	Q.42	A
Q.43	B	Q.44	B	Q.45	C	Q.46	B	Q.47	B	Q.48	A	Q.49	A

Printed by Libri Plureos GmbH in Hamburg,
Germany